Hugh We

NO COWARD SOUL

The remarkable story of Bob Appleyard

NO COWARD SOUL

The remarkable story of Bob Appleyard

Stephen Chalke
&
Derek Hodgson

with illustrations by Susanna Kendall

a cover portrait by Ken Taylor

and a foreword by Dickie Bird

FAIRFIELD BOOKS

Fairfield Books
17 George's Road, Fairfield Park, Bath BA1 6EY
Tel 01225-335813

First published 2003

ISBN 0 9531196 9 6

Printed and bound in Great Britain by
Bath Press Ltd, Bath

for

the Sir Leonard Hutton Foundation Appeal

for the advancement of cricket among young people in Yorkshire

No coward soul is mine,
No trembler in the world's storm-troubled sphere;
I see Heaven's glories shine,
And faith shines equal, arming me from fear.

Last lines written by Emily Bronte
before her death from tuberculosis in 1848

ILLUSTRATIONS

The picture of Bob Appleyard on the jacket is by **Ken Taylor**, who played cricket for Yorkshire and England and football for Huddersfield Town in the old First Division. Ken trained as an artist at the Huddersfield College of Art and at the Slade in London. He now works as a teacher of art in Norfolk, where he is building up an extensive collection of portraits of sportsmen. He has also contributed portraits of cricketers to three other books by Stephen Chalke: *Runs in the Memory*, *Caught in the Memory* and *One More Run*. Fairfield Books is planning to publish a book that combines his art work with his memories of life as a professional sportsman.

The eight black-and-white drawings that appear through the pages of this book are by **Susanna Kendall**. Susanna trained as an artist at the Camberwell School of Art in London and has illustrated a number of children's and natural history books. She has also contributed drawings to three other titles published by Fairfield Books: *One More Run* and *At the Heart of English Cricket* by Stephen Chalke and *The Appeal of the Championship* by John Barclay.

The photographs reproduced in this book come from Bob Appleyard's own collection. If any photographic source believes that it holds the copyright of any of them, it should contact the publisher to rectify the matter.

CONTENTS

FOREWORD

by Dickie Bird

I met Bob Appleyard on the first occasion that I was admitted to the Yorkshire dressing room. You can imagine how overawed I was to be among all these great men. Bob was an England bowler, and I was just a lad up from Barnsley. I was properly respectful: Mr Appleyard, I called him.

He could not have been more helpful to a youngster, which is why I have always held him in the greatest respect. There have been tales that the Yorkshire dressing room in the 1950s was not the happiest, with so many egos, but I can only say that I never sensed anything like that. Bob sat me down, and he more or less told me what I would have to do if I wanted to be a first-class cricketer.

Practice, he emphasised. When you go to the nets, he told me, treat it as seriously as if you were playing in a Test match. Don't fool around. Play every shot seriously. No slogging. And if you're bowling, he said, think of it again as a Test match. In your mind, set your field placings, even though you are in the nets. Don't be afraid to ask anyone if you have a problem.

Johnny Wardle – Mr Wardle – was equally helpful although you had to pick your time with Johnny. There were moments when he would talk and laugh and joke with you and others when he could be very quiet, reluctant to say a word. If you could get Johnny talking, you could learn so much about cricket.

In the end I knew I would never be more than an average player, but the lessons I learned, mostly from Bob Appleyard, were to be invaluable as I turned to umpiring: concentration, application, determination. He drilled those words into me, and they have stood me in good stead right through my career.

If there is one thing wrong with many of the younger players today, it is that they don't seem to know the value of talking to the great players of yesteryear. They are the ones who have done it and know how it's done. Of course the game has changed, but the basics are the same. Some of these lads seem to think they live in a different world where the past means nothing.

I wish I could say that I had been a regular in the Yorkshire team with Bob, but in fact we only played together once for the first team. It was early in 1956 when we played Scotland at Hull in what was a three-day first-class fixture. It was a spinners' pitch and Bob, Johnny and Ray Illingworth had 'em out in no time for a lowish score.

I had to bat behind some big names. Frank Lowson and Doug Padgett put on a lot for the first wicket, with Frank getting a quick hundred, and we declared and bowled them out to win in two days. I came in at number seven and scored eight before I was bowled. Somewhere there's a photograph of me walking out with Bob and Johnny in that match.

Dickie Bird
Barnsley, August 2003

CHAPTER 1

WITH HOPE IN HIS HEART

The Summer of 1950

'Dear Sir, You have been selected to play for Yorkshire first eleven versus Surrey on July 22, 24 and 25 at The Oval. Please reply by return of post and oblige.'

The postcard from John Nash, the county's secretary, is among the many mementoes of his cricketing career that Bob Appleyard has retained. It informed him that a room had been booked for him in a temperance hotel in Queen's Gate for four nights, starting on Friday the 21st of July.

"To play for Yorkshire," he looks back. "It was the realisation of an ambition that I'd had from seven years old."

How dramatically his cricketing star had risen! Four weeks earlier he had not even had a game for the Yorkshire second eleven. He was a 26-year-old Bradfordian, living with relatives in Manningham. He had been working for nearly three years as a commercial representative for Short's Lifts, selling cranes, lifts and mechanical handling equipment, and playing cricket on Saturday afternoons for Bowling Old Lane in the Bradford League.

Now suddenly in the last month his cricket had taken over. Every week he had had to negotiate time off to play: first, for the Yorkshire second eleven, then for a match against Scotland, now to play in the county championship. He had reached 26 years of age with little hint of a career as a full-time cricketer, and now it was happening so fast. What on earth did his employers make of it? "They were fine," he recalls. "One of the directors was involved with Undercliffe, another club in the Bradford League. He was delighted that I'd been chosen."

So on the morning of Friday the 21st of July 1950 he boarded the trolleybus from Manningham Lane to Forster Square and from there took the train to London. He sat alone in the carriage, gathering his thoughts, as the steam train sped him towards the capital. There he alighted to find the pavements still wet from torrential rainstorms earlier in the day.

Carrying a mackintosh, a single case of clothes and a cricket bag, he made his way across central London to reach the hotel around four o'clock. It was a simple establishment and, as a teetotaller, the lack of alcohol did not trouble him. He had a cup of tea and waited quietly for his team-mates to arrive.

"It was a big moment in my life."

There would be no Norman Yardley. The gentleman skipper was at Trent Bridge, captaining England. No Len Hutton, out of action with a bad bout of lumbago. No Willie Watson, still with England's World Cup football side in South America, and no Brian Close, on National Service. But even without this quartet, the county had disposed of Leicestershire in two days at Harrogate and were close on the heels of Lancashire in the championship table.

Bob Appleyard had been born in 1924, the son of a railwayman. His interest in cricket had developed in the 1930s, when Yorkshire had won seven championships in nine years. Then in 1946, while he was still in the Royal Navy, he followed their scores as they made it eight titles out of ten. He was typical of his generation; he expected the White Rose county to finish every summer in first place.

Now he sat on his own in the temperance hotel. That pre-war team – with Hedley Verity, Herbert Sutcliffe, Bill Bowes, Maurice Leyland and the young Len Hutton – were the heroes of his growing years, and now he was to pull on the sweater himself.

"I hung around till about 6.30, and nobody arrived. Then I thought I'd better go for a meal so I wandered up into Knightsbridge."

Restaurant meals were still subject to rationing. He ordered meat and two veg, ate slowly and returned to Queen's Gate. "When I got back, there was still nobody there."

It was Friday the 21st of July, 1950. In London there was a two-year plan to convert the capital's tramways to buses, and road repairs were everywhere, in preparation for the following summer's Festival of Britain. Petrol had just come off rationing, rising to three shillings a gallon, while the Ford motor company was launching two new models, the Consul and the Zephyr.

For entertainment that night, there was a new Rodgers and Hammerstein musical, 'Carousel', at Drury Lane, and the songs were already whistled and sung in the streets. 'When I Marry Mister Snow', 'June is Bustin' Out All Over' and, of course, 'You'll Never Walk Alone'.

Walk on through the wind, walk on through the rain,
Though your dreams be tossed and blown.
Walk on, walk on, with hope in your heart,
And you'll never walk alone.

Meanwhile the world's highest paid singer, Frank Sinatra, was on his first visit to England, appearing at the London Palladium. 'A trim, well-spoken, gay young man,' the *Times* newspaper called him. 'The best of his songs deal in scraps of popular philosophy about falling in and out of love.'

But the quiet Bradfordian, waiting on his own in the temperance hotel, was in no mood for such diversion. Apart from keeping in touch with the Test match score at Trent Bridge – close of play: England 223 all out, the West Indies 479 for three – his thoughts were on the day that lay ahead of him.

"Being my first match, I wanted an early night," he recalls, "but nine o'clock seemed a bit too early. So I stayed up till ten."

There was still no sign of the rest of the Yorkshire side at ten so he went upstairs to the twin-bedded room that he and Alec Coxon had been allocated, changed into his pyjamas and settled himself for a refreshing night's sleep.

What a turn his life had taken in the last month!

In mid-June he had been just another bowler in the Bradford League, working all week for Short's, then on Saturday afternoons taking wickets for

Bowling Old Lane. He bowled medium-fast, with a run-up of 16 paces, and, although he had his share of good days in the league, there were others who took more wickets and at a lower cost. Even in this summer of 1950, when he made his breakthrough to the county side, he only finished in 22nd place in the Bradford League averages.

"He was just another seamer," Norman Horner, a young batsman with Queensbury, recalls. "There were plenty like him."

Like so many men of his age, Bob had lost six vital summers to the war. In 1938 he had been a star in the Bradford Schools side, a 14-year-old who might have caught the county's eye. But by 1946 he was 22, he was starting again, and his performances in the league were not special. Now four years on, there was a new generation emerging, spearheaded by the extra quick Freddie Trueman, the 19-year-old miner's son from Maltby. It was probably only the fact that Ernest Holdsworth, Chairman of the county club, was president of Bowling Old Lane that led to Bob's being invited to play for the Yorkshire second eleven. The Colts, as they were called.

"I wouldn't say that I thought my chance had passed. I was trying to be a better bowler for Bowling Old Lane. As far as I was concerned, I was serving my apprenticeship in cricket."

On June the 28th, the day after his 26th birthday, he travelled to York to play for the first time for the county second eleven. It was his first two-day match. It was also his first two-innings match, though in the event Cheshire only batted once, making 311 for six. The other bowlers – Aspinall, Barraclough, Mason, Smales – had all played for the first team, but it was the debutant from Bradford whose figures stood out at the end of a long day in the field: 24 overs, four wickets for 29 runs. 'From the Colts' point of view,' the *Yorkshire Post* wrote, 'the outstanding feature was Appleyard's bowling.'

The following week he took another two days' leave to play at Knypersley in Staffordshire where, by a happy coincidence, he was introduced to the great Sydney Barnes, nearing eighty years old but still an erect and alert man, still copying legal documents for Staffordshire County Council in his beautiful copperplate handwriting.

Barnes was a legendary figure from cricket's Golden Age before the Great War, and he was still in 1950 England's greatest wicket-taker in Test history. A tall man with a high bowling action, he perfected so many variations of grip and flight that he could trouble the best batsmen on any type of pitch. He played for Staffordshire into his sixties, but his appearances in the first-class game had been few. He preferred to earn his money in the leagues, bowling with unparalleled success for Saltaire in Bradford from 1915 to 1923. In those nine summers he took 904 wickets at an average of only 5.26, and he almost bankrupted the club with his wage demands.

In 1928, at the age of 55, he turned out for Wales and took twelve wickets against the touring West Indians, who reckoned him the best bowler they faced all summer. The following year, playing for the Minor Counties against the South Africans, he bowled 32 overs in three hours and took eight wickets for

41 with, according to his fellow bowler R.J.O. Meyer, 'the kind of stuff I had not thought existed outside of dreamland.'

Fred Trueman recalls a story John Arlott told of Barnes when he was coming to the end of his Staffordshire career in the 1930s. "There was a hold-up in play, and people were asking him about all his different grips. And in the finish one of them said, 'Well, can you show us with the stumps?' He said, 'Yes, for a pound.' He was very money-conscious, was Sydney Barnes. So they went in the nets and put up one stump, and he said, 'I'll bowl you the off-cutter.' He ran up, bowled it and knocked down the stump.' 'Can you do it with the leg-cutter as well?' they asked. 'Yes, for another pound,' he said. So they scratched around for another pound, and he hit the stump again with a leg-cutter. He must have been one of the greatest bowlers there's ever been."

"People were still talking about him when I was playing in the Bradford League," Bob says. "He was a legend. Leonard, George Hirst, Bill Bowes, they were all of the opinion that he was the best bowler of all time. For me, as a young man, he was in a bracket with Wilfred Rhodes and George Hirst. It was like meeting God. It was a very special moment in my life, to have met him."

Who knows what they discussed that day at Knypersley? Bob has no memory of the old man demonstrating bowling grips, but by a magical coincidence, perhaps inspired by Barnes, it was in this game against Staffordshire that Bob began to extend his bowling repertoire. 'SF' was a relentless bowler, probing the batsman with constant changes of pace and flight, the master of a multitude of grips, and that was the type of bowler that Bob would aspire to be.

At this stage of his career, however, Bob was just an honest-to-goodness medium-fast bowler, with few of the subtleties that he would later acquire.

"It was a quantum leap, going from Bowling Old Lane to the Yorkshire second team, and in many ways it was to my advantage. The game was longer, and the fielders were better. Somehow I found it easier to play a better class of cricket. But I realised that it wasn't enough just to come in and bowl as fast as I could. I had to be doing more with the ball. It was in that match that I experimented with bowling off-breaks. I still took my full run, and I started slipping them in. The grip was very different so I didn't fool the better batsmen, but the ball still had to be played."

He had learned how to spin the ball as a boy before the War, but he had never bowled spinners in a match. "I just fiddled about with them in the nets." Yet at Knypersley, on a pitch that was taking some turn, he mixed seam with spin, all off a 16-pace run, and he captured seven first innings wickets, all bowled, for 41 runs.

"I bowled well," he says. "I was in control."

When Staffordshire batted again, Yorkshire's new-ball bowlers – Freddie Trueman and the experienced Ron Aspinall – again made no headway, and this time the newcomer from the Bradford League bowled 20.5 overs and took eight wickets for 21 runs. His match return of 15 wickets for 62 runs remains to this day the best ever recorded by a Yorkshire bowler in second eleven or minor county competition.

An 18-year-old Ray Illingworth also played in that match at Knypersley. "Bob had a tree behind him," he says, "and there wasn't much of a sight screen. He suddenly started bowling an off-cutter as a slower ball and, with the dark background, the batsmen weren't picking it up."

It is a romantic tale, a great bowler whose breakthrough came as a result of a badly positioned tree, a tree that has long since been removed, but the older members of Knypersley Cricket Club are insistent that it is not true. "It was an oak tree," says Ron Cooper, then first eleven captain. "The tug-of-war team used to practise on it. It was nowhere near behind the bowler's arm. It would have been at wide long on. And there was nothing wrong with the sight screens."

Whether there was or was not a tree to assist his bowling, Bob took his opportunity in those two days in July 1950. "That match at Knypersley really started him off," Ray Illingworth says.

Fortune plays its part in cricket, as it does in life. At the other end from Bob at Knypersley was Ken Smales, an off-spinner who had started the summer in the Yorkshire side, capturing the headlines in the match against the West Indian tourists at Bradford, a game he still recalls.

"It was a sticky wicket," he says, and he can still recite his exact figures. "I took five for 44 and two for 29, including the wickets of Weekes and Worrell. But the selection committee picked the teams for the next games before we bowled, and they put Alan Mason in instead of me. And I never got back in."

At Knypersley, while Bob was taking his fifteen wickets, Ken Smales – later to play with success for Nottinghamshire – managed only two in each innings. "I got seven wickets against the West Indians," he says ruefully, "and I never played another game for Yorkshire."

After his success at Knypersley Bob Appleyard received a summons to travel the next week to Edinburgh. Yorkshire were playing a three-day friendly against Scotland, and Freddie Trueman had pulled a leg muscle. He and the young batsman Norman Horner were being given their chance.

Just a fortnight had passed since his Colts debut at York. Now he was going to be changing with the Yorkshire first team – with Norman Yardley and Len Hutton, captain and senior professional, the last survivors of that great pre-war side that he had idolised.

"You went into the dressing room, and you spoke when you were spoken to. And you sat in the corner. You made sure you didn't sit in the senior professional's place. Wherever you went as a side, people had their favourite places in the dressing room. You found that out by trial and error. If you put your bag on the wrong seat, it would soon be out in the corridor."

"There was a real sense of regime," his fellow debutant Norman Horner recalls. "There was a certain pecking order, and you didn't interfere with it. I went to Warwickshire the next year, and it was totally different. With Tom Dollery as captain, you just enjoyed yourself."

"In a way, it was easier for me," Bob thinks. "I was already 26. I had a good job, and I knew the ways of the world. I'd been in the Navy in the War, after all, so I was used to a certain regimentation."

At Edinburgh Norman Horner opened the innings alongside Len Hutton, making 36 to the great man's 79 as Bob looked on with admiration. "Leonard was my hero," he says. "He was everybody's hero."

Never mind Don Bradman. When in 1938 Hutton broke the Test record with his innings of 364 against Australia, all Yorkshire was of one mind. "He was the best in the world. And he was a Yorkshireman. And that meant that we had the best in the world."

But Hutton was suffering at Edinburgh. "He had lumbago, and he couldn't field. We had a masseur, Bright Heyhirst. He was just a rubber. And he got him on the table. There was a gas ring in the room and a big iron kettle, and he boiled up some water. He opened up all Leonard's pores with hot towels and rubbed all this hot stuff into his back. On the train going back, his back was so hot and painful that he had to stand most of the journey against the open carriage window."

Hot stuff? "That's what we called it. When Bright retired and some bills came in, they were from an equestrian supplier. They used this stuff on horse's fetlocks. Whether it was to make the horses jump, I'll never know. It certainly made us jump."

Norman Horner scored 43 in the second innings while Bob Appleyard finished with match figures of 26 overs, five wickets for 41. As a result both were selected to play at The Oval the following week.

For cricket statisticians, the pair of them made their first-class debuts in Edinburgh. But that is not how Bob thinks of it. The game at Scotland was not an important one. All his life he has thought of the Oval match as his first appearance for Yorkshire.

As a Bradford schoolboy before the War he had imagined himself playing for the county and, though his life had taken many turns since then, he had never given up on the dream.

"I still wanted to play for Yorkshire, but the ambition didn't dominate everything."

Now, in a remarkable four weeks, he had been catapulted from Saturday afternoon cricket against Baildon Green and Queensbury, villages that stood on the hills above the city of Bradford, to a place in the Yorkshire side, taking on fellow championship contenders Surrey in front of a great Saturday crowd. His mind was racing as he lay in the temperance hotel bed. He was on the eve of his greatest challenge.

Sleep did not come easily, and it was gone midnight before he drifted off.

Then at about one o'clock the door crashed open, the electric light was on and his room-mate was blundering about.

Alec Coxon was to be Bob's new ball partner in the morning, a kind man whose rough edges and outspoken manner had led him into several altercations with authority.

"He was chuntering away. He'd been out somewhere. Some girl had given him a Queen Anne lighter, and he was going to mend it for her. He was a bit of an engineer."

The night remains alive in his memory, though fifty-three years have passed. "He's in the sink, cleaning his teeth. Then he's in bed, and two minutes later he's snoring. And I'm awake. And I don't get to sleep for a long time after that. He's snoring away in the other bed. Then at seven o'clock he's up, fresh as a lark, and in the bowl again. 'Come on,' he says, 'it's time to get up.' And off we go. That was my first introduction to Yorkshire cricket."

It was Saturday the 22nd of July 1950. The *Times* newspaper, running to only ten pages as a result of print shortages, reported American forces being driven back by Communist fighters in Korea. "Dark shadows hang over the progress of mankind," the Conservative leader Winston Churchill declared.

There was a proposal for an X certificate for films 'wholly adult in conception and treatment' and a declaration by the Methodist Conference in Bradford that inter-racial marriage 'did not break any law of God'. At a public meeting in Liverpool, called to discuss the spread of tuberculosis, a Doctor C.O. Stallybrass said that the pre-war levels of sanatorium accommodation were no longer adequate. 'The long waiting lists for hospital treatment are in the highest degree tragic.'

But none of this was on the mind of Yorkshire's newest cricketer as he arrived in the dressing room at The Oval, waiting for the stand-in captain Don Brennan to call him up to the table to collect his remuneration.

As an uncapped player his wage for this away match was fifteen pounds, less National Insurance, and out of that he had to pay his travel, hotel and meal expenses.

"But really money didn't come into consideration. You'd have given your eye-teeth to play for Yorkshire. You thought you were privileged to be playing."

"Normally twelfth man was responsible for getting all the luggage onto the train and to the ground," Norman Horner remembers. "But for some reason on that occasion I was doing it. I had to take it by taxi to The Oval and pay all the fares and the tips. Then, after the captain had paid us, it was my job to go round and get back my expenses."

Did that take long? "I got most of it eventually, but it could be a little difficult with one or two of them."

At half past eleven, with the atmosphere damp and the pitch green, the Yorkshire team took the field. The left-handed Laurie Fishlock took guard, and Alec Coxon ran in to bowl the first over from the pavilion end.

Coxon was not a fast bowler, but then few were in the immediate post-war years. Yorkshire had resumed in 1946 with their pre-war opening attack: Bill

Bowes, 37 years old and still recovering from his time as a prisoner-of-war, and Frank Smailes, 36 and never more than medium pace. Coxon was their first new recruit in that summer of 1946, and even he was 30, though he only admitted to 29. 'He was impressively industrious,' according to J.M. Kilburn in his history of Yorkshire cricket, 'but he was always nearer the artisan than the artist.'

One Test appearance against the Australians in 1948 marked his progress, but in the dressing room there was an altercation with Denis Compton and he was never selected again. "He was all right with me," Bob says, "but he could be bombastic, very aggressive on and off the field. He didn't take any prisoners."

Coxon played a prominent part in the Yorkshire team that shared the championship with Middlesex in 1949. Now in 1950 at the age of 34 – or 33, as he would have it – he was enjoying his best season, high in the national averages and carrying the new ball attack.

"He could go on all day. He was like Glenn McGrath: fast-medium, very accurate, a whippy kind of bowler. He didn't charge in like a lunatic. He bowled within himself, and he was very economical. He didn't give anything away. I learned a lot from him about pacing myself."

The two of them, the new recruit and the hardened professional, bowled without a break for almost the whole morning session. Coxon conceded only two runs from his first eight overs, having Fishlock caught at short leg, while Bob, coming in from the Vauxhall end, took his first wicket when he slipped in an off-break. "I took my full run, with the field still set for out-swing, and I bowled this off-break. It landed right on the spot. Fletcher was batting and, because it was slow and different and because he'd never seen me bowl one before, he took a swipe at it, missed and was bowled."

It was a magical moment, though not all captains in the Yorkshire tradition would have appreciated it. There was a story from the 1930s that Bill Bowes, as a young man, sent down a slower ball, only to be confronted by his captain Brian Sellers. "You're paid to bowl fast," he was told. "I've got others in the team who can do that."

Leg-spinner Eddie Leadbeater also recalls experimenting with an off-break in the 1951 Roses match at Sheffield. "It was just before lunch, and I'd never done it before. I ran up to bowl to Geoff Edrich, and I bowled this off-spinner. It just pitched nicely, turned and bowled him. Norman Yardley came up. He said, 'I've set your field for leg-spin, not off-spin.' It was the only time I got a rollocking from him."

By contrast, Bob received no admonishment for his off-break to Fletcher, and he followed his first success by bowling the promising Cambridge undergraduate Peter May for a duck. Then he moved the ball away to have Bernie Constable caught in the gully. He was in his eleventh over, and he had taken three wickets for 18 runs. The *Times* reporter was impressed: 'Appleyard, who has a high and virile action, is distinctly fast, and he was able to make the ball come off the pitch at varying heights.' 'He bowled like a veteran,' the *Yorkshire Post* reckoned. 'His command of length was remarkable for a debutant. His run was smooth, and he showed splendid stamina and zest.' By three o'clock Surrey were all out. Coxon, five for 51. Appleyard, four for 47.

Rain on Sunday made the pitch on Monday ideal for the spinners, and wickets fell so fast that Yorkshire were travelling back to Bradford that evening, victors by seven wickets and leapfrogging Lancashire at the top of the championship table. Bob was only required to bowl two overs in the second innings, but he was a contented man on the train back to Bradford. Once again he had raised his game to cope with the demands of a higher level.

"Often I felt that the better the opposition, the better I bowled. For some reason I didn't always bowl well when the opposition was less than top grade. If a young lad came in, first match, I could never get him out."

He pauses to reflect on the reason, offering a suggestion that will surprise those who only know him by reputation. "Whether I was too soft, I don't know."

He played for Yorkshire in the next match at Hull, taking the wickets of Crapp and Milton in an innings victory over Gloucestershire.

The Yorkshire team at Hull, July 1950

Standing (left to right): Vic Wilson, Frank Lowson, Johnny Whitehead, Bob Appleyard, Billy Sutcliffe, Ted Lester, Herbert Walker (scorer)
Seated: Bright Heyhirst (masseur), Eddie Leadbeater, Jackie Firth, Johnny Wardle, Geoffrey Keighley, Alec Coxon, Harry Halliday
Norman Yardley and Don Brennan were playing for the Gentlemen at Lord's, Len Hutton was unfit

But as at The Oval he spent the second innings in the outfield, his medium-fast bowling superfluous as the two spinners Leadbeater and Wardle shared all ten wickets. Such inactivity was a new experience, one that gave him further food for thought.

"That was a turning point for me. I felt I could be bowling, and I didn't enjoy standing at fine leg and long on. I wanted to be part of the action. I wanted to be a strike bowler in all conditions, on all types of pitches."

So what was his solution?

"Had I been an 18-year-old I doubt if I would have recognised the signs. But I decided that I had to have a second string to my bow."

Up to this point he had been a medium-fast bowler. He had experimented with a few off-breaks. Now the thought was hatching that he could bowl spells in both styles. All he needed was practice time, and he could get down to that in the winter.

On the Saturday he returned to Bowling Old Lane, taking just one wicket as Great Horton made 200 for five. The following week he spent all five days, selling lifts and cranes. With no further triumphs in the Bradford League, he needed to take only two more days' leave, for one last Colts match at Scunthorpe.

His golden spell had lasted just one month.

Nevertheless, when *Wisden* was published the following year, the full Minor Counties averages showed him in first place, with 29 wickets at an average of 7.89 each. More remarkably, he also appeared in the full first-class averages, his 11 wickets at 16.09 sufficient to put him in fifth place, between Jim Laker and Brian Statham. They were good figures, but they gave no hint of what was to follow in that remarkable summer of 1951.

When the summer of 1950 ended, Yorkshire finished in a disappointing third place in the championship table and J.M. Kilburn, in his season's summary, failed to spot the potential of the 26-year-old from Bowling Old Lane. 'Yorkshire,' he wrote, 'were always in need of a fast bowler and an off-spinner.'

Their need was even greater when the committee decided to dispense with the services of Alec Coxon. "I thought that was a bad decision," Bob says. "Alec had ruffled a few feathers, and he was a bit abrasive. But it didn't make sense. He was such a good player, not past his best at all, and he was a good bat – and a good catcher. I know he was supposed to have thumped Denis Compton, but he was just a hard-working, hard-playing Yorkshireman. He was very helpful to me."

By January, Bob was driving across to Leeds to attend nets at Headingley's Winter Shed. Maybe, as he suggests, if he had been 18 years old, he would have thought that his game was already sufficient for success. But he was not 18, he was 26, and he was determined to improve his bowling. It had always been his dream to play cricket for Yorkshire, not just two or three times in one summer but as a vital performer in the side. He had quickly realised the limitations of his medium-fast bowling, and he wanted to develop his repertoire so that he could bowl on all pitches, not spend long sessions in the outfield while the spinners were in action. He was an intense man, a thinking cricketer, and he was preoccupied with the challenge that had been posed by his first experiences of county cricket. As J.M. Kilburn was to write of him, 'He was never a self-satisfied bowler, content with what he was doing and could do.'

"Why did Yorkshire take so long to find Bob Appleyard?" Trevor Bailey, later his England team-mate, was wont to ask. But Bob rejects the question.

"I was a late developer. That's why I'm always suspicious of people writing youngsters off, especially spin bowlers. Hardly a decent spin bowler has completed their apprenticeship before 25 or 26 years old. Spin bowlers are going to get a lot of stick. So, if a youngster comes into the game and has one or two bad days, he can have the confidence knocked out of him. Whereas if you are like me and you've played a few years as a seamer, you know the drill. You can cope with the bad days without losing confidence. My late arrival was to my advantage, really. I was a more mature cricketer."

His entry in the *Playfair Cricket Annual* for 1951 was brief. Just three short lines, where Les Ames above him had 32:

> **APPLEYARD, Robert** (Yorks.) B. Brad-
> ford 27/6/1924. Right medium-fast bowler.
> Right-hand bat. Debut 1950 – 2 matches.

Little can any of the young Yorkshire hopefuls in the Winter Shed have realised what was to come, how quickly his *Playfair* entry would expand. No bowler in the long history of cricket has had such a remarkable first full summer as Bob Appleyard enjoyed in 1951, and so much of it followed from his hard work on those winter evenings at Headingley.

"Net practice is so important," he says. "That's where you learn your skills, then you go out and do it in the middle. A lot of cricketers don't spend enough time working in the nets."

> *Walk on, walk on, with hope in your heart,*
> *And you'll never walk alone.*

A keen mind. A determined spirit. And a heart filled with hope. Another summer lay ahead.

BOWLING FIGURES 1950

for Yorkshire

			First innings				*Second innings*			
July 12,13,14	Edinburgh	Scotland	10	3	19	2	16	7	22	3
July 22,24	The Oval	Surrey	23.4	3	47	4	2	0	2	0
July 26,27,28	Hull	Gloucestershire	28	5	73	2	4	0	14	0

Matches	*Overs*	*Maidens*	*Runs*	*Wickets*	*Average*
3	83.4	18	177	11	16.09

for Yorkshire Second Eleven

			First innings				*Second innings*			
June 28,29	York	Cheshire	24	8	29	4				
July 5,6	Knypersley	Staffordshire	20.3	3	41	7	20.5	10	21	8
July 10,11	Thirsk	Northumberland	16	6	39	2	24	8	53	4
August 17,18	Scunthorpe	Lincolnshire	29	13	46	4				

Matches	*Overs*	*Maidens*	*Runs*	*Wickets*	*Average*
4	134.2	48	229	29	7.89

CHAPTER 2

LIVING LEGEND OR BLOODY-MINDED YORKSHIREMAN

The Genesis of this Book

This book was sought by several publishers in 1955.

Bob Appleyard had just returned from a triumphant tour of Australia and New Zealand. It had been a dramatic series, with England winning the Ashes down under for the first time since the Bodyline controversy of 1932/33, and interest was so great that no fewer than fourteen accounts of the tour were on sale during the following English summer.

Twelve men represented England in the three Test victories, and all but one have told their stories in autobiographies, some two and three times. Ten of them have also been the subject of full-length biographies, not to mention all the books – technical, historical, humorous – which they have written or to which they have lent their names.

Hutton, Cowdrey, Compton, May, Tyson, Evans, Statham, Bailey, Graveney, Edrich and Wardle. The eleven of them have spawned more than fifty titles. Yet the twelfth, Bob Appleyard, has never gone into print.

"I'd have been more attractive to a publisher in 1955," he admits. "When I was in Australia, I got a letter from an agent, offering me an advance payment of £250, which was a lot of money then, and I did consider it. But at the time I didn't feel I knew enough about anything."

The years passed. All too soon his playing days were over, and he became immersed in the challenges of a business career. His family was growing up, and his work took him all over the world. There was no time for looking back.

Retirement might have provided the moment to settle to the book, but he preferred to re-engage with Yorkshire cricket, joining the county club's committee. There were battles to be fought with Geoffrey Boycott and his supporters, a campaign to bring cricket back to the Bradford Park Avenue ground, the establishment of the Yorkshire Academy and the raising of funds for the Sir Leonard Hutton Foundation Appeal.

Bob Appleyard turned seventy in 1994, and there was still no sign of his story being committed to paper. Don Mosey, the *Test Match Special* commentator, wanted to write it, but ill-health prevented him. Then Derek Hodgson, cricket writer on *The Independent*, met Jack Sokell, long-time chairman of the Wombwell Cricket Lovers' Society.

"Surely somebody's going to do Bob," Jack said, "while he's still with us."

At the time Derek lived in the Cotswolds, but the remark spurred him to make a series of visits to interview Bob in Ilkley. The shape of a book emerged, then a synopsis was sent to several publishers.

Forty-five years earlier they would all have said yes, but now the replies were depressingly similar. "Robson Books were the most encouraging," Derek recalls. "We sent them some sample chapters, but in the end they said that the reps felt that it would be difficult to sell. Some of the other publishers even asked, 'Who's Bob Appleyard?'"

Derek returned to Yorkshire, to a house only three miles from Bob, but the project was put on hold. They still met, however. "Well, if we ever get back to the book," Bob would say whenever their conversation took an interesting turn, "we must remember to include that."

So who is Bob Appleyard?

Because his career at the highest level was so short, because he did not stay in the eye of the media in his later life, because – in the words of Don Mosey – 'he did not court personal popularity and did not achieve it', Bob Appleyard has slipped into the background of cricket history in a way that belies the greatness he attained in those few extraordinary years in the 1950s.

In January 1988, to coincide with Australia's bicentennial celebrations, England's cricketers agreed to visit Australia to play a single Test match at Sydney. Prince Charles flew out with the Ashes urn, and the Gestetner Company organised the playing of a parallel Test on computer, the English and Australian teams to be chosen from all those cricketers who were still alive. Living Legends, they were called.

The England team was selected by Len Hutton, Colin Cowdrey and Ian Botham, and they decided to appoint Hutton as captain. Boycott was chosen as his opening partner. Peter May, Denis Compton and David Gower completed the specialist batting line-up, with Ian Botham at number six filling the all-rounder's berth. Alan Knott pipped Godfrey Evans to the keeper's gloves after the toss of a coin. Fred Trueman and Harold Larwood were the fast bowlers, bringing disappointment to Alec Bedser, and the final two places were set aside for a pair of spinners for the turning Sydney wicket.

Colin Cowdrey summarised the selectors' deliberations:

> **Derek Underwood** is one of the great England bowlers, yet it was felt that **Tony Lock**'s exceptional record in Australia in the later part of his career put him marginally ahead of Underwood.
>
> **Titmus**, **Illingworth** and **Allen** all laid claim to a place, each had good records, but **Bob Appleyard**, in the short period that health allowed him to play for England, was able to demonstrate without doubt that he was one of the greatest bowlers that there has been. He possessed astonishing accuracy, bowling from a great height. A slow medium off-cutter was his stock ball, interspersed with a seamer, an away-swinger and, by way of contrast, a genuinely spun slow off-spinner – and he could throw in a lethal yorker. He pursued each batsman's weakness with a tenacity and zeal all his own. In the way that English batsmen found O'Reilly difficult to master and score against, Appleyard

was rarely mastered and it was a desperate blow, to both Yorkshire and England, that ill-health cut his career so short.

And so, for this particular match in these particular conditions, **Appleyard** wins the first spinner's place.

And, because he is so accurate and can be guaranteed to hold an end for the captain, we can afford the luxury of playing **Doug Wright**, a match-winner capable of bowling out the best players at any time. If he could be expensive, his record shows that he took his wickets in less overs than most other bowlers.

So **Appleyard** and **Wright** comprise the selectors' choice of spinners.

Unfortunately the computer programmer did not share the same view of the bowlers' strengths and, though Bob dismissed both Neil Harvey and Greg Chappell, he proved more expensive than his fellow spinner.

"At all the intervals," Bob recalls, one of several England 'legends' who flew out for the real match, "they were announcing the score in the computer Test. On the first day Bradman was out cheaply, and there was a real groan all round the ground."

Bradman, caught Botham, bowled Larwood, 8.

"We all knew that he was going to get a century in the second innings."

At lunchtime on the second day, while Hutton was on his way to a computer century, the fourteen living legends on the ground reported to the rear of the Bradman stand where each took his place in a vintage car for a parade around the outfield. Sir Donald Bradman led the way in a 1911 Rolls Royce, followed by Arthur Morris in a 1909 Delage. Further back, Boycott was assigned a 1905 Rover while Bob climbed into a 1911 Star.

Sir Donald Bradman in a 1911 Rolls Royce

"Geoffrey Boycott turned up in a cream-coloured suit, with his traditional panama hat. The driver of the Rover had probably been up all night polishing it but, as Geoffrey got into the car, he took out a big white handkerchief and placed it on the seat so as not to dirty his suit."

Bob chuckles with amusement at the memory of what followed.

"About a quarter of the way round, the Rover decided it had had enough and packed up. Geoffrey had to get out and start pushing. They pushed it to one side. Then, to Neil Harvey's delight, Geoffrey had to get into his car."

The weather was not kind to the real Test and, with Australia following on, David Boon batted out the last day for a dull draw. It was the final day in the press box for Bill O'Reilly, great leg-spinner-turned-reporter, who was retiring after 57 years in the game.

Events on the computer, however, were more exciting with the last England wicket falling with only two overs remaining. Bradman's second innings century left England 287 to win and, despite a 'thrilling' 65 by Compton, they lost by 37 runs, six wickets falling to the bowling of Bill O'Reilly himself.

O'Reilly as a bowler was a great fighter. 'He had the look of a man who might have founded or sacked a city,' Robertson-Glasgow once wrote. 'He had the inspired joy of battle. He would have bowled till his boots burst, and after. If only one cricket ball was left in the world, and that one came to pieces in his hand, he would whiz down a leg-break with the largest fragment.'

The real cricket contained no such fighting finale, but Bob enjoyed his trip hugely and he retains his invitation with pride. Thirty-three years after his only England tour, he had been chosen as his country's best living spinner – and chosen by Len Hutton and Colin Cowdrey. Another fifteen years have passed, and there have been no newcomers to challenge that judgement.

Yet the publishers ask, 'Who is Bob Appleyard?'

Bob Appleyard came late into the Yorkshire team and took 200 wickets in his first full season. The following summer he was laid low by tuberculosis, had half a lung removed and had to learn to walk again. Yet, after two summers of inactivity, he returned, winning a place in the England team and taking part in that memorable tour of Australia, where he topped the Test averages.

In his short career he took 708 wickets at an average of 15.48 runs each. Since the first world war, of all the many bowlers who have taken 200 wickets or more in their first-class careers, only Yorkshire's great slow left-armer Hedley Verity has finished with a lower average.

Bob Appleyard made his dramatic entry in 1951, and he was already in physical decline by 1956. He lost two years to tuberculosis, yet such were his achievements in the remaining four years that there are many who place him in the ranks of cricket's greatest bowlers.

"Bill Bowes told me," Hedley Verity's son Douglas remembers, "that he thought the greatest three right-arm non-speed bowlers in the history of the game were Sydney Barnes, Bill O'Reilly and Bob Appleyard."

"His is a name I would write down immediately if I was picking a World XI from this century," Fred Trueman wrote of Bob in 1988. "There just cannot have been a better off-break bowler."

But Bob's cricketing achievements are barely half the story. For this is a book about a man whose strength of purpose has triumphed over adversities that would have broken the spirit of most of us. And being the man he is, drawing on an inner faith and 'not one to court personal popularity', he has not sought sympathy or admiration for his struggles, certainly not sought to make money from the publication of his story. His share of the proceeds from this book will go to the Sir Leonard Hutton Foundation Appeal, to assist the development of cricket among young people in Yorkshire.

"All through my time in cricket," he says, "both in my playing days and on the Yorkshire committee, I've wanted to leave the game in better shape than I found it. That's all you can do, I think."

I, Stephen Chalke, took on this book from Derek Hodgson in the autumn of 2002. Much work had been done by Derek but Bob, ever the perfectionist, was looking for a further input. So I too have made a series of visits to Ilkley, where Bob has led me carefully through the details of his life.

He reached the age of 79 in the summer of 2003, and his physical stamina is not as great as it was five years ago. Hard sessions in the garden can leave him breathless, and he no longer plays golf. But his mental drive is still exceptional. If we pass more than a few minutes in idle pleasantries after my arrival, he grows restless. "We're wasting time," he interjects. "We need to get to work." A typical session would start at two o'clock and still be going strong at ten. The next morning we would be back in action by nine.

Then, after I have written up each section, he sits with his friend Ron Deaton and checks the text, line by line. Accuracy is vital, as it has always been in his life, whether he be working as an engineer, bowling in a Test match or cultivating his beloved alpines.

"We have a family motto," Bob says. "If a job's worth doing, it's worth doing well."

"On page 35," Ron says, telephoning through their corrections, "in the description of Bertie Buse's bowling, you've got the line, 'The trick is to get it swinging in the last yard.' Bob wants to change that to 'the last couple of yards'."

"Fine," I reply. "I assumed it was just a turn of phrase. I didn't think it was meant as an exact measurement."

"You've no idea," Ron says. "We spent twenty minutes on the floor with a tape measure."

Then there has been the saga of the revolver port door. It was a piece of equipment that Bob was involved in manufacturing during the war. You might think it an incidental detail in the life of a cricketer, but it has taken hours of work by us all to come up with a description that has satisfied Bob's desire for technical precision. "I think it's important to get these things right, don't you?"

he says, and, as an author, having one's work taken so seriously, it is impossible to disagree.

As the writing of the book has neared completion, he has started to make lists of topics that have not yet been included.

Some of them are hard to place in the text: "I don't think we've got in about Pele's last football match in New York. That was a very special moment in my life. ... Have I told you about the time at Bramall Lane when I had to show a delegation of Soviet mineworkers how to bowl off-breaks? ... I would like to say something about the Bedsers. They've put so much back into cricket over the years."

But mostly he is looking forwards, not back, wanting to improve the game now and anxious whether we have said enough about its problems. "I want to say something about four-day cricket. It's been a disaster; it's achieved nothing. The first two days don't mean anything. I'd like to see them try two-day matches with a single innings each. You'd get more starts, more results, and no loss of quality. ... There's too much feather-bedding of cricketers. You don't develop competitive spirit by feather-bedding. We need a tougher approach like the Australians have. These central contracts! Players should be made to earn their places in the England team by their form, not on their potential or past performances. ... County cricket has got to be strengthened. I think we need to say that in the book. And it's not strengthened by spending so much of the money on overseas players. We need to develop our own young cricketers."

For most old cricketers approaching eighty, these would be wistful observations on a game which they can no longer influence, but not for Bob. He is still wanting to be in the thick of it all, wanting to raise money for youth cricket, wanting to affect the development of the Yorkshire Academy and the University of Bradford's Centre of Cricketing Excellence.

Bob is a battler. He has had a tough life, taking many more knocks than most of us, but he has responded to each blow with a single-minded determination to pick himself up and keep fighting. He has been helped along the way by friends and in his adult life he has been blessed with a close and loving family around him – but much of his strength of purpose he has derived from within himself, not least from his deep-rooted Christian faith.

Initially I found him a rather austere character, not somebody who was easy company in a convivial sort of way. We always had to be 'getting on with things' or discussing the schedule ahead of us. Even in the garden, where most men potter about for relaxation, he is always seeking new achievements.

"When I gave up golf, I needed a fresh challenge so I got interested in alpines. I contacted one of the leading growers, Andrew Durance, a local consultant to the Royal Horticultural Society, and I suggested that I went over one day a week and gave him a hand in his nursery. I wanted to learn by doing what he did, not just reading the books.

"The most important thing with alpines is where you put them. Some need sun, some need shade; some need acid soil, some alkaline. And some of the plants are nurseryman's plants; they might last a year and die. Look at this blue Himalayan poppy. It needs a cool root, you've got to plant it in the shade. And this lewisia. It's survived the winter. Lewisias are very difficult, you know. You've got to plant them where the water drains away."

It is a beautifully kept garden, a delightful place to sit in peace on a sunny afternoon, but it is not in Bob's nature to pass time so idly. "There's always something to do. You sit down to relax, and you keep seeing jobs to do."

He is, in the modern terminology, 'a driven man' but it did not take me long to realise that, underneath his relentless drive, there lay great integrity and no mean intelligence.

"Bob's quite a deep thinker," I said one day to Ken Taylor, whose early years at Yorkshire overlapped with Bob's final ones. Ken had enough talent to play both football and cricket professionally and to train as an artist, but he is a more relaxed character, happy to stop the lawn mower and sit down for a chat.

"A deep thinker," he repeats. "Bob's that all right. That's his problem. I sometimes think he thinks too much for his own good. He's always thinking."

There have been plenty of people over the years who have found themselves at odds with Bob's thinking. He has a strong sense of right, and he is not one who gives way readily when he believes in something. That is an integral part of his personality, the same resolute personality that brought him back to triumphant fitness from a potentially fatal disease. For some, he was not an easy team-mate or fellow committee member, and perhaps as a result he has not been accorded the credit he has deserved, either for his playing career or for his unstinting contribution to Yorkshire cricket in more recent times.

Even now, in telling the story of his life, he is not seeking affection. He wants simply to put the record straight and to argue once again for the things in which he believes.

"This book will give you your proper place in cricket history," I suggest one day, and he is not impressed.

"No, that's not important," he retorts with energy. "I want to do something for Yorkshire cricket. There's so much going on. The game is at a threshold." And he is away again. "The Academy has been under-performing. I warned them five years ago. They've been playing too many matches and not doing enough skill training."

I am only 55 years old, but keeping up with him can be hard at times.

Bob has engaged at every stage with the words that I have sent him. He is a man whose trust has to be earned. There have been occasions when I have submitted chapters containing controversial material, and he has sought to have his own viewpoint expressed more strongly. We have locked horns, and at such moments I have begun to realise how formidable an opponent he can be, whether with a ball in his hand or on the other side of a committee table. He can be relentless in probing for the weaknesses in my argument.

Bob's trust in me has grown, however, and I have come to appreciate his battling spirit, how it is founded on a hard rock of personal integrity, how it has been forged out of great emotion.

There has been pain for him in revisiting certain episodes in his life, and he is not comfortable with the expression of too much feeling. More than once, I have seen tears well up in his eyes, sentences stopped as he fights down deep waves of feeling. He has not wanted the book to reveal that, but it is there.

"He is a very emotional man," his younger daughter Liz says. "He just doesn't like to show it. We always knew when he was close to tears, he used to lift up the newspaper so that we couldn't see his face."

He has fought so many battles in his life, and of course he has not won them all. But he does take great pleasure in recalling the victories.

"I'm not sure we've covered the Maxwell business properly," he says again, and he recounts more stories of his unhappy eighteen months as an employee of Robert Maxwell, the business tycoon and Labour MP. The two of them ended up in a legal dispute that generated 93 solicitors' letters and was set for a High Court hearing. Most people, confronted by the magnate's bullying tactics, buckled eventually – but not Bob.

"I know that Appleyard," Maxwell told one of his confidants. "He's a bloody-minded Yorkshireman. He'll take me all the way."

'A Bloody-Minded Yorkshireman.' Bob is proud of the epithet, and for a while we thought that it might make a good title for this book. Bob has been a thorn in the side of many over the years. He is a combatant, tackling his opponents with the same zest with which he has tackled the adversities of his health and personal life, determined that they would not get the better of him. He is single-minded, obdurate, a man who will fight all the way for what he thinks right. A Yorkshireman through and through.

But bloody-minded? I will leave that to you, the reader, to decide.

CHAPTER 3

THE BEGINNINGS OF BOWLING

May & June 1951

To take 200 first-class wickets in one summer is a great achievement, one that requires high skill and immense stamina. Only three bowlers have reached this figure since the second world war: Tony Lock, Tom Goddard and Bob Appleyard. In fact, in the last forty years, even adding in all the wickets from one-day cricket, no bowler has exceeded 160 in one summer.

To take 200 first-class wickets as a bowler with a long run-up is a feat of even greater stamina. Of the seven bowlers to reach 200 in the last 75 years, five have been spinners – Charlie Parker, Tich Freeman, Hedley Verity, Tom Goddard and Tony Lock – while just two, Alf Gover and Bob Appleyard, have arrived at the wicket after run-ups of fifteen yards or more.

To take 200 first-class wickets in one's first full summer, as Bob Appleyard did in 1951, is a unique achievement. No other bowler in the history of cricket has made the step up to the first-class game with such immediate success, his tally exceeding by 46 the record set by Wilfred Rhodes in 1898.

But to take 200 wickets in one's first summer off a 16-yard run-up and to be suffering all the while, unawares, from a life-threatening lung infection, it must rank as one of the most extraordinary achievements in all sport.

And it probably would not have happened if Bob had not arrived for his weekly net one cold February evening with a blister on his right index finger.

The Winter Shed at Headingley was a primitive building with a wooden floor and no heating. It contained just two cricket nets, with room for the bowlers to run in only seven yards. But this was where the Yorkshire players gathered two evenings each week from early February, along with their coaches, Emmott Robinson and Arthur Mitchell.

Robinson had been a character in the great Yorkshire side that won four consecutive championships in the early 1920s, while Mitchell grafted most of his runs in the '30s in a team that won the title seven times. Between them they had played with so many Yorkshire greats – Rhodes and Hirst, Sutcliffe, Leyland and Verity – and they passed on their keen technical awareness with an expectation that their successors would bring further triumphs.

"I couldn't wait to get started," Bob recalls, "so I used to go across in January. That winter especially. The previous summer I'd played three times in the first team, I'd smelled the first-class game, and I wanted to do everything I could to get in the side regularly."

He was still working in Bradford as a representative for Short's Lifts, and he was due to be married on the 28th of March to Connie Ledgard, whom he had met at the Bradford Dance Club. Her father had run a shop and wholesale business in Four Lane Ends, specialising in confectionery, but he had died in 1943 and now her mother kept it going. They were strong Methodists, and

Connie ran the Sunday School at the Methodist headquarters at Eastbrook Hall. Connie worked and lived with her mother on the premises of the business, and the plan was for Bob to move in after their marriage while they saved up for their own house.

On the evenings when he was due at the Winter Shed, he borrowed his future mother-in-law's 1937 Wolseley 14 and drove across to Headingley.

"Neither Emmott nor Arthur Mitchell ever had a car, they used to travel by train and bus, so I started asking them, 'Would you like a lift?' I used to drop Arthur at Baildon, in time for the last pint, then I'd take Emmott on to Bradford. And all the time I'd be picking their brains."

And what did they tell him?

"I remember Emmott saying to me, 'If tha's to be a bowler, tha knows tha hasta bowl five good balls an over, and the sixth hasn't to be a bad 'un.' I've never forgotten those words. During a long spell it's so easy to lose concentration and to send down a loose delivery at the end of an over. I kept remembering his advice in Australia, when it was hot and humid and we were bowling eight-ball overs."

Bob with Emmott Robinson in the Winter Shed

Bob was learning from his passengers, and he even found them of benefit when one evening, overtaking a slow trolley bus, a newly-fitted wheel on the Wolseley came off. It spun away, hit a wall and rolled off down the road, the passengers on the bus watching with amusement as Bob jumped out and headed after it.

"Unfortunately there was a police sergeant on the back step of the bus. He rang the emergency bell and booked me for driving an unroadworthy vehicle."

In court he was fined five shillings, the minimum amount for the offence. "My solicitor had mentioned the names of my passengers, and the magistrate asked me to pass on his best wishes to Emmott and Arthur."

It was in the Winter Shed during one of those evenings in early 1951 that the accident happened that transformed Bob's cricketing career.

Yorkshire's bowling attack was in transition. With Alec Coxon gone and Brian Close still on National Service, only Johnny Wardle of the bowlers in the Winter Shed was a capped player. Even with the young Freddie Trueman being pencilled in for an extended run in the first team, there were still vacancies for an off-spinner and a second new-ball bowler.

Bob knew that his medium-fast bowling would not be sufficient for him to hold his own at county level, and his first experiments with off-spin had intrigued the captain Norman Yardley. "He got me to bowl it more often, and he encouraged the coaches in the Winter Shed to help me to develop it."

After a few such sessions his spinning finger developed a blister, but neither Yardley nor Bob himself can have anticipated what would happen on the evening that the blister prevented him from bowling as usual. The batsman in the net was the 16-year-old Doug Padgett, and Bob still recalls his first delivery to him.

"So as not to stop bowling, I thought I'd bowl it off the middle finger. I ran up, and I found that I could bowl it much quicker than the normal off-break. I didn't even have to change my action. The wickets were on springs, I hit them, and they went all over the place. Arthur Mitchell came over. 'What's going on here?' he said. I said, 'Just watch this, Arthur,' and I did it again. He looked at me. 'If you can bowl like that, you can bowl any bugger out.'"

Now he was a two-in-one bowler. He could swing the new ball, he could bowl off-breaks at some speed, and he did not have to change his run-up. Little did he realise it as he drove Arthur and Emmott home that night, but his blister had created the solution to both Yorkshire's bowling vacancies.

It was the Spring of 1951. The War, in which Bob had served in the Royal Navy, had been over for nearly six years, but England was still rebuilding. Meat was rationed to eight pence worth per person per week, enough for just four ounces of rump steak; fuel prices were rising, with the National Coal Board importing coal; and the Labour Government suffered Cabinet resignations when it introduced prescription charges for false teeth and spectacles.

English cricket had drawn great crowds in the post-war years, but the Test side was still waiting for a new generation to emerge. The previous summer the West Indians, inspired by the young spinners Ramadhin and Valentine, had won for the first time in England, and in the winter England's tour of Australia ended in a crushing 4-1 defeat.

Yorkshire's Len Hutton, a survivor from pre-war years, carried the batting, averaging almost 80 in the two series, while the bowling depended heavily on the medium-pace of Alec Bedser.

The Yorkshire team, meanwhile, had a solid look to its batting, the first six the same as they had been when the championship title was shared with Middlesex in 1949. That was the summer in which Len Hutton hit 1,000 runs in both June and August and, though there were many in the South who preferred the debonair improvisation of Compton, purists in the North had no doubt who the premier batsman in England was. His opening partner Frank Lowson had modelled himself on Hutton, and on his best days it was hard to tell them apart.

Bob and Frank Lowson padding up in front of the old pavilion at Headingley
"The photographers used to leave their pictures in the dressing room, and it was considered a bit egotistical to take home photographs of yourself. But I've always been a bit of a collector so, when everybody else had gone, I'd put them in my bag."

Frank had played with Bob at Bowling Old Lane but, although he was a year younger, he was now starting his third summer in the Yorkshire side, his well-organised technique attracting so much attention that he played in a Test trial only three weeks after his debut. "He really was a star," Bob says, "especially on turning pitches. Anyone can play on a flat pitch but, if you wanted two batsmen to play for your life on a turner, against Laker and Lock, you'd pick Len and Frank."

The next three in the order were Vic Wilson, Ted Lester and Willie Watson. The hard-hitting left-hander with farmer's forearms, the wristy but unorthodox right-hander who could score as fast as any, and the calm, quiet left-hander who had missed most of the 1950 season playing in England's World Cup football team.

Then came the amateur captain Norman Yardley, a veteran of the triumphant pre-war days and now leading the side with all the quiet authority of one who had captained England in three of the previous four summers.

The wicket-keeper Don Brennan was the team's second amateur. Unusually tall and wearing distinctive white gloves, he kept with panache on wet pitches, his name starting to be mentioned as an alternative to Godfrey Evans in the England side. "He was as good as anybody when he was standing up to the wicket," Bob reckons.

Johnny Wardle had inherited the golden mantle of Yorkshire's slow left-armer from the legendary Hedley Verity, who had died in Italy in the war and who in turn had replaced Wilfred Rhodes, the greatest wicket-taker in all cricket history. "Personally I think Hedley Verity must be the best spin bowler this country has ever had. I talked to Bill Bowes, Len Hutton and Don Bradman about it, and they all agreed. The only question really was whether Hedley was better than Wilfred."

So did Johnny suffer by comparison? "Yes, of course he did. That's what happens in Yorkshire – like everybody compared Boycott with Hutton. At this time Johnny was a left-arm orthodox spinner but by 1956, when he'd perfected his chinamen and googlies, he was the most dangerous bowler in the country. He was deadly that winter in South Africa when he bowled his chinamen. Lock might have been better on a real turner, but Johnny could bowl on good pitches, when it was dry and the ball wasn't turning. If you asked Peter May who was the better on all wickets, he'd say Johnny Wardle."

The ninth man in the side was a Yorkshire rarity, a leg-spinner. Eddie Leadbeater – "a chirpy character" from the Huddersfield League – was fighting against a deep Yorkshire prejudice against such bowling. "They preferred to pin their faith in the left-arm orthodox spinners. The trouble with leg-spinners, throughout the history of the game, is that you can say to yourself, 'Keep five out, and you're going to get a long hop or a full-toss.' They were thought to be too expensive, and it wasn't the Yorkshire way to give away runs."

Bob pauses to reflect on the exceptions: "Eric Hollies and Bruce Dooland – but the best exception of course is Shane Warne."

That was nine men on the team sheet for the first games: Hutton, Lowson, Wilson, Lester, Watson, Yardley, Brennan, Wardle, Leadbeater. It was the remaining two bowling places that were not yet settled.

At Lord's, against the MCC, they tried out Trueman and Foord, the bespectacled schoolmaster from Scarborough, but, on an easy-paced pitch, they managed between them just one wicket in fifty overs. At Oxford it was the turn of Foord and Appleyard and, in a rain-ruined match, Bob was the first to make his mark, taking four undergraduate wickets. So it was he and Trueman who found themselves picked to play the South Africans at Bradford.

The poor South Africans. Their one-day match at Luton had been lost to the snow. They had suffered thunderstorms at Worcester. Now at Bradford rain washed away all play on the Saturday and, when they did get on the field on Monday, according to J.M. Kilburn in the *Yorkshire Post*, 'the wind was cold, the skies were dark, and dampness lay upon the field and its surrounds.'

"That sounds like Bradford in May," Bob chuckles. "I've played there in June when it's been snowing."

Yorkshire declared on 214 for four on the rain-affected pitch, and there was time in the evening for Bob to bowl his first spell for Yorkshire in his home city. "It was always my favourite ground," he says.

In his first over he had Eric Rowan playing on. "That wasn't a bad wicket. He was one of *Wisden*'s five cricketers of the year." Then, taking the place of Fred Trueman at the pavilion end, he removed in successive balls Endean, bowled off his pads, and Fullerton, caught at short fine leg. With the pitch still damp and five fielders around the bat on the leg side, he bowled McLean to reduce the South Africans to 27 for five. At this stage his figures were twelve overs, four wickets for nine runs.

He continued till the end of the day, 'lapsing from length only once or twice', by which time the South Africans had recovered to 67 for six.

"When it was dry, Bradford was a superb pitch to bat on. It was the favourite ground of Herbert Sutcliffe – and Leonard. But, if it rained and the sun came out, you got stickies. Jim Laker ruined a Test trial there."

The Test trial had been the previous May. Bowling for England against the Rest, Laker had taken eight wickets for two runs, thus preventing the selectors from viewing the young batsmen they had summoned. For that match the selectors also called up the young Fred Trueman but, as on this Monday evening against the South Africans, the conditions did not greatly suit him.

"It wasn't just that the pitches were not covered in those days. People forget that the run-ups weren't covered, either. So somebody like Fred couldn't run in."

On Tuesday morning, Bob took two more wickets as the South Africans were bowled out for 76. In the biggest match of his short career he had bowled 25 overs and taken six wickets, three more than the experienced Wardle at the other end.

"The ball lifted, which suited my style of bowling better than Johnny's. I bowled it quicker and from a steeper angle so it bit into the pitch and made an impression. That's how you get the ball to climb. Johnny relied more on revolutions so he'd spin it, and it would just skid through. Time after time that season, when I got wickets, he'd miss the boat."

Even amid their successes the new bowling partners were developing a rivalry. "There's nothing like a bit of healthy competition in the team."

In the *Yorkshire Post*, limited to only six pages, J.M. Kilburn found room for both praise and warning:

> Appleyard's final achievement was six wickets for 38, which was a distinguished performance and represented excellent bowling, even in favourable conditions. The figures should, however, be regarded with due sense of proportion and not transmuted into a millstone of inflated reputation for Appleyard. He bowled well, he does bowl well, but as yet he is scarcely beyond the beginnings of bowling, which is a difficult craft not learned in a day.

The beginnings of bowling? Bob laughs. "You should send that to the England selectors."

'Yorkshire and England,' Kilburn continued, 'cannot afford any more wastage through the arrested development of players from whom too much is expected too soon. "Give the man a chance" would be fair plea to those whose business or pleasure is to pass judgement.'

"The senior players always made sure we didn't go too far, too fast," Bob says.

The second innings brought no further success for Bob. This time, in a day of near-freezing temperature and intermittent rain and hail, Wardle and Trueman reduced the South Africans to 86 for nine. The few shivering spectators watched with mounting excitement as the last pair survived the final four overs. According to Kilburn, 'the South Africans are chilled to the marrow, so chilled that they could be forgiven, as one of them suggested, for thinking Bradford only a few miles from the North Pole. It has not been weather for English cricketers, let alone South Africans.'

Little improved in the next fortnight. The first two days at Hull were lost. The Roses match at Old Trafford drifted into a draw that caught the mood of the 'cold, grey weather'. At Fenner's J.M. Kilburn was moved to write, 'North and South and East and West, the cold winds blow through cricket.' Then the night before their match at Chesterfield more heavy rain fell, and Norman Yardley, winning the toss, found himself inspecting yet another sodden pitch.

"You couldn't rely on the weather forecasts. They weren't like they are today. And the pitches would change so much during a match. But Norman was an exceptional reader of pitches. He liked to put sides in, too. He thought it gave us a psychological advantage. There were many times when he put them in when other sides wouldn't have done. But, if he was thinking of doing it, he'd take the bowlers out and he'd say, 'What do you think?' And we'd say, 'Yes, send them in, we'll get them out.' And of course, as we'd made the decision, the onus was on us to do it. It was very clever captaincy."

As Bob talks, his mind makes comparisons with the present. "I don't know if Hussain would do that. He'd probably take out Fletcher, the coach. I can imagine what Fred would say. 'Well, send bloody Fletcher out to bowl then.'"

At Chesterfield Derbyshire were soon all out for 114, and by the end of the next day Yorkshire had won by seven wickets.

Kelly, caught Hutton, bowled Appleyard, 0
"Len would catch them behind him sometimes."

Bob's contribution was eight wickets in the match, his best tally to date, but his only memory is of a wicket he did not have to take. "Denis Smith had given us a bit of stick in the first innings and, as he was coming out in the second, Len said to me, 'Drop your quicker one on his boot.' Well, I was just a rookie. Len was the senior professional. So I did as I was told."

The fast yorker was another wicket-taking variant in the newcomer's armoury, and *Wisden* records the outcome: 'Smith, retired hurt, 0.'

Bob had been in the team for only three weeks, and he was still learning the etiquette of county cricket. "I ran up to bowl in one game and the batsman was backing up. In the league you ran him out so, instead of letting go of the ball, I swung my arm over and broke the wicket. Harold Elliott was the umpire. He just bent down and picked up the bails. 'Don't be so bloody silly,' he said and put the bails back on. If I could have crawled into a hole in the ground, I'd happily have done so."

Unlike most of the counties, Yorkshire did not own a ground, travelling between seven venues for their home matches. Hull and Scarborough were categorised as away games, with the players having to find overnight accommodation, while the second eleven were sent to places as diverse as Redcar and Doncaster, one hundred miles apart. Headingley staged a Test match but only three county games.

Bob drove his second-hand SS Jaguar to Huddersfield for the next match, against Warwickshire. Heavy overnight rain forced the groundsman to improvise a new pitch and, according to J.M. Kilburn, 'batting first was a speculation.' For the first time Bob took ten wickets in a match, but the pitch suffered further rain and, when Yorkshire batted a second time, needing 136 to win, they slumped to 49 all out.

It was Bob's seventh game of the summer, his tenth appearance in all for the county. "It was a disaster. It was the first time I'd ever played for Yorkshire and lost. I was devastated. We were brought up to win. I just didn't believe Yorkshire should ever lose."

On the face of it, defeat had been brought about by Warwickshire's leg-spinner Eric Hollies, bowling what he considered to be the best spell of his life against indifferent batting, but in the corner of the deflated dressing room Bob was sitting in silence, critically assessing his own performance.

Five for 71 in 26 overs, then five for 39 in 20. The county averages in the *Yorkshire Post* had him leading the way, with 38 wickets at 11.55 each. It was a start that would have thrilled most newcomers, but in the aftermath of this painful defeat he was not satisfied with his bowling.

"I thought I should have bowled better, especially in the first innings."

The next day at Bramall Lane, Sheffield, in front of 21,000 spectators – "We were disappointed if we didn't get 20,000 on a Saturday." – he removed both the Somerset openers and was described as 'much the most troublesome bowler'. But luck was not with him – 'He was edged or missed with regularity in each of his spells.' – and the West Countrymen, who had not beaten Yorkshire since 1903, were satisfied with a final score of 234, especially when Hutton was bowled before the close.

Only an hour and a half's play was possible on Monday but, hard on the heels of defeat by Warwickshire, it has left a deep mark in Bob's memory. "Bertie Buse came on, bowling little seamers, and they went like boomerangs. I've never seen a ball swing so much in my life – and late, too. Some bowlers get the ball to swing from the arm, but that's not the trick. The trick is to get it swinging in the last couple of yards."

Yorkshire subsided to 76 for nine, Buse taking six wickets, and the Somerset batsman Eric Hill recalls what followed in the evening. "We went to a stage show. We had our own box. A conjuror in orange tights with beautiful blondes and God knows what. We'd all had a few, celebrating Bertie's success – not at Bertie's expense, I should add – and all of a sudden he stood up unsteadily, looked at the audience, then at us, and he made this great announcement. I can still see him. 'Just like my f---ing bowling.'"

The next day was even more dramatic. The Yorkshire batsmen, following on, took the score to 269 for seven. 'The match was in balance again,' J.M. Kilburn wrote. 'Neighbour was speaking to neighbour, and spirit was so restored that Yorkshire, offering the reasonable proposition of 113 in 110 minutes, declared for their own interests, not Somerset's.'

Bob bowled Harold Gimblett – "He was my rabbit; I got him out all four times that summer" – and had his fellow opener Les Angell caught at short leg. Within ten minutes Somerset were five for three – 'They batted like panic-stricken schoolboys,' was Kilburn's verdict – and, when Bob bowled Stuart Rogers, they were 39 for five. Wardle did the remaining damage and, 'by six o'clock the unbelieving spectators were cheering their heroes to the dressing room.'

Kilburn's pen was flowing with the excitement:

> From the depths of distress and indignity Yorkshire rose to an astonishing victory. Writers of fiction would scarcely have dared to present quite so fantastic a picture, though no doubt the psychological novelists would have found material for two or three thousand pages. This was one of the times to remember with Crispin's Day and August 1926. It was such stuff as dreams are made on, and cricket to perfection.

"It was a wonderful declaration," Bob reflects, "and a great match to be playing in."

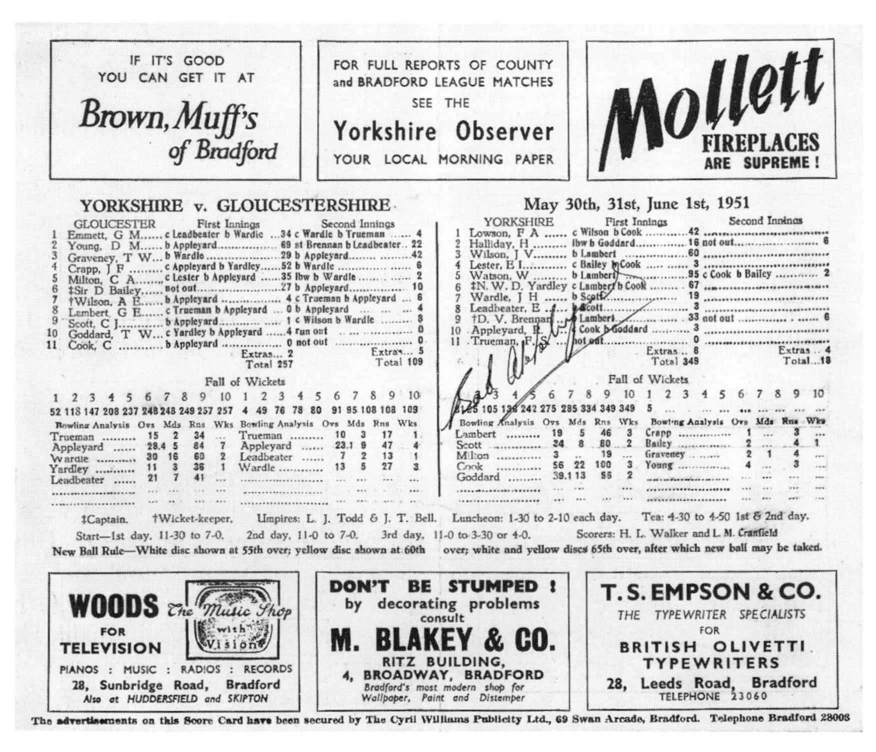

YORKSHIRE v. GLOUCESTERSHIRE — May 30th, 31st, June 1st, 1951

	GLOUCESTER	First Innings		Second Innings	
1	Emmett, G M	c Leadbeater b Wardle	34	c Wardle b Trueman	4
2	Young, D M	b Appleyard	69	st Brennan b Leadbeater	22
3	Graveney, T W	b Wardle	29	b Appleyard	42
4	Crapp, J F	c Appleyard b Yardley	52	b Wardle	6
5	Milton, C A	c Lester b Appleyard	35	lbw b Wardle	2
6	‡Sir D Bailey	not out	27	b Appleyard	10
7	†Wilson, A E	b Appleyard	4	c Trueman b Appleyard	6
8	Lambert, G E	c Trueman b Appleyard	0	b Appleyard	4
9	Scott, C J	b Appleyard	1	c Wilson b Wardle	8
10	Goddard, T W	c Yardley b Appleyard	4	run out	0
11	Cook, C	b Appleyard	0	not out	0
		Extras	2	Extras	5
		Total	257	Total	109

Fall of Wickets

	1	2	3	4	5	6	7	8	9	10
First Innings	52	118	147	208	237	248	248	249	257	257
Second Innings	4	49	76	78	80	91	95	108	108	109

Bowling Analysis	Ovs	Mds	Rns	Wks	Bowling Analysis	Ovs	Mds	Rns	Wks
Trueman	15	2	34	...	Trueman	10	3	17	1
Appleyard	28.4	5	84	7	Appleyard	23.1	9	47	4
Wardle	30	16	60	2	Leadbeater	7	2	13	1
Yardley	11	3	36	1	Wardle	13	5	27	3
Leadbeater	21	7	41	...					

	YORKSHIRE	First Innings		Second Innings	
1	Lowson, F A	c Wilson b Cook	42		
2	Halliday, H	lbw b Goddard	16	not out	6
3	Wilson, J V	b Lambert	60		
4	Lester, E I	c Bailey b Cook	3		
5	Watson, W	b Lambert	95	c Cook b Bailey	2
6	‡N. W. D. Yardley	c Lambert b Cook	67		
7	Wardle, J H	b Scott	19		
8	Leadbeater, E	b Scott	3		
9	†D. V. Brennan	b Lambert	33	not out	6
10	Appleyard, R.	c Cook b Goddard	3		
11	Trueman, F. S.	not out	0		
		Extras	8	Extras	4
		Total	349	Total	18

Fall of Wickets

	1	2	3	4	5	6	7	8	9	10
First Innings	[illegible]	[illegible]	105	13[illegible]	242	275	285	334	349	349
Second Innings	5	...	...	...	...	...	...	...	...	...

Bowling Analysis	Ovs	Mds	Rns	Wks	Bowling Analysis	Ovs	Mds	Rns	Wks
Lambert	19	5	46	3	Crapp	1	...	3	...
Scott	24	8	80	2	Bailey	2	...	4	1
Milton	3	..	19	...	Graveney	2	1	4	...
Cook	56	22	100	3	Young	4	...	3	...
Goddard	39.1	13	96	2					

‡Captain. †Wicket-keeper. Umpires: L. J. Todd & J. T. Bell. Luncheon: 1-30 to 2-10 each day. Tea: 4-30 to 4-50 1st & 2nd day.
Start—1st day, 11-30 to 7-0. 2nd day, 11-0 to 7-0. 3rd day, 11-0 to 3-30 or 4-0. Scorers: H. L. Walker and L. M. Cranfield
New Ball Rule—White disc shown at 55th over; yellow disc shown at 60th over; white and yellow discs 65th over, after which new ball may be taken.

The scorecard for the next match – against Gloucestershire at Bradford

The next morning he was back at Bradford Park Avenue, his favourite ground, with his home town weather much as he had grown used to enduring. 'A bitter wind drove bowlers into their sweaters at the end of every over and huddled as many as possible of the 4,000 spectators into the lee of the sheltering walls of Park Avenue.'

"That's at the Horton Park end," he explains. "That's where the knowledgeable spectators used to go and sit. It's where the wind came from."

Gloucestershire reached 237 for five, with Bob's contribution only two wickets for 81 runs. "I had diarrhoea, and I had to keep coming off the field. After three or four times Arthur Mitchell gave me some browny-coloured liquid. 'Here, get that down you,' he said. I had no idea what it was."

In no time his figures were transformed, two for 81 became seven for 84, and he came off to discover that his medicine had been port and brandy. "I was teetotal at the time."

Four more wickets in the second innings were followed by twelve at Taunton. "We only used to book in two nights at the hotel there." Making his debut in that match was the 16-year-old Doug Padgett, whose unbeaten 25 was, according to Eric Stanger, 'as good as many a fifty'. "It was a splendid innings," Bob remembers. "He played for Idle in the Bradford League. He was quite a classical player, and he looked very good."

On one of the mornings of that match at Taunton, Bob and Frank Lowson arrived at the ground. "We were walking between the gate and the pavilion, and we met Bill Bowes talking to an elderly, white-haired gentleman and his daughter." Bowes was now a journalist, and he introduced the pair to the two Yorkshire players. "The father was a retired marine insurance assessor, living near Taunton, and his daughter worked in the Admiralty as a statistician. They were great Yorkshire supporters." Some cricketers brushed away such contacts with the public, but Bob and his room-mate Frank Lowson stopped to talk, making an impression that would lead to the start of a fascinating correspondence the following year.

In the match Bob's figures of twelve wickets for 94 runs were the best to date in his short career. With ten more in the next match against Surrey at Headingley, he took his season's total to 67, and it was only the twelfth of June.

"I owed so much to Norman Yardley's captaincy," he reflects. "I was terribly green. The cricket was so different from the Bradford League, and I didn't know any of the batsmen. But, as they came down the pavilion steps, Norman would wander over, and he'd tell me something about them. 'This chap's a bit strong with the right hand, I think we ought to have a mid-wicket,' or 'Don't bowl short, he's a back-foot player.' That was all. He had so much knowledge. I suppose these days it's all on computer, but he was brilliant. He gave me three years' worth of experience in one summer."

It was all success upon success, but the *Yorkshire Post*'s Eric Stanger was sounding the first alarm: 'Appleyard, I thought, showed signs of tiredness.'

In the last three weeks he had bowled 270 overs, taking one end for more than two-thirds of the time Yorkshire had been in the field, and for most of his spells he had been in tandem with Johnny Wardle.

"It wasn't so bad when Fred was bowling at the other end, with his long run up. But Johnny was only bowling off three yards, and a lot of the time he'd bowl maidens and field off his own bowling. It only took him two minutes, maybe a minute and a half, and I'd be bowling again before I'd got my breath back. I was tired every match by then."

A year earlier he had not even graduated to two-day second eleven cricket. All he had played had been afternoon matches – in the Bradford League on Saturdays, for the nomadic Yorkshire Owls on Sundays – with the annual treat of a six-day Southern tour with the Owls, playing all-day games at Tunbridge Wells, Sevenoaks Vine and Haywards Heath.

Yet now he was bowling 90 overs a week, first choice with the new ball and in partnership with Wardle when the pitch was taking turn. The weather was cold and damp for much of the time and, although he did not yet know it, he had a tubercular hole in his lung.

Michael Barton, the Surrey captain, recalls batting against him at Headingley, making a steady fifty before Bob got a ball to stop on him and he pushed a catch back to the bowler. "I do remember thinking how pasty his complexion was. And I thought, 'That is the sort of pastiness that tubercular people have.'"

Ten years older than Bob, Barton had grown up in Liverpool in the 1920s, and he had encountered the ravaging disease at several points in his childhood. "But then I thought to myself, 'It can't be so. Nobody with tuberculosis could possibly do the things he's doing.' So I never came to the conclusion that he had tuberculosis. But when I read the next year that he'd got it, I wasn't as surprised as I might have been."

The travel schedule for the cricketers was punishing, too. No sooner had the Yorkshire team completed the match at Headingley than they were on the train for a week at Brentwood and Lord's, each of them taking two bags, one for their cricket equipment, the other for clothes.

"They weren't the sort of clothes you could throw in a washing machine," Bob reflects, "not that we had washing machines. I used to get my shirts made from fine wool taffeta by Thomas Cullen in Shipley, and they were terribly difficult to iron. My trousers were made from cream-coloured wool gabardine by Garnetts of Bradford. I had quite a few pairs of them. Then we had wool pullovers that used to shrink like mad. You couldn't take the field in dirty clothes so, if you were away for a week or ten days, you had to take an enormous bag of clothes and, of course, you came home with a great bag of washing."

Bob had been married for less than three months to Connie. Was it a shock to her, all the hard work of being a cricketer's wife?

"It was hard work being a cricketer."

In 1951 Brentwood was a small market town surrounded by flat Essex countryside, and on its pretty, tree-lined ground a healthy midweek crowd had hardly settled in its seats when Len Hutton drove Trevor Bailey's first ball through the covers for four.

"There were several batsmen on the circuit who played shots from the word go. Dickie Dodds, George Emmett, Roy Marshall. If the first ball was a half-volley, they didn't mess about. And Leonard, too, though he liked to build an innings, got some pretty fast scores at times."

This Wednesday was once such day, with Hutton often advancing down the pitch during Bailey's run-up, and by mid-afternoon his 97th century was being applauded. On the Thursday Essex's Paul Gibb, a Yorkshireman himself, replied with a workmanlike hundred of his own. Then on the Friday the visitors pressed for the victory that would take them to the top of the table.

In the final over the ninth Essex wicket fell, Bob's fifth of the innings, 'to bring the day to its highest pitch of drama. Preston, no batsman by repute, had three balls to play, and the encircling fieldsmen scarcely left him breathing space.' He survived, and the Yorkshire players set off for Lord's. In the championship race Warwickshire remained in the lead.

"At that time, as an uncapped player, I got fifteen pounds for an away match. We were paid during the game. Norman Yardley used to go to the bank and draw out the money. When you got three of those big white fivers in your hand, you thought you were a millionaire. But of course we had to pay all our own expenses out of them: the train fares, the digs, the meals. So we didn't eat well, and we stayed at fairly cheap places. When we went to Lord's, we stayed at a nearby pub."

As an uncapped player he was taking home less than in the job he had given up for the summer, but that was not a calculation that worried him.

London was celebrating the Festival of Britain – 'the people giving themselves a pat on the back,' the Deputy Prime Minister Herbert Morrison called it – and there were several social engagements for the Yorkshire team. On the Monday morning, before the match at Lord's resumed, they accepted an invitation from Schweppes to go on an elevated walk through the trees in Battersea Park's Festival Gardens, then in the evening there was a Society of Yorkshiremen dinner at the Café Royal. Between the two events Bob captured another four wickets, though that of Jack Robertson for 91 was a struggle to achieve.

"I'd rather have bowled at Peter May than Jack Robertson. Peter was a better bat, but Jack Robertson played me better than anybody. He was so correct on the off-side and, if I pitched it on his leg-and-middle, he'd just flick me over square leg. Certain batsmen – Cyril Washbrook was another – you knew you were going to struggle against them. Others, like Harold Gimblett and Dennis Brookes, they were good bats, but it's funny, I ran in and I expected to get them out. That game at Taunton, in the second innings, I remember Harold Gimblett. 'Oh that's buggered it,' he said when I took the ball. I bowled this long hop, and he pulled it. It should have gone for four, and

Vic Wilson just put his hands together and caught it. It's funny how you get a hold on certain batsmen. It gets established very quickly. He's got something up there when you run in to bowl, just like you have with the ones you can't get out."

Robertson scored 2,000 runs in each of the first seven summers after the war, yet his Test career consisted only of tours to India and the West Indies, when the leading players were missing, and two home Tests, in the second of which he scored a century.

"He never got the recognition he deserved. Leonard was the number one batsman, and Washbrook always got preference because they made a good opening partnership. Then, with Compton and Edrich, they probably didn't want to pick another player from the same county. He was unlucky. He was good enough to have been in the side for years."

Yorkshire at Lord's, 1951
Standing (left to right): Fred Trueman, Frank Lowson, Billy Sutcliffe, Vic Wilson, Bob Appleyard, Doug Padgett (12th man), Eddie Leadbeater
Seated: Willie Watson, Don Brennan, Norman Yardley, Len Hutton, Johnny Wardle

On the final morning at Lord's Len Hutton underlined his pre-eminence with the 98th century of his career, then in the afternoon it was Denis Compton's turn. This match marked Bob's first sight of him, and he still winces with shame at his dismissal of him in the second innings.

"Obviously I'd heard a lot about him, the Brylcreem Boy and his 3,800 runs in 1947, but I'd always been playing at Bowling Old Lane on Saturdays so I'd never seen him. He hadn't got many in the first innings and, when he came in,

Johnny and I were bowling pretty tight and it was a good pitch. And I could see him getting itchy. When he made a move to come down the pitch, Johnny dropped it short, and we kept him quiet. Then somehow I had a premonition that, on the first ball of my next over, he was going to come down at me.

"It had been in the news that J.J. Warr had bowled a beamer for Middlesex so, when I ran in, I held the ball loosely in my fingertips and, when Denis came down as anticipated, I let go this beamer. It would have knocked his head off, but he ducked and put his hands up, and Don Brennan, who was standing up to the wicket, caught it off his gloves. I wasn't happy about it afterwards. I had a word with Leonard and Norman Yardley, and we agreed that it wasn't the way to carry on. I never bowled another after that."

And Compton? How did he react? "I became quite friendly with Denis later, and neither of us ever said another word about it."

It was June the 19th, and the county averages in the *Yorkshire Post* told the story of Bob's astonishing start:

	Overs	*Maidens*	*Runs*	*Wickets*	*Average*
R. Appleyard	504.3	145	1146	90	12.73
J.H. Wardle	477.2	209	907	47	19.29
E. Leadbeater	223.1	61	606	29	20.89
F.S. Trueman	279.4	63	773	34	22.73

With the *Post* made up of only six pages, there was little opportunity for journalists to shine the limelight on the rising stars of county cricket, but Eric Stanger did find room for nine column inches entitled 'Bowler of the moment':

> The man of the moment in the Yorkshire side is undoubtedly Bob Appleyard, who has not only stepped so well into the breach left by Alec Coxon but has become shock-bowler, stock-bowler and wicket-taker-in-chief. He may not have equalled Hedley Verity's feat of 100 wickets by June 19, but there seems to be no reason why he should not be around that mark on June 27, when he celebrates his 27th birthday. I could imagine no better birthday present, unless it be the county cap which, at present rate of progress, must inevitably come his way.
>
> But if, and when, Appleyard does become a capped player I do not think that it will be found that he will require an extra size in headgear. I have seen a lot of him recently and I am very much struck by his approach to the game and his manner. He has the right temperament, I am sure, and the bowler's correct philosophy.
>
> Temperament and philosophy go hand in hand. Appleyard confesses that he found county cricket, with its hard grind of day-after-day bowling, something of a trial at first, but he has quickly, thanks to physique and good sense in resting on every conceivable occasion, adjusted himself. That he has the right outlook is, I think, borne out by what he had to say to me on the

subject of dropped catches. "I never let them worry me," he declared. "They are all in the game. Besides, I always think that they are counter-balanced by the cheap wickets you get from time to time." That, to my mind, is the ideal outlook for any bowler.

As for modesty, Appleyard is the first to admit that so far the wickets have been in his favour and he has the good sense to learn something from every game. As for false modesty, which can be almost as bad as swollen-headedness, and certainly, if persisted in, may give a bowler an inferiority complex, he knows that he has bowled well so far – knowledge which gives him confidence for the hard days ahead.

The one ball in his armoury which is really devastating is that which, contrary to expectations, when pitched on or just outside the leg stump zips back to take middle or off – a fast leg-break, though Appleyard bowls it without conscious variation of his normal off-cutter grip and action. How does he do it? He would like to know himself but he is wise enough not to dissect his action to attempt to find out. Many a bowler who had the knack of sending down the unexpected and tried to discover why, has done so with disastrous results.

Harold Gimblett was a victim of this fast leg-break at Taunton. So was Laurie Fishlock of Surrey. If Appleyard does not know that he is going to bowl it when he runs up to the crease neither does the batsman. It is not a "secret weapon" or any such nonsense; it just happens and when it does it is just about unplayable.

Bob Appleyard is learning fast and his reputation among county batsmen is spreading fast. As one of the Somerset players said to me: "He is always at you, attacking the stumps the whole time, and he never seems to send down two deliveries alike in any one over."

Already I find a fear among Yorkshire followers that he may be over-bowled, and that he may be stale before the end of the season. He has strength and stamina; the rest, I think, we may safely leave to the good sense of the people who handle him. It has never been the Yorkshire way to burn out any bowler in a season or two.

"I had an ability to go through the pain barrier. It was happening all the time. It's one of those amazing things. You can bowl twenty overs, you can feel tired, you struggle on. Then by sheer persistence you get a wicket and suddenly you get a new lease of life. And you start all over again. If you don't get any wickets, you get more and more tired.

"But by this time I expected to get five wickets every innings. At least five. I wasn't counting them. You just go and do what you've got to do. Every match is different, every batsman is different, and circumstances change. The only thing that doesn't change, if you're on a roll, is that your expectancy is high."

He was on a great roll, 70 wickets in four weeks, more than three times as many as Fred Trueman, and the youngster, after a poor match against Middlesex, was feeling twinges of self-doubt.

"Freddie didn't do all that well at Lord's," his room-mate Eddie Leadbeater recalls. "We were in the hotel bedroom at night, and Frank Lowson came in to us. We were all going to go out. And Freddie said, 'I don't think I'll go out.' He was really upset, was Fred, almost in tears. 'I don't think I'll ever make it,' he said. And I said, 'Oh don't talk so silly, Fred. It's only one match.' And of course he never looked back."

Fred confirms the essence of the story in his book *Ball of Fire*: 'By the middle of the 1951 season my patience was wearing thin with Yorkshire. I began to think I would never get anywhere.'

The previous summer he had played a Test trial at the age of 19, now he was struggling to hold his Yorkshire place alongside the newcomer from the Bradford League.

"Fred was quick," Bob says, "and, when he got it in the right place, he took wickets. But he was erratic at that time. I think they persevered with him because he had this marvellous out-swing, and it swung late. He obviously had the potential to become a great bowler – his run-up was smooth, he had everything really – but, when he was young, he always bowled as fast as he could, and that was a problem. He hadn't developed the control."

In Bob's view there are very few bowlers who should strain for maximum pace. "Brett Lee and Shoaib are athletic enough and quick enough to bowl flat out all the time," he says, "but the faster you bowl, the more inaccurate you become. These speed measurements that they're putting up are no good for the game. The bowlers look up at them. They try to bowl as fast as they can, and most of the time they're bowling too short."

Back in Leeds Bob was given a rest, as the county side played a two-day match against Yorkshire Past. He travelled across to watch, and he saw the 50-year-old Wilf Barber hit a hundred before being bowled by Trueman, the young man's only wicket.

The next fixture was against Nottinghamshire at Sheffield. Notts batted on the Saturday, making 244, and Yorkshire replied with 408, thanks largely to an attacking century by Ted Lester. Late on Monday, he and Eddie Leadbeater put on 127 in quick time, the young leg-spinner approaching his first century as the day drew to a close. "Don Brennan was captain," he recalls. "He told me he was going to declare overnight and, if I wanted my ton, I should hit out. So I had a go and got out."

Leadbeater, caught Harvey, bowled Richardson, 91. 'He was caught at slip,' the *Yorkshire Post* reported, 'trying to force the necessary nine runs off the last three balls of the day.'

He had more than doubled his previous best, but it was not the Yorkshire way to bestow excessive praise on its young players. "The vice-president Ernest Holdsworth came into the dressing room, and he congratulated Ted. Then he turned to me. 'What were you doing, Leadbeater, getting out for 91?'"

The next day the cricket committee selected the teams for the following matches, and during the afternoon they announced to the press that they were giving the more experienced Johnny Whitehead a longer run in the side and sending Fred Trueman off to Grimsby to play for the seconds.

What strange games Fortune can play!

For the first time in his extraordinary Yorkshire career Bob Appleyard, averaging almost seven wickets a match, failed to take even one. 'There will be times when he will bowl worse and take wickets,' Eric Stanger thought.

"Bramall Lane wasn't my happy hunting ground. It was a good track, and the ball didn't turn a lot. It favoured the quick bowlers."

But, while the press was digesting the return of Whitehead, the Bramall Lane pitch bestowed all its favours on Fred Trueman as Notts subsided to an innings defeat. 'Recently he has been very erratic,' Stanger wrote, 'but today he bowled with much greater control of length and direction, hitting the stumps five times.' His final figures of eight wickets for 68 were the best of his short career, and he left the field, dreaming of an England call-up, only to discover that he was at Grimsby the next day with the Colts.

'As it turned out,' he wrote in *Fast Fury*, 'I was twelfth man at Grimsby and so peeved that I slept through most of the match in a deck-chair.'

Meanwhile at Headingley, against Glamorgan, Bob moved from 90 to 99 wickets. Jim Laker had reached 90, but he was due to rest during Surrey's next match against Oxford University. So the 27,000 Yorkshire spectators, who filled Bramall Lane to capacity on Saturday for the visit of the touring South Africans, were all prepared to cheer the remarkable success of their 'bowler of the moment'. He would be the first bowler in the country to 100 wickets, as Johnny Wardle had been the previous year and as Hedley Verity, Wilfred Rhodes and George Hirst had all been in their time.

But the sun beat down, the pitch provided 'delectable batting circumstances' and Bob drove home wicketless, conceding over 100 runs for the first time in his life. The South Africans finished the day on 358 for five.

"It was a batsman's paradise," Bob reflects. "I wonder how many wickets I'd have taken that summer if every pitch had been like that one."

But worse was to follow.

"I had a temperature of 103 over the weekend. I stayed in bed all Sunday and, when I took the field on Monday morning, I came off after an over. Bright Heyhirst the masseur said, 'Get on the table. I'll give you a rub.' And I said,

'Can't you get a doctor?' So they asked for one over the tannoy, and this Yorkshire supporter came in. 'You'd better get off home,' he said."

Back in Bradford he was visited the next morning by a locum.

"He came at 8.30, and he was smelling of whisky, either from that morning or the night before. He was a retired doctor, and he was very keen to get me back on the field to get me my 100 wickets. So was I. So I came back far too soon."

And the locum's diagnosis? "He said I had pleurisy. There was no x-ray or anything. He just told me to stay in bed and gave me some cough mixture. I rested for a few days, the temperature went down, and I came back. I only missed two matches – though one of them was at Bradford."

Wisden, along with all the books on Yorkshire cricket, has been happy to accept the locum's diagnosis: 'Appleyard took 99 wickets before the end of June and, had it not been for an attack of pleurisy which kept him out of two matches, he almost certainly would have been the first bowler to take 100 wickets last summer.'

Pleurisy is an inflammation of the membrane that covers the lung. It is not pleasant, but it is an infection that soon clears up – unlike the tuberculosis that was diagnosed the following summer by Geoffrey Wooler, a thoracic specialist in Leeds.

Tuberculosis can kill. It creates permanent holes in the lungs, holes that spread. Only the previous year George Orwell had died of it, and the medical world was still experimenting with drug treatments that could arrest its development.

How long had Bob had tuberculosis when Geoffrey Wooler saw him for the first time in May 1952?

"At least two years," he says. "Probably longer. I don't know why it wasn't diagnosed earlier."

CHAPTER 4

SOMETHING HEDLEY NEVER DID

July & August 1951

Bob Appleyard had taken 99 wickets with a well-advanced tubercular infection, and he was back within ten days of a major warning, striving again for his 100th.

In the match he had left early, Hutton and Lowson had put on 286 for the first wicket. They both hit hundreds, Hutton's his 99th and Lowson's 'rivalling his partner in fluency of stroke-play'. "I heard the score when I was in bed, and it cheered me up. Clearly it wasn't a pitch for the bowlers."

Then at Bournemouth Vic Wilson began a golden spell of his own, six centuries and an average over 100 in the next dozen matches.

"Vic was so powerful. We played at Lord's one year, and J.J. Warr thought the way to get him out was to bowl short outside his off stump. The ball was rattling the boards and bouncing back, almost before the fielders could turn around."

Bob was still out of action for the Middlesex match at Bradford, but he was not much missed as rain washed away the final day. It rained also on the other side of the Pennines, at Old Trafford where England needed 139 to beat South Africa. When their innings did get under way, Cuan McCarthy – the Springbok fast bowler – got vicious lift from the wet pitch, repeatedly hitting Ikin, the Lancashire opener, about the body and hands. Len Hutton, his partner, was asked to agree that the Lancastrian had shown great courage and skill. 'Aye,' he said mischievously, 'but the better player was at the other end.'

The next day, as black clouds gathered overhead, Hutton found himself on strike with 94 not out and just one run needed for victory. A six off slow left-armer Tufty Mann would make him the first batsman to hit his 100th hundred in a Test match. He lofted the ball high over cover, and to the groans of the expectant Manchester crowd it fell to earth just inside the boundary.

The spectators arrived the next morning at Hull in the hope that they would be the ones who would cheer his 100th hundred and, with Bob Appleyard returning, there was the further prospect that they might also celebrate the first bowler to 100 wickets.

In the end they suffered double disappointment. Hutton's second innings fifty was brought to a halt by rain on Friday, while Bob's first wicket did not arrive till Thursday afternoon, by which time Jim Laker had lifted his tally from 94 to 100, taking six wickets on Wednesday evening as a wet Worcester pitch dried in the sun. 'At almost exactly the same time as Laker took his 100th wicket,' the *Yorkshire Post* noticed, 'Appleyard had a difficult catch dropped by Hutton.'

Hutton's hundred was not long coming. They journeyed down to London for the next match at The Oval, and on Saturday evening he left the field with

61 not out. Monday morning brought 15,000 expectant spectators to the ground, a local headmaster even inspecting the queue for truants.

"William Harrison was a great benefactor to the Yorkshire team," Bob remembers. "He was a solicitor from Settle, and he'd moved to London as chairman of a firm of paper manufacturers. He used to give a dinner for the Yorkshire team whenever we played in London, and he got his friend who was surgeon to the royal family to come and speak. Arthur Dickson Wright, his daughter is Clarissa the television cook. He was a brilliant speaker.

"William Harrison came in the dressing room on the Monday morning, and he said to Leonard, 'If you get a hundred today, I'll give you 100 guineas.' Well, Len was keen enough to get the hundred in any case, but he was on the same pay as the rest of the capped players. And 100 guineas was a lot of money, compared with the £17 the capped players were paid for an away match. So he went out, and he scratched around for ages.

"We used to watch him. He'd go in with his long-sleeve sweater on. After about half an hour he'd take it off, and we'd say, 'He's going to get a hundred today.' As if he'd decided on the day. And he did more often than not. He was the greatest of batsmen. I bowled for hours at him in the nets, and I tried like hell to get him out. And he tried like hell to stop me. I don't know that I ever did get him out."

J.M. Kilburn described the events of that morning at The Oval:

> His batting had the calm and concentration characteristic of his approach to any important occasion. His habitual touch of the cap before he takes up his stance, his constant examination of the pitch between overs, his refusal to play any but the strokes of his choice or run any but the most carefully judged of runs, betokens a Hutton on business bent. All the signs were there, and after 70 minutes of the day Hutton's score was 96. A half-volley outside the off stump was driven through the covers for four, and the spectators were on their feet, applauding, before the ball had reached the boundary. Hutton raised his bat and lifted his cap in acknowledgement, and settled down to play the next ball.

"He threw his bat after that. He played some magnificent shots. The next fifty came in a quarter of the time. He played shots all round the wicket. He was a master."

'He is the greatest classic player in the world today,' Jack Hobbs said.

'I always knew he would do it,' George Hirst added, recalling the 14-year-old he had coached in the Headingley nets in 1930.

'Given good health, he must have a chance of beating Jack Hobbs' world record of 197 centuries,' Herbert Sutcliffe suggested.

Given good health. Hutton was 35. He had one arm shortened as a result of a gymnasium accident in the war, and he could no longer play the pull shot with freedom. And his lower back was starting to trouble him.

Len Hutton, with Bob

The master's back was not improved in the Surrey second innings, either. "I'd got three in the leg trap, Len in the middle of them, and I bowled this long hop to Bernie Constable. Bernie's eyes lit up, the leg trap all turned their backs, and he cracked it straight into the middle of Len's back. The ball jumped up in the air, and Vic Wilson turned round and caught it."

Constable, caught Wilson, bowled Appleyard, 47.

"It's the last thing you want to do to instil confidence in your short legs. They didn't wear helmets or padding, like they do now. But fortunately incidents like that were a rare occurrence."

Moving on to Maidstone, Fred Trueman was demoted to twelfth man, and Bob and Frank Lowson set about putting him more at ease in the environment of county cricket.

"Fred used to come in a royal blue suit with a maroon-coloured roll-neck sweater. He was in and out of the side, and we said, 'Fred, you've got to smarten yourself up. You've got to get yourself a shirt.' So we marched him into a gents outfitters and got him a blue airforce-coloured shirt, matching his suit, and a tie.

"The following year, when I was in hospital and he bowled the Indians out, there was a picture of him receiving an illuminated address from Maltby, his home village, and he was wearing a bow tie and a smart suit. He'd moved on from the maroon roll-neck pullover. In fact, he became one of the best-dressed cricketers of the lot. He certainly never appeared in stubble. If anybody had turned up like Atherton or Hussain, he'd have been sent off to shave."

The step up to county cricket, with men like Ernest Holdsworth and William Harrison laying on dinners, was not so hard for Bob. He was 27 years old, married and working in a responsible job. He had served in the war. But Fred was young, his father worked at the coalface, and he was entering a new world.

"One year William Harrison came in the dressing room and offered him a Rolls Royce for 100 guineas. Freddie didn't know what to say. He turned it down. I think he thought it would be a bit too pretentious for him."

With his new shirt and tie, Fred was back in the side for the next match at Trent Bridge and, as at Sheffield, when he took eight for 68, he showed his liking for the Nottinghamshire batsmen.

He took a hat-trick, he had figures of five for four and, though the afternoon sun made batting easier and his eight wickets finished up costing 53 runs, 'nothing could change the glory of his morning.'

"Well done, Fred," he remembers Hutton saying to him. "I think I'll go in and get my 101st now." And Hutton did, with a 'masterly' 194 not out. Even if Bob's wickets were coming more slowly since his return from illness, the team was in good spirits and victory at Edgbaston in a week's time would put them hard on the heels of Warwickshire in the championship race.

First, however, they had to play a friendly match against Scotland at Scarborough. The fourth Test was taking place at Headingley, and England had called up four Yorkshiremen: not only Hutton and Watson but newcomers Lowson and Brennan. The selection of Brennan, in place of Evans, created some surprise – but not for Bob.

"It wasn't unexpected from my point of view. He was keeping so well. A lot of my attack was on leg and middle, and sometimes the ball went down the leg side. Also I bowled a quicker one. But Don always stood up. He used to grumble a bit, but he took everything. And, when he finished playing, his hands were remarkably unblemished. He could have been a surgeon."

Without his travelling companion Frank Lowson, Bob set out alone in his beloved Jaguar. "All our cars were second-hand. You couldn't get new cars in those days, even if we could have afforded them. There were huge waiting lists." It was seventy miles to Scarborough, and he was due there an hour before the start.

"We didn't have warm-up routines or play football like they do now. We'd have a net for about ten minutes or so, though there were grounds, like Park Avenue, where there weren't any nets. We used to play up against the white wall in front of the members' stand. It was just to loosen up. The batsmen got their feet moving, and the bowlers attuned their muscles."

And what about the bonding, and the motivational team talks?

He shakes his head in incomprehension. "You put the Yorkshire sweater on, and the cap with the white rose. You don't need any psyching up."

Alas, at 10.30 a.m. at Scarborough, he was not there for any of it. He was stranded on the road between York and Malton, with a punctured tyre. "There was a problem with the changing of the wheel. The central locking nut wouldn't unfasten. It was a quiet road, and I couldn't get any assistance. In the end I was two hours late."

He missed much of the Scotland first innings and found himself dropped for indiscipline from the team to play Warwickshire in the crucial match at Edgbaston.

It was the top-of-the-table decider but, with Yorkshire missing four players at the Test in addition to Bob, their batsmen struggled in vain against the leg-spin of Eric Hollies while their bowlers failed to stop Tom Dollery, the Warwickshire captain, from taking a century off them. Earlier in the summer Hollies had bowled them out for 49 at Bramall Lane, and this second defeat – by an innings and 16 runs – dealt a terminal blow to their championship aspirations.

"I have to say that, watching the match, I felt that, had I been bowling, I'd have done better. The pitch seemed to suit me ideally."

Bob did not even have the luxury of a rest, with twelfth man responsible for all the errands required to be run, be they for the captain Norman Yardley or the teenage Doug Padgett. There were drinks to be taken out, baths to be run, and afterwards there were all the bags to be collected and put in a taxi to the railway station, where they had to be loaded onto the guards van.

July was over. The bowler, who had come so close to being the only man since the last war to reach 100 wickets by the end of June, had still not reached 120. The talk in the county now was of the promise of the young Trueman. The *Yorkshire Post* set out the details.

	Overs	*Maidens*	*Runs*	*Wickets*	*Average*
R. Appleyard	801.5	229	1845	119	15.50
F.S. Trueman	528.1	112	1427	75	19.02
J.P. Whitehead	181.2	38	476	24	19.83
J.H. Wardle	836.2	360	1610	79	20.37
E. Leadbeater	543.1	121	1520	67	22.68

The pitches had become harder, the 'pleurisy' had taken its toll on his frame, and even his great mental strength, his expectation of wickets, was not as it had been in June. At Harrogate on the first of August he took one wicket for 118 runs in the Derbyshire first innings, and he sat watching Vic Wilson and Willie Watson scoring hundreds.

"I remember thinking to myself, 'Where's the next wicket going to come from?' I'd got to that stage."

Then on the final morning came the moment that seemed to turn his luck once more.

"Guy Willatt, a left-hander, was batting. I was bowling over the wicket, as always, fast off-spinners, and this ball, for some reason, pitched on his off stump and, instead of spinning away from him, it hit leg. It was one of those things I had no control over. Perhaps it was something in the pitch, or the position I got myself in. I wish I could have done it regularly, but it really was just a fluke."

Such a ball bowled today would attract endless close-up replays, with expert analysis, but Bob just smiles. "I'd love to have heard David Lloyd explaining it. 'That was a miracle ball,' he'd have said."

It was the 'secret weapon' that Eric Stanger had described back in June: 'it just happens and when it does it is just about unplayable.' And it had come when it was most needed. "It set me off onto a quite good spell after that."

Five wickets in the Derbyshire second innings, three in a rain-ruined Roses match at Bramall Lane, then twelve at Leicester where he bowled 38 overs in the second innings. Success had brought fresh energy, and it would carry him through the closing weeks of the summer.

Back at Park Avenue, the rain returned, washing away Saturday's play against Essex and falling most of Sunday as well. When the match finally started on the Monday, Doug Insole the Essex captain won the toss and was persuaded by Trevor Bailey to ask Yorkshire to bat first on the soft surface.

Here was the joy of cricket on uncovered pitches: the reading of the playing strip, the selection of the bowling attack, the decision on the roller.

"The heavy roller at Park Avenue had a wooden frame," Bob recalls. "It needed three at the front and three at the back to push it, and of course there wouldn't be the ground staff for that. So, if it needed doing, we'd go out and do it ourselves. We all did it. I can remember pushing it alongside Leonard."

That day at Bradford runs came so freely for Yorkshire that, by the time the sun came out and the drying pitch became treacherous, there were already 295 on the board and Yardley was able to declare. Then, according to J.M. Kilburn, 'Appleyard thoroughly enjoyed himself. He had Gibb caught at short leg when the ball "popped"; he had Insole lbw when it kept low; and in four successive balls he clean bowled Horsfall, Smith and Vigar.'

It was a great shock to Essex's Trevor Bailey, who was always quick to sum up his opponents and who could not match this fast off-spinner with the seamer who had taken wickets down at Brentwood.

"At Brentwood I'd put him down as another highly efficient in-swing bowler. There were a number at that time: Reg Perks, Derek Shackleton, Cliff Gladwin. But at Bradford he bowled fast off-breaks, and on that soft, drying pitch he came as close to being unplayable as any bowler I have ever faced."

"I had the best of both worlds," Bob says. "I could bowl with the seam, then if necessary I could revert to spin. So it meant that we could play an extra batsman. I mean, what's the point of being a quick bowler or a slow bowler when you can't get on because it's the wrong type of pitch? If I had my way, I'd take half a dozen bowlers, and I'd teach them every discipline. You'd have to start with those who can bowl quick.

"It can't be all that difficult, really. Lots of folk could have done what I did. But for some reason you've got to be one or the other."

It is a view that challenges all the conventions of cricket coaching, delivered by one of the game's most remarkable bowlers. "Lots of folk could have done what I did," he thinks.

"Why do you have to be one type of bowler or another? It's something that baffles me. Jim Swanton wrote about me, and he tried to put me in a category. But why do you have to be in a category?"

'Sometimes he bowled like Alec Bedser,' Johnny Wardle wrote, 'and sometimes like Jim Laker, and you hardly realised the difference till you were out.'

Against Essex at Bradford he bowled 17 overs and took six wickets for 17 runs. It was sufficient for Norman Yardley to take him and Freddie Trueman aside and to present them with their county caps.

"Fred always claims he got his cap before me because in the picture he's got it on his head and Norman Yardley's passing mine over to me. But I say that this was a retake for the photographer. We're still arguing about it fifty years on."

With six more wickets in the second innings, he finished with match figures of 41 overs, twelve wickets for 43 runs. 'The Yorkshire committee,' Kilburn suggested, 'might have awarded him gown as well as cap to mark graduation (with honours).'

He had taken 24 wickets in a week, but he added only six at Scarborough where Worcestershire's Don Kenyon – "another one like Jack Robertson who never got the recognition" – hit 145 and condemned Bob to only his second experience of defeat while wearing the white rose.

"We didn't perform on the day. I had played so little cricket at the seaside, and I was realising for the first time how conditions could change in an hour. The tide comes in, and the ball starts moving about. Worcestershire used the conditions much better than we did."

Bob was last man out, caught and bowled by Roley Jenkins, with only nine runs wanted. Coupled with Warwickshire's victory at Coventry, Yorkshire's defeat brought to an end their last mathematical chance of the championship.

'For most counties second would be a happy place,' Johnny Wardle wrote, 'but Yorkshire are frankly not satisfied.'

At Headingley there were ten more wickets for Bob – 40 in a fortnight – and Eric Stanger enjoyed commenting on the Hampshire captain Desmond Eagar's choice of headgear. In the first innings, 'his gay Harlequin cap caused a buzz of envy among the juvenile spectators.'

"That would have interested Fred," Bob chuckles. "A fancy cap, or a cap with rings round, made him ten miles an hour faster. Did he get a bouncer?"

Eagar, caught Wilson, bowled Leadbeater, 0.

In the second innings, 'Eagar, changing his Harlequin cap for a sober blue, but not his luck, was bowled by Appleyard and bagged a "pair" for the first time in his career.'

The season was entering its last fortnight. Bob had bowled over 1,100 overs, but there were plenty more to come. At Northampton – "That was a good, dry pitch. Freddie Brown got a few runs. I was bowling well by then." – he completed 40 overs in an innings for the first time and took his wicket tally from 168 to 179.

From Northampton they took the train to Hove. Twelfth man loading the bags at the railway station was Eddie Leadbeater, and Bob's quest for 200 wickets encountered a fresh obstacle.

"There were two trains, one on each side of the platform. He put all the bags on our train, then he put mine on the other one. I don't know what he was doing. I suppose it was his idea of a joke."

"Was it heck?" Eddie replies. "How it got misplaced, I don't know. But I can assure you that I didn't do it intentionally."

Whatever the explanation, Bob's equipment sped away northwards, and he found himself playing at Hove in borrowed boots. "Johnny Whitehead lent me his. And they were half a size, or a size, too small for me."

Despite this, he took five wickets in the Sussex first innings – 'another distinguished performance in his truly wonderful season,' Kilburn wrote – but he added only two in the second before rain washed away the third day.

According to *Wisden*, 'Sussex might have lost in an innings but for admirable play by Sheppard, who hit nine boundaries in a well-nigh faultless display.' It was David Sheppard's last innings in a summer in which he had scored more than 2,000 runs with seven centuries, and it still stands out in his memory. "That first year, when he was fit, Bob was a very great bowler. He had such variation of pace, and we were batting on a real sticky wicket at

Hove. I think I made 67 not out, and I was prouder of that innings than any other that summer. Bob Appleyard was a very formidable bowler."

The early abandonment on the final day 'offered the Yorkshire team the consolation of a comfortable journey to Bristol', but it left Bob frustrated. He had completed 1,200 overs in less than four months, and he still wanted to bowl.

"Tuberculosis is a funny disease," thoracic surgeon Geoffrey Wooler says. "You often find that the patients are elated until it gets really bad. At the early stages their morale seems to remain pretty good."

At Bristol he managed to take just three Gloucestershire wickets in their first innings. Then Len Hutton stepped out to bat.

"They were the only county he hadn't made a hundred against. I remember Bomber Wells saying, 'He won't get one here.' And I said, 'Don't bet on it.'"

By close of play Hutton was 110 not out, the second Yorkshireman – after Herbert Sutcliffe – to achieve the distinction of a century against all the other counties. Then the rain returned, the last two days were lost, and the Yorkshire players returned home, their championship programme at an end. There was just one festival match – against MCC at Scarborough – still to be played.

Bob had had 186 wickets when the game at Hove had been abandoned, and now he had 189. There had been plenty of talk about his 200 in the press, but the prospect seemed to have disappeared over the horizon.

"For some reason it didn't mean all that much to me. I was tired, and I was just playing each day as it came. It's only in later years that it's come to seem so important."

Scarborough was 'first-class cricket on holiday'. "All the families used to go over to the Festival. Connie and I stayed at Mrs Hogg's, a little bed-and-breakfast place that Bill Bowes recommended."

The MCC put out an attractive batting side, starting Simpson, Edrich, May, Doggart, Insole, but there was little carefree stroke-play for the holiday crowd to enjoy, as J.M. Kilburn noted:

> The rains of the week had defeated the most elaborate of protective covering or the most tender care of groundsmen, and batsmen had to struggle for their holiday living. Appleyard looked the part of the outstanding bowler of the season. He bowled 33 overs with only the lunch interval and the change of ends for rest. On the whole his analysis of eight for 76 was fair reward for a fair day's work. His ambition of 200 wickets in his first full season draws close to realisation. His tally is now 197.

'What a ruddy summer it was,' Fred Trueman declared in *Fast Fury*. 'Fit only for flipping ducks.' And Saturday's play came to an early end, the light darkening as rainstorms gathered. Yorkshire batted most of Monday, and the last day of the season arrived with nine MCC wickets to be taken and the crowd willing Bob to claim three of them.

"It was a fine, warm day, and Bill Edrich was not out overnight. As we took the field, Leonard said to me, 'The third ball of the over, bowl it a foot outside his off stump, fairly well up.' – which I did. Len positioned himself at long on, in front of the scoreboard, and the ball went straight down his throat. I don't think he'd to move a yard. There aren't too many occasions when you put a man in a certain place, and the ball goes down his throat like that. It was definitely Len's wicket. He knew Bill. He knew his style."

That brought Bob to 198, 'but, though he bowled nearly all morning and most of the afternoon, no other success came his way before tea.'

All eyes, all hopes, were on the newcomer from Bradford – "They seemed more concerned about it than I was." – but among the spectators, there was a gathering fear of disappointment.

> His run-up was a dark and curving pathway across the green, his leg-trap crouched in co-operation and occasionally the bat was beaten but when wickets fell they fell to other bowlers.

"200 wickets. Why should it mean so much more than 199 or 198? At one point I asked Norman Yardley to take me off. 'It's spoiling the game, skipper,' I said. And he just smiled. 'Keep going,' he said."

'Eventually MCC had only two wickets left, and Appleyard needed both of them.' At the end of a long, long summer he had bowled 45 overs in the innings, nearly 40 of them in this one day. "I really was tired then. I was on my knees."

"It was an amazing feat," his team-mate Ted Lester says. "He bowled virtually the whole day. And it all came down to the last two wickets. I remember thinking at the time, 'I hope nobody hits a catch to me.'"

Finally there came the joyous ending. He went back to his mark and ran in for his 46th over of the innings, his 79th of the match, his 420th of the last four weeks, his 1,323rd of the season.

> With excitement high, he had Hall caught by Yardley at mid-on off the first ball, and Tattersall, a left-hander, caught at mid-on by Trueman off the fifth. Both fieldsmen showed obvious relief, Yardley fanning his face with his cap.

"We all trooped off," Ted Lester says, "with a great sense of relief."

It was all over. Bob Appleyard of Bradford had become the first man in the history of cricket – and almost certainly the last – to take 200 wickets in his first full summer. They had all been for Yorkshire, too, unlike Hedley Verity, whose 200s had all included England wickets. These things mattered in Yorkshire and, when he had enjoyed the warm but orderly congratulations of spectators and fellow players, he sat down in the dressing room and received from Bill Bowes the highest compliment the great bowler could give the young man.

"Well, you've done something Hedley never did."

J.M. Kilburn's pen was flowing freely for the last time that summer:

> From May to September Appleyard has been both attack and defence in Yorkshire's bowling, storm-trooper and guardsman, in fair weather and foul. Whatever may develop in his subsequent career nothing can tarnish the glory of his first full year and there is every prospect of great things to come, for Appleyard's bowling has the basic principles of length and direction as foundation for his sharp off-spin and skilful variation of pace. He leaves the fields of 1951 as a tired but deservedly happy man.

Leaving the field at Scarborough
Photo taken by Lawrence Byford, Yorkshire President in the 1990s

There were no television cameras to be faced, no champagne for the teetotaller to drink. He climbed into his second-hand Jaguar with his wife Connie, and they made their way home to Bradford.

"We stopped to eat between Tadcaster and York. Not dinner in the strict sense of the word. Just refreshment. It might have been beans on toast."

And had they set some time aside for a holiday at the end of it all?

"No, that was the holiday. We'd been to the Scarborough Festival."

The final Yorkshire averages spelled out the detail of his summer's work.

	Overs	*Maidens*	*Runs*	*Wickets*	*Average*
R. Appleyard	1323.2	391	2829	200	14.14
J.H. Wardle	1279.1	576	2333	122	19.12
J.P. Whitehead	185.2	40	482	24	20.08
F.S. Trueman	740.4	167	1852	90	20.57
N.W.D. Yardley	265	79	562	26	21.61
E. Leadbeater	693.3	152	1959	81	24.18

Eleven times that summer a Yorkshire bowler took ten wickets in a match:
Wardle once, Trueman once and Appleyard nine times.

The national averages underlined the same story.

	Overs	*Maidens*	*Runs*	*Wickets*	*Average*
R. Appleyard	1323.2	391	2829	200	14.14
J.B. Statham	714.2	178	1466	97	15.11
A.V. Bedser	1100	338	2024	130	15.56
J. McConnon	862.4	238	2186	136	16.07
J.J. Warr	449.2	119	1011	59	17.13

The next highest wicket-taker, Jack Young of Middlesex, had 157.

Later that week he received a letter and a telegram.

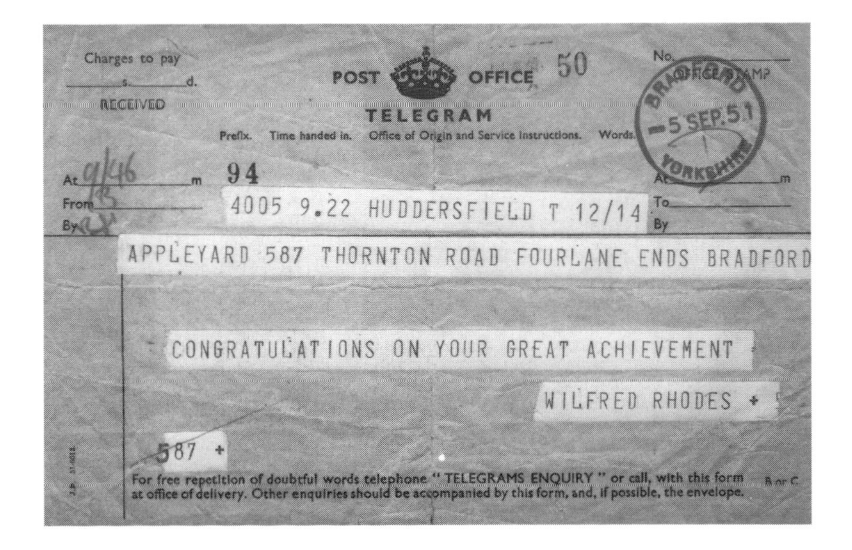
Charges to pay s. d.
RECEIVED
POST OFFICE 50
TELEGRAM
Prefix. Time handed in. Office of Origin and Service Instructions. Words.
No.
BRADFORD
5 SEP 51
YORKSHIRE
At 9/46 m 94
From
By
4005 9.22 HUDDERSFIELD T 12/14
APPLEYARD 587 THORNTON ROAD FOURLANE ENDS BRADFORD
CONGRATULATIONS ON YOUR GREAT ACHIEVEMENT
WILFRED RHODES +
587 +
For free repetition of doubtful words telephone "TELEGRAMS ENQUIRY" or call, with this form at office of delivery. Other enquiries should be accompanied by this form, and, if possible, the envelope.

The letter was from Anne Hirst:

> My father G.H.Hirst has asked me to write to you and give you his most hearty congratulations on your splendid achievement. He's watched your progress with great interest and says that I'm to tell you you've done well and will find that all the hard work is well worthwhile.

Bob was short-listed by the Cricket Writers' Club to be its Young Cricketer of the Year, but the award was presented at a London dinner to Peter May. "I remember Bill Bowes getting up and making a speech and, in the nicest way, suggesting that I should have won it."

Then the following Spring he emulated Wilfred Rhodes by being named, after just a single summer of first-class cricket, as one of *Wisden*'s five cricketers of the year. The tribute in the almanack was written by Bill Bowes, and he ended it with words of warning:

> With such a fine utility bowler in the side, Yorkshire need to be careful they do not give him too much work to do. At times last season he was overbowled. Some Yorkshire officials say: "We hope he never takes 200 wickets again." But when a man can be used as opening bowler, spin bowler and stock bowler combined, the temptation to use him to the full is hard to resist.

That winter an MCC side sailed to India for a five-Test tour that spread over six months, and in November Derbyshire's 'Dusty' Rhodes returned home ill. He was another like Bob who could bowl in two styles, in his case seam and leg spin, and Yorkshire received an enquiry about Bob's availability to fly out as a replacement.

"I hate to think what would have happened to me if I'd gone out there in that climate. But I was lucky. It transpired that Nigel Howard, the captain, wanted a leg-spinner."

In the end the figure that climbed out of the aircraft at Bombay was none other than Bob's chirpy team-mate Eddie Leadbeater, the only cricketer in modern times to play for England and never win a county cap.

Meanwhile, back in Yorkshire, Bob set about improving his fitness, spending every weekend at Halifax Golf Club. Set on Ogden Moor, with two streams running through it, it is a testing course, with undulating hills that rise steeply from the clubhouse and spongy turf that makes climbing hard work. Nothing but open moor separates the course from Haworth and Bronte country to the North, while on a clear day you can see from the high 13th green all the way to Meltham and the Peak District. The curlews circle overhead, and the mill chimneys of the industrial towns seem but distant specks in the valleys below.

"I often played two rounds on a Saturday and two on a Sunday, all through the winter, on my own sometimes. One of the holes is twelve hundred feet above sea level, and it can be pretty wild and windy. Sometimes, I remember, I was playing in the snow."

The windswept figure high on the moor was determined to maintain, even to improve on, the standard he had set in his first summer of county cricket. But, alas, he was fighting a losing battle, a battle with the hole that was spreading in his left lung.

"I thought I wasn't fit. I was trying to build up my stamina and strength, but I was always feeling tired."

BOWLING FIGURES 1951

			First innings				Second innings			
May 2,3,4	Oxford	Oxford Univ	20.4	7	26	4				
May 5,7,8	Bradford	South Africans	25	13	38	6	11	4	17	0
May 9,10,11	Hull	Northamptonshire	12	2	35	2				
May 12,14,15	Old Trafford	Lancashire	25	7	48	2	11	2	36	1
May 16,17,18	Cambridge	Cambridge Univ	14	6	14	2	19	6	35	3
May 19,21	Chesterfield	Derbyshire	15.3	6	31	4	21	7	49	4
May 23,24,25	Huddersfield	Warwickshire	26	4	71	5	20.2	10	39	5
May 26,28,29	Sheffield	Somerset	27	7	49	3	13	3	35	3
May 30,31,Jun 1	Bradford	Gloucestershire	28.4	5	84	7	23.1	9	47	4
Jun 6,7	Taunton	Somerset	25.3	7	59	6	16	4	35	6
Jun 9,11,12	Headingley	Surrey	30.2	6	81	5	33.2	4	93	5
Jun 13,14,15	Brentwood	Essex	27	5	60	2	27	10	51	5
Jun 16,18,19	Lord's	Middlesex	27	8	68	4	16	3	45	2
Jun 23,25,26	Sheffield	Nottinghamshire	35	14	66	0	5	2	9	0
Jun 27,28	Headingley	Glamorgan	18	9	24	4	22.2	11	44	5
Jun 30,July 2,3	Sheffield	South Africans	36	5	104	0				
July 11,12,13	Hull	Sussex	35	8	77	2				
July 14,16,17	The Oval	Surrey	21	8	53	3	23	5	54	2
July 18,19,20	Maidstone	Kent	20	3	53	2	26	5	82	4
July 21,23,24	Trent Bridge	Nottinghamshire	10	2	36	1	20	5	44	1
July 25,26,27	Scarborough	Scotland	5	1	17	3	21	6	42	2
Aug 1,2,3	Harrogate	Derbyshire	35	7	118	1	27	12	42	5
Aug 4,6,7	Sheffield	Lancashire	28	6	63	3				
Aug 8,9,10	Leicester	Leicestershire	17	8	36	5	37.5	16	57	7
Aug 11,13,14	Bradford	Essex	17	8	17	6	23.4	10	26	6
Aug 15,16,17	Scarborough	Worcestershire	35	11	53	3	26	7	35	3
Aug 18,20,21	Headingley	Hampshire	29	8	55	4	29.2	14	32	6
Aug 22,23,24	Northampton	Northamptonshire	22.5	8	43	5	40	12	84	6
Aug 25,27,28	Hove	Sussex	18.4	5	31	5	22	3	60	2
Aug 29,30,31	Bristol	Gloucestershire	24.2	9	45	3				
Sept 1,3,4	Scarborough	M.C.C.	33	6	76	8	45.5	12	105	3

Matches	*Overs*	*Maidens*	*Runs*	*Wickets*	*Average*
31	1323.2	391	2829	200	14.14

CHAPTER 5

THE VALLEY OF THE SHADOW OF DEATH

1952

The capped professionals reported to the Winter Shed at the start of February each year, but so keen was Bob to get back into training that he was there with the Colts and other young hopefuls from early January 1952. He may have taken 200 wickets the previous summer, but he was looking for personal improvement. On the Halifax golf course he worked to increase his stamina while in the nets he attempted to integrate a new delivery into his repertoire.

In 1951 he had occasionally bowled a leg-cutter, a ball that pitched and cut away to the off. Eric Stanger in the *Yorkshire Post* described it as a 'secret weapon', but it happened unconsciously and he had no notion of how to do it deliberately – until one night that winter when he travelled to Sheffield to give out the prizes at a cricket dinner and found that the main speaker was George Pope, the former Derbyshire and England bowler whose leg-cutter was legendary.

He drew Pope aside, the two men retiring to the cloakroom. He always carried a cricket ball in the pocket of his long raincoat, to keep hard the skin on his spinning finger, and he asked the old bowler to demonstrate his action. Pope, like Bob, was a large man with large hands; he held the ball in a classic seamer's grip, the index and middle finger on top of the ball, and he showed how an upward flick of the third finger could impart the necessary rotation. "It was almost impossible for the batsman to detect it," Bob says. "But you have to have very strong fingers to bowl it like that."

Bob, however, had a different grip, the ball wedged between middle and third finger, but quickly he realised that he, too, with no change of grip, could impart an upward flick with the third finger. There would be no great rotation of the wrist and therefore no signalling of the variation to the batsman. In the Winter Shed a year earlier he had chanced on a method of bowling fast off-breaks off his middle finger. Now he saw how he could slip in an equally fast leg-cutter with no discernible change of action. Used sparingly, it could be a deadly delivery, and he could not wait to test it out in the Winter Shed.

As a bowler, how should he be classified? As an off-spinner or an off-cutter? It was a distinction that Jim Swanton, the *Daily Telegraph* correspondent, sought to clarify when they found themselves on the SS Orsova, sailing to Australia in the autumn of 1954.

"We had quite a technical discussion. We were trying to establish where the dividing line was between spin and cut."

But Bob, though a technical man who was happy to analyse his wrist position or the angle of his shoulder, was not as bothered by his bowling category.

The conventional grip for an off-break

Bob's grip

"The key to it all is the speed at which you bowl the ball. Because I bowled with the middle finger behind the ball, it gave me more power and I was able to bowl it much faster than most off-spinners. And the faster you bowl, the less time your finger is on the ball so the less spin is imparted. You get more bounce, more pace off the pitch, and that gives the batsman less time to play. The extra spin comes from bowling slower, keeping the finger longer on the ball. But there are pitches where you can spin it too much. After all, who needs to turn the ball two feet when the bat is only four inches wide?"

Here was a technician at work. 'A bowler's bowler,' J.M. Kilburn called him:

> He had no striking mannerisms of run-up or delivery. He was not obviously beating batsmen by pace or by sharp spin or by the hypnotism of swing. Pulling off his sweater, he did not rouse excitement or anticipation. Dismissed batsmen seemed to have been at fault rather than left in helplessness.

His skills were those of a proud craftsman: 'consistent accuracy', 'a care never to bowl below the best of which he was capable' and a relentless probing of batsman and pitch. 'His first overs in any match were given to search for the pace likely to extract most response from the condition of the pitch.'

"Emmott Robinson umpired a Yorkshire match during my first summer, and apparently he said to Bill Bowes, 'Ah've seen bowlers with two changes of pace, sometimes three, but nivver one with five, like this lad Appleyard.'"

Fifty years on, Bob still watches the cricket and thinks how he would bowl at the batsmen. "You take this Australian Adam Gilchrist. The only way you can bowl at someone like him is to change your flight and pace. So that the ball isn't where he thinks it is. It's all very well teaching someone to bowl line and length but, if all you bowl is line and length, a batsman like that will know where it's going to be. You can bowl the best length ball in the world, and he can move his feet and get runs from it. You've got to change your flight, change your pace."

In May 1951, after his triumph against the South Africans, J.M. Kilburn wrote that Bob was 'scarcely beyond the beginnings of bowling, which is a difficult craft not learned in a day.' That was a judgement the bowler was happy to share as he sought to perfect the leg-cutter that George Pope had shown him, the same leg-cutter perhaps that had made Sydney Barnes great.

"He took batsmen by surprise in 1951," his team-mate Vic Wilson says. "Batsmen facing him had no idea what to expect. He would have had to work much harder for his wickets the following summer."

"The batsmen were already getting wise to my fast off-breaks," Bob recognises, "and were playing me much more cautiously. That's why the leg-cutter would have had such an explosive effect. It would have given me an enormous psychological advantage, but I knew I had to use it sparingly – because you can't set a field to good batsmen on good pitches and bowl too great a variety of deliveries."

His sense of anticipation was great. He wanted to bowl even better than in 1951. He wanted to be part of a championship-winning side. But most of all, "The ambition which burned in my heart was to play for England."

Eventually, with Connie eight months pregnant, the season started with a fortnight of away games down South: at Lord's against the MCC, at Taunton where he had taken twelve Somerset wickets the previous year, then at Oxford and Cambridge.

With Freddie Trueman on National Service, Yorkshire blooded two Colts, George Padgett and Brian Hall, in the Lord's match, preserving Bob for the start of the championship season at Taunton. There the rain fell all Saturday, hiding the hills around the town, and, when play did get under way on the Monday, he was short of energy and troubled by a persistent cough. He had had the cough for more than a fortnight, and it was becoming debilitating. He rested in the dressing-room while his team-mates batted. Then in the late afternoon he took the field, bowling 16 overs for the one wicket of Maurice Tremlett.

"It was cloudy and damp. I bowled for about ninety minutes, and I was really struggling. I had a high temperature and a very bad cough. It was an effort even to get back to the hotel and into bed. Frank Lowson my room-mate wanted me to see a doctor, but I told him I'd see how I felt in the morning."

Lowson did not wait when he got up. He summoned a doctor, who told the feverish cricketer to go home and see a specialist. Further rain swept across the town, washing out the final day's play, but by mid-morning Bob was gone. "I must have driven down for those games, because I had my car there and I drove back all on my own to Bradford. In those days, before motorways, it was a long journey, and I was in a lot of difficulty. I was feeling terrible, but I had no idea what was wrong."

A specialist? He had a sense of misgiving, a premonition of trouble, as he drove 270 miles through the rain. He had had a hard childhood, with setbacks a-plenty, so perhaps he was more prepared than most for bad news. He had started the summer with so much hope – the confidence borne of his previous success, the knowledge that he had almost been called up for England's winter tour of India, the acquisition of the deadly leg-cutter – but now he was no longer in control of his own future. He drove on, fearful of what the doctors might be about to tell him.

T.L. Taylor, the Yorkshire President, referred him to Leeds General Infirmary where he was examined by the thoracic surgeon Geoffrey Wooler. "He sounded my chest and called for an x-ray, just like any normal examination. Then he asked me to stay in for a more detailed examination."

It was May 1952. Doctors at that time did not speculate about possibilities, and Bob lay that night in bed, fearing the worst.

Tuberculosis. Consumption, as many still called it. In the early 1950s there were 50,000 fresh cases a year in the UK, and the newspapers all carried articles on how the war had increased its prevalence. A survey in the British

Medical Journal calculated that there was one tuberculosis patient requiring a hospital bed for every 700 of the population.

The BCG inoculation had not been introduced, but there were now treatments: surgery and a drug called streptomycin, developed in 1944. Bob, however, had grown up in Bradford knowing it as a killer disease, a by-product of poverty and over-crowding. Its victims were sent into isolation in special sanatoria, and those who returned were often shadows of their former selves. That night at Leeds Infirmary he lay alone and in fear.

"When I came to Leeds after the war," Geoffrey Wooler recalls, "I was responsible for 250 beds, and I should think 200 of them were tubercle. I had a sanatorium near Selby and another out near Bainbridge and Aysgarth. All these places had young people in them.

"People were frightened of the disease. Even when people had had part of their lung removed, if we hadn't had available the drugs, it may well have cropped up again. In the early days I used to say that you were fighting a losing battle. But the main thing was to try to make the patients fight as long as possible, by surgery, by removing the worst part of the disease and by giving them drugs. Of that two hundred, at least ten per cent would die. And many of the others were invalids. They'd probably go on for another ten years and gradually succumb to it."

Mary Dobson, now Mrs Mary Braithwaite, was a medical social worker who regularly visited tuberculosis patients, and she confirms this. "The new drug treatments did cause great excitement. I remember one young man. 'I'm going on rimiform next week,' he said. He'd been in the sanatorium for five years, it had been rest and rest only, and suddenly there was a light."

The following morning in Leeds Infirmary Bob was holding hands with the heavily pregnant Connie when Geoffrey Wooler arrived. Fears raced about the young cricketer's head. Would he recover? Would he play cricket again? And would their unborn baby be infected?

Two years later he told his story to the *Daily Express*. For five days in August 1954 they spread his inspirational tale across a middle page.

'A narrative to inspire all who have been ill or who have feared illness.'

> Slowly the specialist said: "You have a tuberculin infection, but it's nothing we cannot cope with...." This was grim. But his words – "it's nothing we cannot cope with" – softened the blow and increased my confidence. He went on: "I may have to do a little surgery. But please you will help us both if you don't worry: that is the most important part, and something you can do for yourself."
>
> He gave my wife the answer to our unspoken question: "There's nothing to worry about, Mrs Appleyard. No child is born with tuberculosis." I put my arm round Connie. She was very brave. I shall never know the despair she must have felt.

"The writing's a bit soppy," Bob interjects fifty years on.

> My next concern was for my future – all that I had planned for, in Yorkshire cricket. Were my playing days over? Slowly the surgeon said: "You will play again, Mr Appleyard. In fact, I shall come to Headingley to watch you bowl."
>
> The surgeon's confident promise gave me faith. And fear was moving out to make room for it.

"Bob was first-class," Geoffrey Wooler says. "His main object was to get well and to get back into playing cricket. I used to hate dealing with anybody who was always depressed. They gave me the idea they didn't really want to be well. I remember operating on one lady. We did a pretty good job on her heart valve and, when she got back home, the family were all expecting her to be 'mother' again and to do the washing – and you see she didn't want to. She resented being fit again. Nobody was going to look after her. Bob was quite the opposite."

In mid-May Bob took up residence in a TB ward at Killingbeck Hospital, Leeds. The operation was scheduled for October so that the streptomycin could work to arrest the growing hole in his lung. It was his first experience of hospital life, and he asked Geoffrey Wooler what he could do to help himself get back to normal.

The *Daily Express* continued the story:

> The surest way would be to lie in a plaster cast, but that was impracticable. The next best thing was to lie on my back, or left side, for five months.
>
> Five months … It needed will power to carry this through, for I had just left a life of great physical activity.
>
> The mental approach of a TB patient is vitally important. I saw chaps who could not reconcile themselves to their condition, who lost their sense of proportion because they feared tuberculosis. I was not going to be one of them.

"I insisted on lying on my back or my left side. It took me a while to get used to it. Sometimes the staff, to make it easy for themselves, would try to get me up for the bedpans. But I wouldn't. It might sound a bit crazy today. Probably nobody would do it. But I wouldn't get up for anything. For five months."

Visitors called. Some sat beside him. Others stayed awkwardly at the end of the bed, fearful of catching the infection. John Nash, the county secretary, was one who sat on the bed – "Now, Bob, you get well again. Your salary will be paid into the bank." – and so did his employer, Reuben Short: "Don't worry, we'll look after you." Then there were Herbert Sutcliffe, Bill Bowes, Frank Lowson, Len Hutton, all bringing a buzz of excitement to the ward.

But his thoughts were mostly with Connie who was now in a maternity home, being cheered by visits from Dorothy Hutton, Barbara Watson and others.

> Then on June the first at eight o'clock in the morning a nurse came up and said, "Congratulations – it's a girl." We had hoped for a boy (another cricketer, perhaps) but Connie and the baby were well so I was more than content.
>
> At ten o'clock a newspaper photographer walked in with three enlargements of photographs he had taken of my wife and daughter.
>
> And inside the envelope was a small lock of hair my wife had snipped from the baby's head.

That was Sunday morning. Six days later, on the Saturday afternoon, the world of cricket discovered a new sensation. England had selected Freddie Trueman for the first Test and at Headingley. Less than five miles from the hospital, he tore in to bowl to the nervous Indian batsmen, removing Roy, Manjrekar and Mantri in a 14-ball spell that had the scoreboard showing a total of no runs for four wickets. "They weren't the bravest at that time," Bob chuckles, though he must have wondered about the turn of Fate that had left him, a *Wisden* Cricketer of the Year, lying immobile on his back while his young county colleague, who had bowled in his shadow the previous summer, was blazing his name across all the newspapers.

Three weeks later Bob was being carried on a stretcher to an ambulance that drove him to the Gateforth sanatorium, near Selby.

"The coughing had stopped by then and, with all the resting and the hospital food, my weight was starting to go up. Normally I was 13 stone 10, but by the time I left hospital I had got up to 16½ stone."

Connie had brought him a cricket ball which he kept under the bedclothes, working his fingers against it so that he did not lose the hardness of skin, the 'hoof', that would be so necessary if he ever made a comeback.

"He kept that secret from me," Geoffrey Wooler says.

Bob had set his mind on returning to cricket, and his surgeon had given him encouragement. Not all his visitors, however, were as optimistic.

"You know, lass," Bill Bowes told Connie, "he'll never get back to the first-class game."

"Please don't tell him that," she replied. "He believes he's going to play for Yorkshire again."

Gateforth had opened in 1901 as the Leeds Sanatorium for Consumptives, an old manor house surrounded by a series of single-storey buildings, set in quiet countryside. With the female patients and the hospital administration in the Hall itself, the males were in the out-buildings, in two- or three-bedded rooms with french windows that opened out onto a grassy terrace. It was an environment much more congenial than the large wards at Killingbeck.

Mary Dobson, the medical social worker, recalls the ripple of excitement when the hospital staff heard that they were to care for the Yorkshire cricketer. "Bob Appleyard's going to be admitted ... Bob Appleyard's just come in."

Bob did not have the domestic or social problems that would cause her to work closely with him, but she was a keen follower of Yorkshire cricket, Bright Heyhirst was a friend of the family and she always stopped for a talk. "He was very much liked by the staff and the other patients. There was no side to him, no 'I'm Bob Appleyard'. He was just one of the lads."

His room-mate was an inspired choice. John Isherwood was a First Secretary in the Foreign Office, and their conversations helped to pass the long days. "We got on like a house on fire," Bob says. "He'd been in Tehran and in Rabat in French Morocco. He loved it out there, and he was full of fascinating stories. Also he was a Lancastrian, and he was a great cricket fan. On Sundays they used to pull our beds outside so that we could watch the hospital cricket team. They were long days. We hardly saw anybody but the people who brought the meals. So having him there was a great stroke of good fortune."

Mary Dobson recalls her conversations with them. "They were very intrigued by my knowledge of Yorkshire pubs."

The previous summer two senior Foreign Office diplomats, Guy Burgess and Donald McLean, had fled to Moscow, tipped off by an unidentified 'third man' that their spying had been discovered.

"After I left hospital, a fellow from the Foreign Office came to see me, to check that John Isherwood hadn't told me any secrets."

The summer passed. Trueman took 29 Indian wickets in the four Tests, but National Service limited his county appearances and Yorkshire, deprived of two key bowlers, finished once more in second place. Their 17 victories yielded them sufficient points to have won the title in each of the previous four summers but Surrey, outright champions for the first time since 1914, were victorious 20 times.

Bob sought to keep in touch with the world of county cricket as best he could, and he was aided in this by the receipt of letters from Lorna Smart, the Admiralty statistician he had met with her father at Taunton the previous summer. "Her father had given her three passions in life," Bob says. "Music, mathematics and cricket." She combined two of these passions by developing systems of cricket scoring that she then analysed on the train from Bishop's Stortford to London each morning and which she sent to cricketers who she thought might be interested: the Australian Keith Miller, Lancashire's Len Wilkinson, Frank Lowson and now Bob.

Fifty years have passed, and Bob retains not only the letters – full of chatty observation about his fellow cricketers – but the many pages of figures in various coloured pens. With her father she had watched every day of the 1948 Ashes series, using a complex system of scoring to identify every ball faced by each batsman: which bowler it was from, where the ball finished up and whether it had hit the bat, the pad or nothing at all. From this she was able to devise complete summaries of the series. It is the sort of data generated with ease by the modern computer, but it was years ahead of its time in 1948.

'The standard method of scoring suffers from a complete separation between the batsman's scores and the bowling analysis,' she explained in her first letter, 'though neither means very much without the other.' Using the example of Bob's debut match at The Oval in 1950, she then used her system to reconstruct his first over in county cricket:

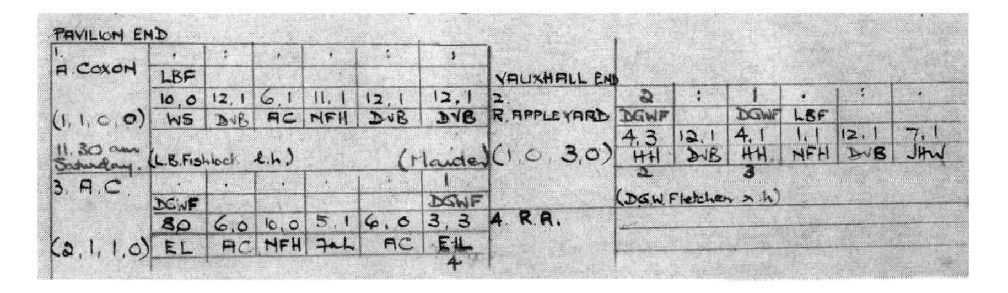

Fletcher's two was hit to mid wicket where Harry Halliday fielded it (?after chasing it out); it went between 66 and 88 yards, roughly. Next ball he didn't touch and it passed outside the off stump to Brennan, standing back. Third ball Fletcher got a single to mid wicket, where Harry again fielded it but appears to have been quicker so it must have been nearer to him. Fishlock, then the striker, turned the next ball to Horner at fine leg, and the fifth ball went through to Brennan untouched. The sixth ball he played to Johnny at mid-off.

She then explained how this method provided valuable insights into each batsman's preferences for different types of bowling, the pattern of their run-scoring and their rate of scoring measured in balls received rather than – as was normal at that time – by runs per hour.

For the 1948 series against the Australians, her figures of scoring rates reveal some surprising results. Washbrook, 43 runs per 100 balls faced. Compton, 40. Hutton, 33. Edrich, 29.

"You couldn't read these letters and ignore them," Bob says. "She knew more about the game than I did. She'd grown up with it; she'd observed it."

More followed at regular intervals, the letters becoming less formal – 'Dear Bob' in place of 'Dear Mr Appleyard' – and her report from Yorkshire's match at Lord's in June 1952 was full of asides about the various players:

> I could watch Len and Frank till the cows come home. My family has a stupid habit of attaching nicknames (generally zoological ones) to their favourite players and my brother christened Frank "Tadpole", on account of his infinite promise of developing into (as one newspaper aptly but inaccurately put it) "more like Hutton than Hutton is himself".
>
> Len's hundred was cheered resoundingly in a way I've never heard him get from the supercilious Lord's spectators, and he really seemed to have become a national possession, not just Yorkshire's pride and joy. Perhaps his captaincy of England has made a lot of difference but at last even Middlesex supporters are beginning to assess the realistic merits of our Len and their Denis, whom no one can truthfully claim as what he once was. Like Edrich he has aged much more in the past few years than Len has.
>
> There are times when Willie looks wide awake and fully conscious of his surroundings, but Saturday was one of the other times. He just wasn't with us at all.
>
> Master Close looks a very lonely, fed-up and disillusioned chap at the moment, but whether he is learning more sense and unlearning his previous know-it-all errors I don't know. That episode in the nets at Taunton didn't look very promising. You probably remember the way he hooked a ball over the back of the net out into the road, which you went to fetch (where anyone else would have asked a bystander to fetch it). Eddie tore a brisk strip off him but two minutes later, while you were still retrieving the first ball, the young chump did exactly the same again, with the air of a boy who thinks he has done something clever. That time he really did catch it. Eddie took the bat away and made it clear that he'd had it, under the oldest rule in the world: "Six and Out".
>
> Here at Lord's he eventually got out off the most feeble caught and bowled to Young. Johnny came in for the last ten minutes, and a good time was had by all. The six balls he connected with

> were all well into the air, fine blows, two of them sixes. I get very sniffy down at Taunton with the local idea that sixes are all that matters – they seem to think the game should be awarded to the side hitting most sixes. However when it is our dear old Johnny I howl with delight as much as the rest of the mob.
>
> I so badly want Johnny to become a great bowler in the true tradition of Yorkshire left-handers, but he is usually a sad disappointment. He produced 30 maidens out of 48, which sounds marvellous until you begin to think that it took him 288 balls to get one wicket. The average is around 55, and real bowlers such as Verity and Rhodes and you come out about 38 or 39.

"Of course Johnny bowled his overs twice as fast as everybody else," Bob says, engaging immediately with her data, "so he created more winning time."

Sitting on the train without a calculator or computer, and with cricket reference books less comprehensive than now, she could not follow through this idea as easily as we can, but her general observation contains insight. In the summer of 1952 Johnny Wardle bowled 63 balls for each of his wickets where Bob the previous year had taken one every 39. Across their whole careers, Wardle needed 55.5 balls for each wicket, Rhodes 44.0, Verity 43.0 and Bob 42.4.

"I had nothing to do all day in the sanatorium," Bob says. "There were an awful lot of hours between visits, and there was no television like there is now. We used to be avid listeners to *The Archers*, the quarter of an hour before meal time. So I lay in bed, hour after hour, digesting all Lorna's information. It helped me to keep in touch, not to feel isolated from the game."

The operation drew near. He developed an interest in yoga, learning breathing and relaxation exercises from a book and discovering that twenty minutes of deep relaxation could be as valuable as a full night's sleep. "I became so involved with meditation," he recalls, "that I succeeded in frightening myself. There were times when I felt I might be entering another dimension. It does concentrate the mind when you're in danger."

One week before the operation, he was transferred to Pinderfields Hospital in Wakefield, and there he lay in a ward with eight other tubercular patients. Most mornings one of them would be wheeled away to theatre, only to return in the evening with various tubes attached. For some, there would be recovery. For others, the prospect only of a short life as an invalid.

His own moment of reckoning was drawing near.

'FAITH CONQUERS FEAR' was the title of the *Daily Express* article that told that part of his story:

> There are times when people turn to prayer for help. That ward at Wakefield was no exception. We all talked freely about religion, of the need for total faith: faith in yourself, faith in your surgeon and, most important, faith in God. I do not regularly

> attend church or chapel. Nor did most of the others in the ward. Yet we shared a common basic loyalty.

One day he flicked open a magazine on his bed, and he found himself reading and re-reading the words of the 23rd Psalm.

> *The Lord is my shepherd; I shall not want.*
> *He maketh me to lie down in green pastures: he leadeth me beside the still waters.*
> *He restoreth my soul: he leadeth me in the paths of righteousness for his name's sake.*
> *Yea, though I walk through the valley of the shadow of death, I will fear no evil: for thou art with me; thy rod and thy staff they comfort me.*
> *Thou preparest a table before me in the presence of mine enemies: thou anointest my head with oil; my cup runneth over.*
> *Surely goodness and mercy shall follow me all the days of my life: and I will dwell in the house of the Lord for ever.*

Fifty years on, I read the lines slowly to him one evening. He was brought up in that tradition of unflinching toughness that Yorkshiremen pride themselves on, yet in the silence that follows I can see him struggling to hold down the waves of emotion that have welled up inside him.

"'Yea, though I walk through the valley of the shadow of death,'" he repeats eventually. "That was the prominent line, prior to the operation. 'Thy rod and thy staff they comfort me.'

"It's such an imperfect world. There's got to be something better. I can't believe that this is the beginning and end of everything. When you've gone through the experiences I have in life, if you don't have any faith, what have you? What's going to pull you through?

"People don't go to church anymore. Yet, as soon as there's a rail crash or some other tragedy, that's where they turn. People don't demonstrate their faith, but I suspect that deep down they still have it."

> *Yea, though I walk through the valley of the shadow of death, I will fear no evil: for thou art with me; thy rod and thy staff they comfort me.*

As they wheeled him into the operating theatre, the words ran round his head. He was determined that his faith would conquer fear.

CHAPTER 6

YOU'LL BE A MAN, MY SON

1924-51

Bob Appleyard was 28 years old when he was wheeled into the theatre for surgery. An active man all his life, he held on steadfastly to the words of Geoffrey Wooler. "Don't worry. You will play again. In fact, I will come to Headingley to watch you bowl." There was nothing that he could do for himself but to lie quietly and to have faith in his surgeon. But, beneath this faith, there must have lurked fear: fear that he had bowled his last ball, fear that he faced a life of invalidity, fear of an early death.

What gives one man the strength to overcome such fear where others lose their will?

"I used to go to see him at Gateforth," Geoffrey Wooler recalls, "and he was always looking on the bright side, saying 'Will I be able to come back?' I would have thought that he would have been wise not to have done much for some time, but you couldn't tell him. His main object was to get back and bowl again. He was never depressed, even though he had such an extensive disease."

Robert Appleyard was born in Bradford on Friday the 27th of June 1924, the first child of John Lucas Appleyard, a railwayman, and his wife Maud. His parents' marriage had been "frowned upon in some quarters" because his father was Church of England, his mother Roman Catholic. Bob took his father's religion, but the enduring detail about his mother that fascinates him is that her maiden name was Swithenbank.

"Len Hutton came to stay with us here in Ilkley the year before he died, and I discovered that his mother's maiden name was also Swithenbank. I haven't explored this any further yet, but it's not a common name, is it? I mentioned it one day after a trustees' meeting of the Len Hutton Foundation. We'd gone for a fish-and-chip lunch at Bryan's in Headingley, and Richard Hutton was there. A fellow trustee Peter Honeyset turned to Richard. 'You'll have to call him Uncle Bob now,' he said."

The young Appleyard began life in a low stone cottage in Wibsey Bank on the southern outskirts of Bradford. Now the district is well inside the boundaries of a great metropolitan conurbation, with the Huddersfield and Halifax Roads forming a vast intersection close by, but at that time their little cottage looked out on open farm fields.

"Bradford is in a basin, and all around are villages high above it. The roads all come out like the spokes of a wheel, only one of them is flat, and we were on the edge. My first recollection is of an old English sheepdog that we owned. I must have been about four years old."

His younger sister Margaret was born in 1926, and the family of four soon moved up the hill to a bigger house. Three quarters of a century on, Bob sits at home in Ilkley and finds in his memory images of the Bradford of those years: "There were gas lights in the street, with a chap who came and lit them. ... The coal came by horse and cart. You had a grate with a metal plate on top and a cellar beneath. ... Also the milk. It came twice a day, direct from the farm. It was warm. You went out at a certain time with your jug, and the man would fill it with a ladle. ... The railway used to employ knockers-up. People with long poles who came round in the early morning and knocked on the window. They'd keep knocking until they'd got a response." He breaks into laughter as he excavates these childhood details. "You're making me sound really ancient."

Bradford was a proud city, built from Pennine stone on the profits of a wool and worsted trade that grew rapidly in the early nineteenth century. There was misery in the mills, with children working 13-hour days and being subjected to beatings to keep them awake, with workers huddled into houses in narrow terraced streets. Then gradually the accumulated wealth created a municipal idealism that saw the erection of the Town Hall and the Wool Exchange, magnificent Victorian buildings created in Italianate Gothic. 'Bradford may not attract,' one guide book wrote, 'but it cannot fail to impress.'

Forster Square, named after the MP who pioneered the country's free education system, was created as an open space in the city centre, with statues and floral displays, and the people were provided with parks, most notably Lister Park with its boating lake, open-air swimming pool, tree-lined walks, large botanical garden and Cartwright Memorial Hall, housing the city's art gallery and museum.

To the north of the city, beside the river Aire, Sir Titus Salt, whose fortune came from alpaca wool in South America, created a model village, Saltaire, with well laid out cottages for his mill workers as well as a school, an evening institute, a Congregational church and two areas of allotments.

"Bradford was the centre of the wool industry," Bob says with pride. "It took in the raw wool. Washed it and cleaned it, because of the soft water supply. Then they combed and spun it. Sometimes they would weave it into cloth, and sometimes send it to Huddersfield or Halifax. And the finished cloth would go to Leeds where the tailors were. They had a large Jewish community there."

Leeds was only eight miles away, but it had a more sophisticated air. Cosmopolitan, built of brick not stone, further from the dales and moors where the sheep grazed, the sheep from which the area's wealth was being created.

Yorkshire County Cricket might have its headquarters in Leeds, but the best club cricket in Yorkshire was played in the Bradford League. 'The keenest in all England,' Roy Genders called it in his 1952 book *League Cricket in England*. 'If not everybody's idea of cricket as it should be played, it is a wonderful school for teaching one the finer points of the game.'

With choral societies, brass bands, two football league clubs and the Bradford Northern rugby league side, the city was a proud one.

Their northern pride, however, came with a strict sense of right and wrong. There were no public houses in Titus Salt's Saltaire, the Methodist Church had its headquarters in the city and, when Bob's mother left her husband and two children, he felt the sense of disapproval around him.

He was seven years old, his sister five, and his only contact with his mother, after her departure, was when she sometimes collected him from school and on Saturday mornings. "I never knew the real reasons for her leaving. You look at things in a different light when you get older, but at the time I blamed her." He fumbles for words, long having learnt to cope with his sense of rejection. "It was a bit embarrassing, to be honest, as divorces were almost unheard of."

The family was now three, and they moved into Bob's grandmother's house at Wibsey, where he lived outdoors like all the children in the area. Playing cricket and football, riding bicycles, roller-skating when they metalled the cobbled street, running to school in the morning. Often, when his father walked down to the city centre market on Saturday, he walked with him. "He'd go down with a sack, fill it with potatoes, other vegetables and apples and walk back up home. Sometimes we'd come back on the tram."

At the age of seven he acquired his first cricket bat. "We had to save 500 Oxo cube coupons and send off for it. It was an Indian bat, with a picture of an elephant on the front. You were a bit special in the street if you had your own bat."

There were few private motor cars and no television to keep a growing boy indoors. "We used to go hiking. We'd get a tram out to the end of the line, for a copper or two, and walk in the woods. That was a special treat for us. Grandma Appleyard used to take us at bluebell time. Unfortunately we didn't have a weather forecast in those days so sometimes we got soaked.

"Entertainments were minimal. We used to have family sing-songs. You had to make your own activities."

By the summer of 1934, Bob was ten years old and playing cricket for his junior school team. On a Friday in late July his teacher took them across to Headingley to see the fourth Test against the Australians. On the previous day England had been bowled out for 200, but Yorkshire's own Bill Bowes had struck back in the evening, leaving Australia on 39 for three.

The boys sat all day on the grass, leaving an hour before the close, but not one wicket fell as Bradman and Ponsford added 388 runs. "We'd just got out of the gate, and a big cheer went up. Ponsford had stepped back and hit his wicket." Ponsford, hit wicket, bowled Verity, 181. The next morning Bradman was bowled by Bowes for 304. "I reminded Bradman of this when I met him in Australia. 'I can never understand why I became a bowler,' I said."

He spent one year at Wibsey Modern School before passing the entrance exam to Priestman Central. It was not as prestigious as a grammar school, but it was a major step up from the elementary schools, offering the opportunity of a specialist commercial or technical training beyond the age of 14.

By this time cricket was becoming a passion. "The school was only about a mile from the Park Avenue ground so, if Yorkshire were playing, as soon as the school bell went, we ran all the way down. We used to get there about tea-time, when members came out for a stroll or arrived from their places of work. Each member could take in a lady or youth so we used to stand outside the gate till one of the members said, 'Come on, lad' and took us in the ground. There was no embarrassment.

"Sometimes the members took us into the stand, behind the bowlers' arm, and talked to us. Other times we sat on the grass, with a bottle of pop. We had freedom."

There were always wickets for Hedley Verity and Bill Bowes, runs for Herbert Sutcliffe, Maurice Leyland and the young Len Hutton, as Yorkshire triumphed repeatedly. "So many heroes. They were winning the championship. And that was the expectancy."

Bob's own cricket was progressing fast. At first a batsman in the school team, he discovered how to bowl and by 1938, the summer of his 14th year, he was taking wickets a-plenty in the Bradford Schools' team. Five for nine against Dearne Valley, six for 26 against Leeds, six for 28 against Huddersfield. Then, in the Yorkshire Schoolboys final, he took five Sheffield wickets for just five runs and they won the County Cup.

"It was held at Undercliffe Cricket Club. My father came and watched. Someone offered me a shilling for each wicket I got, and I got five. And five shillings was a lot of money in those days."

Opening the batting in that Bradford Boys' side were William Deplidge and William Elliott, both of whom went on to play football for Bradford Park Avenue, Billy Elliott later playing for Burnley and Sunderland and winning five caps for England.

"We all played cricket and football. I remember when I was at junior school, we had a football match against Ryan Street Juniors. I was centre-half, and I had to mark Len Shackleton. He ran rings round us, even at that age. He was a brilliant dribbler."

Shackleton, later a hero on Wearside, became the 'Clown Prince of Soccer', one of the great ball-players of the post-war game. "The trouble was, he'd beat somebody, then rather than pressing forward he'd go back and beat them again."

But, if Bob draws pride from having played in the same cricket team as boys who became England footballers, what did they think of his playing cricket? "Len Shackleton was a very good cricketer. He once confessed to me in later life that he'd rather have played cricket for Yorkshire than have played soccer for England."

The Bradford Boys' team, with Bob on the far right, standing
Deplidge is sitting, second from left; Elliott is sitting, second from right

The Bradford Boys' team was asked to serve as ball boys in an exhibition tennis match at Odsal Stadium, starring Bill Tilden, Donald Budge, Lester Stoeffen and Ellsworth Vines. "There would be these great events from time to time in Bradford. The Cossack horsemen also came to the Odsal Stadium and gave this wonderful display of horsemanship." And his memory of the tennis? "I got given one of the match balls, and Bill Tilden signed it."

He has treasured so many mementoes, does he still have the ball? "I was looking for it one day, and it turned out that Connie had given it to the girls to play with. Never to be seen again."

In the summer of 1938 the fourteen-year old Robert Appleyard was a rising star, and the following Spring he was invited to Headingley to Easter coaching sessions supervised by George Hirst. "I remember its raining one day and George leading us under one of the stands, where we listened intently for more than an hour to him talking about cricket."

By then Hirst was nearing 70, one of the last survivors of the great Yorkshire side who had won four championships in the last years of Queen

Victoria's reign, the only man in the history of first-class cricket to score 2,000 runs and take 200 wickets in the same summer. "What a titanic achievement that was – and against some of the greatest players of all time."

When the rain stopped, they all went to change into their cricket clothes. "I can still see the old man in the dressing room, putting on what we called a Doll's red flannel belt around his midriff. Red flannel belts and long sweaters that covered the bum were de rigueur in those days, to keep out the cold wind and to prevent lumbago.

"The clothes were made of wool and other natural fibres," Bob adds, a Bradfordian through and through. "They absorbed the sweat and kept out the chill. I went across to wearing artificial fibres for a while, but I found I started getting backache. You see, there's so much wisdom that can be passed on from the older generations – but people today think everything's changed, don't they?

"When I was working for Short's Lifts, I would call in on George Hirst whenever I was in Huddersfield near the end of a day. He would make two big mugs of tea, and I'd listen to him reminiscing. I remember him saying to me that this business of a bowler being able to pitch the ball on a sixpenny bit was a load of nonsense. He reckoned that, if you spread out a newspaper and put it down, and hit it with five balls out of six, you've done well. I mean, look at Hawkeye on television. With most bowlers, they'd need four newspapers."

Bob has always been in his element learning what he can from experts.

"I'd sit with Wilfred Rhodes whenever we played at Scarborough. He was blind by then, and he'd be guided into the ground by his daughter, walking slowly down the slope behind square leg to the members' enclosure. He always wore a trilby hat, and he carried a white stick. Whispers would go round the ground: 'It's Wilfred', and by the time he reached his seat everybody would be standing and applauding. It was a real privilege to sit with him and to pick his brains about bowling."

Rhodes was nearing eighty by the time Bob's cricket reached its peak in the mid-1950s, just as Bob is nearing eighty now. But do the young Yorkshire players seek him out, as he once sought out Hirst and Rhodes? "'It's a different game now,' they tell you." He shakes his head in bewilderment. "But is it?"

At the age of fifteen Bob was a promising schoolboy cricketer, being inculcated in the great Yorkshire tradition that stretched back through Verity and Sutcliffe to Hirst and Rhodes.

But that was the summer of 1939. "All that had been forgotten by the time war ended. I had to start all over again."

It was not just the war that changed Bob's life. There were great changes, too, at home. His sister Margaret caught diphtheria in the summer of 1937. "She was joining me at Priestman School. I remember one of the teachers saying to me at the start of term, 'I thought your sister was coming.' And she'd already died. She wasn't ill very long. Diphtheria was very infectious, wasn't it? It was my first experience of dying, and it affected me greatly."

By the time of his sister's death, Bob's father had remarried – to Evelyn Child, a younger woman who was to bear him two further children, both girls.

"My father was quite a deep-thinking man. He was a union representative, at the L.M.S. Low Moor branch, though he wasn't a left-wing Luddite. At election time he used to go to all the hustings, listen to the various candidates and vote for the one who impressed him most. It wasn't a question of party for him. He had a friend who used to come over on Sunday, and they'd spend hours talking about the economy and the international situation. He was concerned about Hitler. But I was too young to understand."

And the news? How did they learn the news?

"We had a radio, with an accumulator. It was quite a heavy piece of equipment, and we took it up on a Saturday morning to the local bicycle shop to have it charged up. That was our communication."

Bob breaks off once more to chuckle at the memory. "It sounds like we were back in the Dark Ages."

His father was a religious man and a strict teetotaller. Just old enough to have experienced and been disturbed by the tail end of the Great War, he joined the Quakers for a while and took to writing letters to the *Bradford Telegraph*, expressing his concerns. "He used the nom-de-plume John Lucas, his Christian names. The only line I can remember from any of them is, 'Sheer idleness is the rust which attaches itself to the most brilliant of metals.'

"He also lectured in the evenings on railway engines. I did the drawings for him. It got me interested in technical drawing. He was a railway fireman, but he did become a temporary driver. Sometimes he went down to London and back in a day. He took me on the footplate once or twice, but I was more interested in kicking a football about and playing cricket."

On remarrying, Bob's father had moved to a council house half a mile away in Southfield Avenue. From there Bob continued at school past the age of fourteen, opting for the technical rather than the commercial stream. "I wanted to be a draughtsman. The Priestman School was slightly different from the other schools in Bradford. We took the Royal Society of Arts and the London Chamber of Commerce exams."

Sixty years later he was invited back, their most famous old boy, to attend the opening of a new sports hall at what is now a junior school. "It's 95% Pakistani now," he says, another world from the Bradford in which he grew up. "But I must say, the kids there were all so well-behaved, so polite."

The summer of 1939 saw him joining the Bradford cricket club at Park Avenue. He still has his membership card – price, ten shillings and sixpence, and free entry to county matches there – and he recalls how the professional Stanley Douglas showed him how to bowl off-breaks. "I practised it in the nets, not that seriously because I was an opening bowler, but I got the hang of it. And once you've mastered it, it never leaves you. It's like learning to ride a bike." Too old now for the Bradford Boys' team, he played in the club's third eleven, sometimes the second, but all this dwindled into insignificance as the summer drew to a close.

Sunday the third of September, 1939. At 11.15 in the morning the Prime Minister Neville Chamberlain broadcast to the British people on the radio, and the Appleyards sat beside their recharged set. Chamberlain had demanded that by eleven o'clock the German Chancellor undertook to withdraw his troops from Poland. "No such undertaking has been received," he announced in sombre tones, "and consequently this country is at war with Germany."

It was the news that John Appleyard had been dreading all summer. There was to be another war, one that might be worse even than the Great War which had cast a dark shadow over his own growing years. He was an intense man, given to sessions of serious thought. For a time he had been attracted to the pacifism of the Quakers, and he feared for the future that his young family now faced.

Bob was fifteen years old, starting back at school again and hoping to achieve the qualifications that would allow him to train as a draughtsman. "It is difficult even now to recall the details," he says. "I think I'd been spending some nights at my grandma's. She was on her own, and I spent quite a bit of time with her."

His memory is confused. He has talked so rarely about those twenty-four hours, and he can no longer recall the exact sequence of events.

The *Yorkshire Post* is a more reliable source. On Tuesday the fifth of September, two days after the declaration of war, it carried the following story:

> **BRADFORD FAMILY GASSED**
> **Father, Mother and Two Little Girls**
> A family of four – father, mother and two little girls – were found gassed in the bathroom of their house at Southfield Avenue, Halifax Road, Bradford, yesterday.
> They were Mr. J. Appleyard, a railwayman, aged about 35, his wife, and their two children, Wendy and Brenda, aged about three years and 18 months respectively.
> The discovery was made by Mr. Appleyard's 15-year-old son by a previous marriage, who was living in the house.
> According to a neighbour, Mr Appleyard sent his son to stay with a relative in Bradford on Sunday afternoon, stating that the rest of the household would be away for the night. The two little girls were at that time seen playing outside the house; but shortly afterwards, they were called inside, and nobody saw them again.
> The boy returned to the house early yesterday to see if his father had come back, and found the four persons dead in the bathroom, with the gas ring turned on at full. He ran for assistance, and the police were immediately called.
> A neighbour stated that Mr Applcyard had recently expressed fears about the war.
> The inquest will be opened tomorrow.

The *Bradford Telegraph* carried a report of the inquest:

> Robert Appleyard, aged 15, said on Sunday morning his father, stepmother and the children were at home. Shortly after 3 p.m. his father told him he might have to go to Liverpool and might not be able to get back. His stepmother and the two children would go to a relative at Manningham.
> "He told me to go to my grandmother's. I went and got permission to stay, and I returned home to tell my father," said Robert. "He handed me a box containing a gold watch and gave me four £1 notes. He said I had to keep it if anything happened."
> The Coroner: Did he say that he had no money in the bank and that he had drawn it all out? – Yes.
> Was your father on any sort of Army Reserve? – I do not know.
> Robert said he left the house shortly afterwards and went to his grandmother's at Wibsey. Yesterday morning he returned home about nine o'clock and found the doors locked.
> He waited outside the house for half an hour and smelt gas. Eventually he found the door key in the coal place and went into

the house. Opening the bathroom door he heard a sound of escaping gas.
It was dark inside and, on lifting the curtain behind the door, he realised something was wrong and went for assistance. A neighbour went into the bathroom and turned the gas off from the main.
Questioned by the Coroner, Robert said on Saturday he looked into the bathroom and saw a mattress over the bath. The window was blocked with brown paper. He thought his father was perhaps making air-raid precautions, and did not closely examine the room.
Mary Appleyard, of 11 Holroyd Hill, Wibsey, said the dead man was her son. When she last saw him about a fortnight ago he appeared cheerful and in good health. Last Sunday evening she went to his home expecting he and his family would be there.
She found a piece of paper bearing the words "Back tomorrow" pinned on the back door. She concluded he had gone to visit his wife's mother at Manningham.
Police-constable Kemp, of Bradford City Police, said about 10.30 a.m. yesterday he went to the house and found the bathroom in semi-darkness, the window being partially shadowed with brown paper. He found the man lying on a mattress, on an improvised bed on the top of the bath.
Lying alongside him on his left side was his wife and, next to her, were Brenda and Wendy. All were apparently dead. There was a strong smell of gas, but the gas had been turned off before he got there. There were no signs of a struggle or disturbance and there was no suggestion of violence.

Bob's own mother had left him at the age of seven; his sister Margaret had died of diphtheria six years later. Now, two years on, with the war less than twenty-four hours old, his childhood world had gone for ever.

Yea, though I walk through the valley of the shadow of death, I will fear no evil.

"You're in a state of shock, aren't you?" Bob says. "I was fifteen years old, and I was on my own. My grandmother couldn't cope. So I was taken in by my stepmother's parents."

Billy and Emma Child were devout Christians. "They were working class folk of enormous integrity, uncomplicated people. They'd saved hard and bought their own house. Uncle Billy was an engineering brass turner at Lister's Mills. For fifty years he sang in the church choir at St Paul's, Manningham, and that was where I was confirmed. I suppose I could have rejected my faith at that time, but you need support. And religion provided that support."

For thou art with me; thy rod and thy staff they comfort me.

"Everything changed with the war," Bob says. "Nothing was permanent anymore. So much was happening, and you didn't know what was going to happen next. There was no meaning to anything, no finality."

He left school immediately and started an apprenticeship in the machine shop at Hepworth and Gradidge, a large engineering firm who made pistons and piston rings for car and aircraft engines. There he worked from 7.30 in the morning to 5.30 at night, with a 4½-hour shift on Saturday mornings.

One day, towards the end of his first year there, he caught his right index finger – the finger for spinning the ball – in a milling machine and was lucky to escape with a few stitches. "I was off work a month, I've still got the scar, but it did heal eventually. And, while I was off, I started thinking. I realised that the work I was doing involved too much repetition and that I wasn't going to get on. I needed to get more education. So I started looking for another job."

Such personal ambition was not encouraged during the war, but he managed to secure an apprenticeship in engineering at the smaller family firm of Knowles and Company in Toller Lane near his new home in Manningham. They were a well-equipped precision engineering company, producing machinery for the textile industry, but during the war they became sub-contractors to Rolls Royce and the War Office for essential war work. Bob earned eight shillings and sixpence a week, spending six months in each of the firm's departments: the drawing office, the pattern shop, the iron and brass foundries and the machine and fitting shops.

"It was precision work with very fine limits. As part of the early training, you were given an old file. You took it to the blacksmith. He softened it and hammered it out. Then you ground and shaped it, took it back to the blacksmith to harden, and that was a part of your equipment. I've still got some of them. Filing and scraping, to get the surface correct, was an essential part of every job. It certainly taught me the value of absolute accuracy."

One job required the removal of a burr on a small, armour-plated tank door. "The door weighed about fifty pounds, and it had to be lifted into a bench vice so that we could take off the burr with a two-pound hammer and a cold chisel. It wasn't a precision job, but by the end your arms and legs were almost dropping off. Work like that really built up your muscles and your stamina. We worked all day on that job. Then we stayed through the night and finished at lunchtime the next day.

"We had no idea where the tank itself was being made, but we found out in the end that the part we were making was a revolver port door for the tank commander to open with a lever so that he could fire his revolver."

He also attended night school two evenings a week and joined the fire service as a part-time cycle messenger boy, often spending nights at the fire station. They were demanding times, but his main ambition was to reach eighteen when he could follow in the footsteps of the Childs' son, Norman, by volunteering to join the Royal Air Force. Norman had started out as a policeman, but he had spent 2½ years before the war training to be a pilot and in the spring of 1940 he earned his wings.

"He was a role model for me. I really looked up to him. He was in Coastal Command, flying out of Wick. He was given compassionate leave when his sister died, and while he was home he took me under his wing. I shall never forget the day we went out together on a rowing boat on the Lister Park lake. He couldn't talk about what he was doing, but he said enough that I wanted to be a pilot, too."

It was a pleasant Sunday afternoon. Families strolled about the park as they always did on Sundays. People sat in deck-chairs in front of the bandstand, listening to the brass band. And the two young men rowed in leisurely fashion about the boating lake. This was the Bradford that made them proud, the England they were going to fight to defend.

On the first of May 1941 Flight-Sergeant Norman Child was on a mission out of Wick, and disaster struck. "A fog came over," Bob tells. "The engine failed, and they couldn't land so they had to bale out. Norman was the last man out, and he was too late, the only one killed. By the time it was his turn to bale out, the plane was too low."

Once more sorrow descended on the family. The Childs had had two children, and within a year they had buried both of them: Evelyn and her two little girls, now their beloved Norman. And Bob was bereft as well: he had started to rebuild his life after his father's death, Norman had been such an important part of that, and now he too was gone. All his grief returned.

"He was like an elder brother to me. I felt his loss very deeply. It certainly made me even keener to train to become a pilot."

At sixteen he joined the Air Training Corps, giving up many evenings and weekends in pursuit of his ambition. "I spent my annual holidays at RAF bases. I remember going up one time in a Wellington, with a Canadian air crew. They were a mad lot. I thought I'd never get back."

They were hard years, and the cricket was only a part of them. He played for Manningham Mills team in the Bradford Central League in the first two summers of the war. "We practised Tuesday and Thursday nights, but we were never allowed to bowl until we had rolled and marked the pitch." Then in 1942, realising that he needed to play in the Bradford League itself if his cricket was to progress, he attended nets at Lidget Green. Bill Copson and Tommy Mitchell, both Derbyshire miners who had played for England before the war, were playing for the club, but they were not present on the night Bob turned up. "I hit the wickets quite a few times, but nobody seemed to take any notice. Perhaps there was nobody there who had any influence."

A colleague in the Air Training Corps played at Bowling Old Lane and, when Bob turned up for practice there, he immediately caught the eye of Ernest Holdsworth, the club president. Holdsworth had captained the Yorkshire second eleven in the years after the first world war, nurturing the raw talents of Maurice Leyland and Arthur Mitchell, who would later coach Bob in the Winter Shed.

Mitchell was, in fact, the professional at Bowling Old Lane while the captain was Allan Shackleton, another who had captained the Yorkshire second eleven. Clubs like Bowling Old Lane were a breeding ground for Yorkshire cricketers, and on Saturday afternoons Bob found himself in front of several hundred spectators, pitting his skills against great players: Learie Constantine and Leslie Ames, the Pope brothers Alf and George, Eddie Paynter, even Herbert Sutcliffe and Len Hutton when they were on leave. As in the First World War, when Jack Hobbs, Frank Woolley and Sydney Barnes were all employed, the Bradford League was a magnet for cricket's hungry professionals.

For Bob the hours at Knowles were long, he had evening classes to attend, and he was often away with the Air Training Corps. When he does think back to those years, it is not the cricket he remembers so much as the occasional Sundays he spent cycling with friends. There was little sport on a Sunday, and the morning service at church was at 6.30. So there could be a whole day free to explore beyond Bradford's industrial landscape.

"Occasionally we'd go across to Morecambe and back, about 65 miles each way. There'd be eight or ten of us, all on bicycles with fixed gears, and we had to climb Buck Haw Brow, a huge hill at Settle that's by-passed now. It was a wonderful way of seeing the Dales at that time. We wouldn't see a car all day, because of petrol rationing. When you went uphill, you could tack sideways. And sitting on your bike, you could look over the walls, see far better than you can in a car."

And Morecambe? "I suppose it was the closest seaside. People used to go there during Bowling Tide Week. An attractive town. But we'd only stop a couple of hours. It would take us four hours or more to get there."

It is only sixty years ago – but what a change has come in those years! What a different lifestyle the sixteen- and seventeen-year-old boys of today have.

"The present generation are in cars from being born. Going to school in cars, collected in cars. As soon as they're seventeen, they're looking for a car. We came from a stock who walked or rode horses everywhere. We ran to school, we played football, we rode bikes. It was all natural. We didn't have to train to be fit. We were fit. The stamina was in-built in our growing up. And we came from stock that was fit. Wilfred Rhodes had to walk three miles to the nearest railway station, and he'd be carrying his bags. Then he had to walk to the ground at the other end. He didn't need a training schedule to get fit."

What was it his father wrote to the *Bradford Telegraph*? 'Sheer idleness is the rust which attaches itself to the most brilliant of metals.' Nobody has ever accused Bob Appleyard of idleness.

"I joined the trade union, the AEU. You more or less had to be a member. I went a few times to the meetings. But because it was late at night, half the people who were there were asleep. There were people asking for votes, and people were putting their hands up who were almost asleep. I just thought, 'This is a waste of time.'

"In the shop there was a Communist, trying to convert people, wasting your time when you were on the bench with a pile of work to do. He even got them out on strike for half a day during the War."

At eighteen Bob took aptitude tests for the Royal Air Force and was accepted as a PNB, a Pilot-Navigator-Bomb-aimer. A proud young man, ready to fight for his country, he became 1591383 AC2 Appleyard, waiting on deferred service for his call-up.

RAF casualties were lighter than expected, and the demand for his services never came. He was summoned back for further tests and told that he should look for another service to join. But in a classic bureaucratic muddle, the Royal Navy rejected him on the grounds that he was registered for the RAF. Then, when the Army ordered him to report to Dumbarton, they discovered that he was an engineer, in a reserved occupation, and he returned to Bradford.

He continued to play cricket when he could, and Ted Lester recalls batting against him at Undercliffe in 1944. "He'd got a little bit of a reputation by then. It was a Bank Holiday, I got a fifty. It was the first time I'd ever had a collection, and it was the biggest one I ever had: about 12 pounds, 10 shillings. I never met Bob again till he turned up at The Oval, playing for Yorkshire."

The scorecard survives from that day at Undercliffe:

Lester E.	c Creighton	b Appleyard	72
Wilson J.V.	c Lightowler	b Appleyard	19
Wood A.	bowled	b Appleyard	2
Townsend L.F.	bowled	b Appleyard	5
Dennis F.	c Lightowler	b Appleyard	27

Three of Bob's five victims had been established county players before the war; the other two would become so afterwards.

Bob was cycling to work one morning during the war when he spotted a pair of cricket flannels in the window of a second-hand shop. "Clothing was rationed, and sports clothes weren't being manufactured. So, on my way home, when I saw the shop was still open, I stopped and tried them on." They were a perfect fit, and he carried them home proudly – but not as proudly as he wore them after he had read the label inside. 'H. VERITY'. He still smiles at the recollection: "I wore those trousers until they fell apart."

Eventually, as the war drew to a close, he tried the Royal Navy again, and this time he discovered that they were looking for specialist engineers for ship repair work in the dockyards. Within ten days he was Petty Officer Appleyard, and he was sent to Chatham in Kent and from there to Suffolk where he underwent training on the shore-based HMS Ganges by the River Stour.

"Does anyone play the piano?" one officer enquired at Chatham, and the eager volunteers – expecting a cushy assignment – found themselves lifting a heavy piano up three narrow flights of stairs. So Bob was wary when the call came up, "Does anyone play cricket?" But he soon found himself playing again, though his debut for Nore Command brought him experience of a cricket that was very different from what he had known in Bradford.

"The Navy was very class-structured, and I was the only non-commissioned member of the team. I took a wicket straight away, but I was taken off to give one of the officers a bowl. Winning the game was clearly a secondary objective, not at all like in the Bradford League."

He might have been naturally fit, but the training regime made demands on different muscles, not all of them helpful to him as a bowler. "I struggled with the rope climbing and the parallel bars, and they made me do extra training. It stiffened my arm and leg muscles, which was no good for bowling, but it made me the fittest I've ever been in life. We worked from 6 a.m. to 6.30 p.m., and of course we learned discipline. We learned to execute orders, even if we privately questioned them."

Each Sunday morning, he remembers, the gymnasium with a stage at one end was set out for a church service. On either side of the stage, inscribed on panels, were the words of Rudyard Kipling's poem 'If'.

"It's not all something to follow, to teach youngsters, but it was compulsive to read." And the verse he still recites is one that he has followed.

If you can fill the unforgiving minute
With sixty seconds' worth of distance run
Yours is the earth and everything that's in it
And – which is more – you'll be a Man, my son.

In December 1945 he sailed out to the Bay of Biscay, then down the Mediterranean and through the Suez Canal, spending Christmas Day on an aircraft carrier in the Red Sea. They arrived in January in Colombo in the British Colony of Ceylon, and there he spent three months, repairing ships. He sought out the Colombo Cricket Club. He might have bowled at Learie Constantine and Herbert Sutcliffe in the Bradford League, but such was the importance of rank that his only appearances were for their second eleven.

He spent the summer of 1946 as part of the Reserve Fleet on the River Dart in Devon, where he played cricket for the local Dartmouth club. "The fielding side used to applaud the incoming batsman all the way to the wicket and all the way back to the dressing room when he was out. Well, that had never happened in any Bradford League match I'd ever played."

Compared with the local population, they found themselves well-fed. "We still qualified for overseas rations so we were able to eat bacon and eggs." Then in August he was sent to the HMS Rampura, a repair ship, in the Mediterranean, docking in Malta's Grand Harbour. There he played cricket against the crews of two destroyers, HMS Volage and HMS Samurez.

They progressed to Limassol in Cyprus. "That was a wonderfully peaceful place. Idyllic. It was quite primitive. To have a water tap in a house was a luxury. But the people were so friendly, and there was none of the trouble that built up later."

He volunteered for service in a submarine – "I'd started out trying to be a pilot, and now I was going down in the ocean" – but his stay on board was a brief one. "The captain was doing a spot of fishing over the side when my pal and I went on board. We went down to this compartment for a meal. There were six of us going to sleep in it; there'd be a fuss if you put six chickens in it now. While the captain was eating, someone attached a tin of sardines to the end of his fishing line and, when he came back out, he didn't see the funny side of it all. Fortunately my friend and I were summoned back to the Rampura while he was still trying to find out who'd done it."

Their peaceful break in Cyprus was over. Albanian mines had blown up the Volage and Samurez and, with mine-sweepers ahead of them, the Rampura sailed through the Corfu Channel to their rescue. Almost eighteen months after VE Day Bob was facing the horrors of war for the first time.

"I was in charge of one of the pumping-out crews in the forward compartments, working four hours on and four hours off for 24 hours a day for about a week. We worked all night, pumping out the water, wondering what we were going to find next."

In all, 44 bodies were recovered, many of them men who had played cricket with them back in Malta, but some of their possessions proved even more upsetting to retrieve. "Both ships were going home after two years at sea, and floating in the bilge water were all these toys and dollies the crew were taking home to their families.

"It was all small beer compared to the hardships and losses of all the ships on the Atlantic and Arctic convoys, but it did bring home to us the trauma of war. On Sunday mornings we had a church service on the open sea, and we often sang that hymn:

O hear us when we cry to Thee
For those in peril on the sea."

One of the two destroyers, with its bow blown off
"We took the guns off, blocked up the pipes and made it ready for towing to Malta."

Back in England by December, he underwent the routine medical examination for all forces returning from overseas. On the way home from Colombo, just after they had left Port Said, there had been a panic when there was a suspicion that somebody had caught bubonic plague. Now his x-ray revealed a spot on the lung, enough to confine him to bed for further tests.

"In the end they decided that, whatever it was, it had calcified and would not cause any further problems. I'd completed my service so at the start of 1947 I was discharged."

Was that the start of his tubercular infection?

"There were forty of us in one mess on the Rampura, all sleeping cheek to jowl in hammocks. That was probably the best breeding ground you could find for a tubercule."

Six years later Geoffrey Wooler, his surgeon, obtained the x-ray and suggested that Bob applied for a partial disability pension from the Royal Navy. "But I didn't want to do that. There were people in a much worse state than me, who needed the money more."

So in January 1947 Petty Officer Appleyard became once more a civilian engineer, securing a position with a firm of electrical contractors, Southern and Redfern. "They were frigidaire distributors. I'd done some refrigeration work in Ceylon, and the Chief Petty Officer there said that he was going into refrigeration; there was a big future in it. The fish and meat industry had old sulphur and ammonia plants that hadn't been renewed because of the war. And there were hotels, restaurants, dairies, farms, ice cream plants, even Harry

Ramsden's fish-and-chip shop. They were all having fridges installed. We did some domestic refrigeration but not much. The higher income people had them, but most people just had larders. Our work was mainly commercial."

He found himself in Scarborough, living in digs during the worst winter weather in living memory. Heavy snowstorms and sub-zero temperatures combined with post-war shortages to bring much of the country, especially the North York Moors and the coast of East Yorkshire, to a standstill. This was the time when Bob was visiting business premises and extolling the advantages of refrigeration. He laughs as he looks back: "It was colder outside than it was in the fridges."

By mid-summer he had applied for a vacancy back in Bradford, but his cricket at Bowling Old Lane was handicapped by his work. "The fridges were working full pelt in summer, and they'd break down. So I wasn't able to play as much cricket as I wanted."

Nine years had passed since, as a fourteen-year-old, he had been the star of the Yorkshire Boys' Final, taking five Sheffield wickets for five runs and being summoned to Headingley the following Easter for coaching with George Hirst. "I didn't think about it at the time, but I must have been one of the best schoolboy prospects in the county." But whatever path he had started down at that time had long been lost. County cricket had been suspended for six summers and, when it did reconvene, Bob was away in the Navy, a forgotten figure whose youthful promise belonged with so much else that the war had destroyed. He was in the Navy throughout 1946, then repairing fridges in 1947 by which time he had turned 23 years old. Meanwhile, Yorkshire had found other new-ball bowlers: Alec Coxon, Ron Aspinall, Bill Foord, Johnny Whitehead.

By now he was regretting taking up refrigeration and looked for an opening into a winter-based activity like central heating. However, he spotted an advertisement in the *Bradford Telegraph and Argus* for a salesman at Short's Lifts and, selected from seventy applicants, he embarked on a selling career that would last through his cricketing days and for many years afterwards.

Meanwhile in the summer of 1948 he signed up for Undercliffe, who – like many of the cricket clubs – made payments to most of the amateur players in their first team. "It was called boot money," Bob recalls. "There was no mention of it in the accounts." Promoted that summer from the second division, the club came within a whisker of winning the league but its financial arrangements were contrary to the league rules, a matter that came to a head three years later.

Bob returned to Bowling Old Lane the following summer, this time as an above-board professional. "It was only a few pounds, enough to pay for the cricket gear and the travelling expenses." Ronnie Scarbrough, his friend, was president at Eccleshill club who, falling from the first division to the lower reaches of the second, had an unsettled AGM at the end of 1951.

"Somebody stood up and asked, 'Why aren't we signing any good amateurs?' and Ronnie replied, 'Because we're not prepared to sign these sham amateurs like other clubs.' Ronnie didn't realise the press were present. The next day it was on the front page of the *Telegraph and Argus*, and Ronnie was summoned to a meeting of the league hierarchy to explain his conduct. They were going to ban him."

Ronnie Scarbrough had been the best man at Bob's wedding that spring, and Bob, who was now a Yorkshire player, top of the national bowling averages after his extraordinary first summer, attended the meeting with his friend. In the chair was Ronnie Burnet, whose captaincy of Baildon had led them to the title two years running; alongside him, a solicitor.

"They said the meeting had to be confidential. Nothing was to get in the press. Ronnie was going to be banned sine die from cricket. I stood up and I said, 'When I was at Undercliffe, I was paid five pounds. And there were ten of us in the side that were paid. Just for the record, there was one chap – Les Townend – who wasn't. So you can guess who the others were. It's just hypocritical, is this meeting.' It was the last thing they wanted to hear from me, who'd just taken 200 wickets. So nothing more was said about the matter."

Bowling Old Lane cricket team
Bob standing top right, next to Frank Lowson

Somehow in those years in the Bradford League – "the memory is a bit blurred" – Bob found once more the path towards the Yorkshire team, the path on which he had taken those first steps ten years earlier, before the war had changed everything.

He had lost his family in the cruellest of circumstances. He had formed an attachment to the young pilot Norman Child, only to receive the news of his death. He had seen the bodies of returning sailors floating in the Mediterranean. He was no longer a young boy, playing ball in the street. He had become a tough survivor.

When they wheeled him into the operating theatre at Pinderfields Hospital in Wakefield, he was determined once more to survive.

His religion helped but so, too, did his cricket. "Cricket has always been a bit of a lifeline for me. Without it, what would I have done after my illness? I had a job to go to, but cricket was far more interesting, far more challenging. It was a challenge to get back to where I had been before."

CHAPTER 7
RECOVERY
1952-54

For five months, from May to October 1952, Bob had lain on his side and on his back in the hospital bed, taking streptomycin tablets and resolutely remaining positive. Then the day before his operation at Pinderfields Hospital he was visited by a doctor who had been studying his latest x-ray results.

"I think he was Ukrainian. His English was very limited. He said the results of the x-ray were very good and, if I were you, I wouldn't have the operation. Well, I never really felt ill prior to the operation, and I didn't look all that ill. The coughing had stopped, and I was resting and eating. So his advice put me in a dilemma, because I'd no one else to talk to. But I remembered what Geoffrey Wooler had said. If I wanted to get back to cricket, the quickest way was for him to take out the infected part. So I stuck to what he'd said."

According to the surgeon, the x-rays needed careful viewing. "Unless you took a side view, you wouldn't think there was anything wrong. If you took a straight anterior-posterior view, he looked fine. The lower lobe had expanded up and filled the cavity left by the diseased upper lobe. But when you took a lateral view, it was quite obvious that the upper lobe had gone completely. The lower lobe was adjusting itself to take the place of both lobes."

Eager to return to cricket and placing his faith in the thoracic specialist, Bob elected to go through with the operation. The next day Geoffrey Wooler set about removing the infected part of the lung. He made a large cut all down Bob's left side and, rather than cause further damage by cutting through the ribs, he sprang open the rib cage. Keeping it apart with plastic balls, he pulled out the lung sufficiently to work surgically on it. "He caused the minimum disturbance," Bob says.

"It was just at the beginning of our being able to remove the disease surgically," the surgeon recalls, "and to have drugs to control any post-operative appearance so that it didn't break out anywhere else. Before that, the operations could be terribly destructive, holding onto the shoulder blade of the patient while the surgeon took out ribs to collapse the lung. Many of the patients were left invalids for life.

"Bob had a completely destroyed left upper lobe. The whole lobe was just one large cavity. I took it out, and luckily we managed to save the lower lobe. If I'd had to remove that as well, it would have been pretty grim for him. I don't think he'd ever have attempted to play again. He'd have had a miserable time."

For six hours they worked in the theatre, and the exhausted surgeon left it to a houseman to stitch up the long incision. "It was not the best piece of needlework," Bob says, still carrying a pronounced scar from armpit almost to waist. "Geoffrey did apologise afterwards."

The next day Norman Yardley and Ronnie Burnet arrived at his bedside. "I was doped, and I was in great discomfort because they'd put blocks under the feet at the bottom of the bed so that my head was in danger of sliding into the iron bed-head rails. I had two tubes attached to my chest and two pumps to suck out the residue of the operation. The pumps had a compression motor and a belt drive, and they were going noisily day and night. Norman must have looked at me and thought, 'There's no way he'll ever get back.'"

Within weeks Geoffrey Wooler's skills were on the front pages of the national newspapers. Lord Woolton, the Conservative Party chairman, was taken ill at their conference at Scarborough, and he was close to death when the surgeon was summoned in the night to drain a ruptured abscess on his lung.

Back at Gateforth Bob was reunited with John Isherwood, whose operation had taken place elsewhere, and they began the slow process of recovery. At first there was more lying in bed. "Then once a day they'd take me in a chair to the toilet. And, after about a week, it would be twice a day. Then after another week they'd help me there without a chair, and I'd start using my leg muscles again. Then that would go up to twice a day. We realised that we'd have to learn to walk again; we'd seen other people going through the same stages. It was all very gradual. But it was a wonderful feeling, the realisation that you were starting to get better. Even to get into a chair to go to the toilet, after using bedpans for almost nine months, it was a special moment."

"Being in bed, you lose the tone in your muscles," Geoffrey Wooler explains. "I don't think we should keep them in bed as long as that today. They're all for getting them out as soon as possible."

Meanwhile there were breathing exercises to be done, sessions of sitting up in a bed and working their reduced lungs. The first months of 1953 passed and, though there was no cricket in the newspapers, there were more letters from Lorna Smart to enjoy.

She enclosed five-year figures for the batsmen of each county, revealing their most frequent methods of dismissal and the types of bowler likely to get them out. Even in this, however, her awareness of the game raised difficulties in categorising bowlers:

> You yourself are an excellent example of the problem. Though you do all your bowling with a uniform action, you leave the batsman guessing what he is going to get. I have never been able to make up my mind what your pace really is. It varies so much without the slightest warning perceptible from the boundary. I remember being puzzled over it the first time I saw you play for Yorkshire at the Oval in 1950. I could not decide whether you were quicker or slower than Dumbo Coxon.

"Looking at the speed readings they put up now," Bob says, "I think I bowled at everything between fifty and eighty miles an hour."

Lorna Smart questioned the claim that tail-enders are more likely to be lbw and openers caught behind. She disputed the assertion that leg-sided batsmen are bottom-handed by cataloguing their throwing arms in the field, and she speculated on the dominance of different bowling styles around the counties: 'I often wonder, for example, whether Derbyshire breed fast bowlers because their pitches happen to suit that type or whether that type take most of Derbyshire's wickets simply because they have no-one else who is any good.'

> I enjoy playing with cricket statistics, aside from my wish to find something to help pass the time for you. I still hope that one day by some happy chance something in these statistics might bring about a wicket for Yorkshire earlier than otherwise.

A visit from Len Hutton, John Nash the Yorkshire secretary and Connie. Bob is wearing his second eleven sweater over his pyjamas.

In the previous summer of 1952, in the absence of Bob and of Fred Trueman, Johnny Wardle had bowled an extraordinary 1,857 overs, a figure only ever exceeded by Kent's inter-war leg-spinner, 'Tich' Freeman. As a result Lorna Smart revised her earlier criticism of Wardle:

> As the season advanced I felt more and more humble in my gratitude for his magnificent work. To have got through so many overs is a wonderful feat of physical endurance and a greater feat perhaps of concentrated resolution. Courage and animosity in short bursts are one thing; to keep relentlessly on day after day and week after week takes more doing, as you unhappily know.
>
> When I encountered Johnny at Taunton at the beginning of the season, I told him we were hoping for 200 wickets and 1,000

runs from him (knowing neither is likely but anxious to egg him on). He said in a pathetically wistful murmur, "I'd certainly like to" and it was obvious that he assessed his prospects a good deal less favourably than I did. I wish he had a bit more optimism about his abilities; it might help to induce a more attacking frame of mind when he is bowling.

She is kinder, too, to Brian Close:

His performance of the double again was, we thought, a good thing. He needs encouragement of the right sort and 114 wickets and 1,000 runs are something he knows he has done himself – where newspaper agitation for him to play for England again are still, to my mind, unhelpful and a menace to his gradually growing stability. I suppose one can forgive a Yorkshireman who fails doing his best, but never one who loses his head.

But her greatest eloquence is reserved for Bob and his absence:

The end of the 1952 season brought us mixed feelings. It is always dismal to think of no cricket till the beginning of May: I feel like a camel about to cross the Sahara, storing up all the happy memories of the last season to last me until the next arrives, wondering if it will ever come. There were plenty of happy memories, hours of bliss spent absorbing the batting of our two incomparably lovely opening batsmen, and the many moments of pride in other fine efforts of Yorkshire's players, but it will always remain for me about the most unhappy and disappointing season ever.

All last winter Yorkshire supporters, including me, went around beaming and bursting with pride saying, "Everything's alright, we've got a real bowler now" and thinking gloriously of the massacres ahead, a carnage which we hoped would bring back the glorious days of Verity and Bowes. That it didn't work out like that was enough to spoil everything, but we still fervently pray that the happy days may only be postponed. Get better soon, Bob, we all need you so badly.

Yours sincerely
Lorna Smart

They were the sentiments of all Yorkshire's supporters, and in his *Daily Express* articles Bob recalled his slow return to health:

Gradually at the end of three months I was taught to walk again, step by step. No baby was ever so willing.

Then I was led out to the putting green to make a little white ball creep across the grass. This was exciting. I fingered the putter and felt like slashing at the ball … but restrained. It's restraint you need when health starts trickling back.

Despite these words, he was not content to stay in hospital longer than necessary and, recognising what he was required to do, he decided to discharge himself. "By April I'd had enough. 'Look, I can do this at home,' I said. 'It's only a question of discipline.' The only thing was not to rush things and overdo it."

The cricketing summer of 1952 had passed without him. Len Hutton had been the season's leading run-scorer, Johnny Wardle the leading wicket-taker. Brian Close, back from National Service, had done the double, just as he had in his debut summer three years earlier, and Freddie Trueman had burst sensationally into the England side. Yet for all this Yorkshire success, they had finished second to Surrey in the county championship.

Now the summer of 1953 would also pass without him. It was a happy summer for England: the Coronation of Elizabeth the Second, the news of the conquest of Everest, and in cricket a tense and evenly-fought Ashes series. At Lord's Willie Watson, in partnership with Trevor Bailey, batted almost all the last day for a heroic draw. 'I quite repent of all my past rudeness about Willie's comatose fielding,' Lorna Smart wrote. 'I am determined to appreciate him in future.' Then in August at The Oval, under Len Hutton's captaincy, the Ashes were regained.

But for Yorkshire it was a season like no other in their long history. Joint twelfth place in the final championship table was four positions below their previous worst, with both Leicestershire and Northants finishing above them for the first time ever.

Wisden pinpointed their principal weakness: 'lack of penetration in attack'. Trueman was completing his second year in the RAF, Close was recovering from a cartilage operation resulting from a footballing injury and, though the young Ray Illingworth made progress, the burden of the bowling fell again on the shoulders of Johnny Wardle. His 1605 overs were 20% more than any other bowler in England, but he languished as low as 50th in the final averages, not where Yorkshiremen expected to find their best bowler.

'A general depression seemed to overtake the side,' *Wisden* reckoned.

Out of hospital Bob continued his gradual return to strength. "I was just moving about slowly at first. I was only allowed out of bed for an hour a day. But I gradually got moving. I'm a great believer in following instructions, and I knew I wasn't to rush things. It's hard to explain what it's like when you've been in bed, away from everything, for eleven months. Crossing the road was quite a frightening experience, with all the traffic and the speed of things."

But crossing the road was not his main priority. "I showed the physiotherapist my bowling action, and he gave me a programme of exercises relevant to those muscles." Then he started swimming at Bingley Baths where the superintendent was Jim Wright, who had once been physio to Bill Bowes and Hedley Verity.

He and Connie were still living on the premises of her family's confectionery business in Bradford, but they were able to take a holiday in May in Filey, where they stayed in a flat belonging to a Yorkshire committee member. It was their first time alone together as a family of three, and it was not long before Connie was announcing that they would soon be four.

'That season of 1953,' he told the *Daily Express*, 'I itched to bowl again as I watched most of Yorkshire's home matches.' They were not easy matches for him to watch, with opponents compiling totals that Yorkshire did not expect to concede: Essex 370 for six at Hull, Northants 358 at Headingley, Lancashire 373 at Sheffield, Warwickshire 377 for five at Bradford. He had not bowled a ball since Taunton in May the previous year, he was in no physical state even to turn his arm over now, but his determination was such that he used his time as best he could. 'I had to be content with studying the opposition batsmen, noting their weak shots and the openings against them, memorising their style.'

Then in September, he walked around the boundary at a match near his home in Bradford. Some friends were practising beside the nets, and the ball rolled up to his feet. He bent, picked it up and gingerly bowled it back. It landed on a length. 'It was delightful to find out that I had lost none of my control,' he told the *Daily Express*.

> It was golf that got me back to cricket. First patiently putting, then a few chip shots round the green, resting between outings. After this was a swing with a long iron or two. And by December I was playing nine holes quietly.
>
> My New Year resolution for 1954 was: "I must be fit for the opening of *this* cricket season."

He went back to work with Short's Lifts, and in January Connie gave birth to a second daughter, Elizabeth. They were days of great hope, and he was ready to see if he could still bowl.

"I realised that I wouldn't be able to bowl as I had done. I didn't have the lung capacity. They had an instrument to blow into, to check your capacity. If I remember rightly, mine had been 4,500 originally, where the average individual was only 4,000. But after the operation I was down to 3,000. So I realised I was never going to be as fit as I had been. How could I be?

"The challenge was partly mental. I didn't know how I was going to do. There was no instruction, no yardstick. Nobody could tell me. I switched from bowling off the middle finger back to the forefinger. It took a lot of effort and energy to bowl off the middle finger. I could still run in to bowl off sixteen paces, but I couldn't do the same body work. So obviously I wasn't quite as fast. I had to do more with the ball."

In the Winter Shed, with only seven paces to run up on the old wooden floor, he once more reconstructed his action. With the forefinger now the main spinning finger, the leg-cutter he had developed back in the spring of 1952 was a more noticeable variant than it had been so he realised that he would have to use it sparingly. In its place, he developed variations in his moment of release, including a 'loop ball' that came out before the arm reached its full height. "I could still use the new ball, but my effectiveness became more reliant on the subtleties of spin, flight and change of pace."

For most of us, attempting to return to such demanding physical exercise after major surgery, redesigning a proven action, there would be fears and doubts lingering in the mind – but not apparently for Bob.

"You don't think of failure, do you?" he says.

Norman Yardley, Brian Close and Bob at Lindrick Golf Club

By the end of February he was bowling with confidence. Then the Yorkshire committee sent him to Switzerland for a month's recuperation in Arosa, a winter sports centre. The only condition placed on his visit was that he did not attempt to ski. The last thing they wanted was for their bowler to return with a broken leg.

He took long walks over crisp snow in the mountain air, explored the pine woods and tried his hand at curling. But his venture into horse-riding nearly produced consequences worse than a broken leg.

He was with his friend Ronnie Scarbrough, and they hired two horses from the Swiss cavalry reserve. Bob's was 17 hands high.

"A groom had delivered the horses to the hotel, and Ronnie had mounted his by the time I came down. I climbed on this horse, and it suddenly turned and headed for home, oblivious of me. It charged down the main street of

Arosa, which was covered in ice, and I sat helplessly in the saddle as pedestrians were scattered everywhere, shouting and shaking their fists as I thundered by. We tore along the bank of a frozen lake, and I decided that my best plan was to throw myself off into the snow. But, before I could do it, the horse abruptly changed course again and charged into the stables, all but decapitating me as we galloped through the gate."

The whole experience was too much even for the tough Yorkshireman. "I haven't been much of a horseman since," he admits.

He returned home at the end of March, and home was no longer rooms at Connie's family business. They finally bought their own house, at Thornton, and moved there before the season started.

While he had been in hospital, both Billy and Emma Child had died. "I wish they could have lived to see me get better," Bob says, a little sadly. Only his mother was left from his childhood days, and he was barely in contact with her. His family now was Connie and the two girls.

"She stayed at home with us," Rosemarie says. "She was a traditional mother, and he was the bread-winner."

"She gave him all the love and support that he'd missed as a boy," Liz adds. "She used to say, 'I tried to make it up to him.' She really put him first."

*

Pre-season practice was scheduled for the start of April, and Bob was as keen as any of those who gathered at Headingley.

With Jim Kilburn in Kingston, Jamaica, reporting on Len Hutton's match-winning double century in the final Test, it was left to Eric Stanger of the *Yorkshire Post* to describe the first day of the county's preparations:

> Overnight rain kept Yorkshire to indoor practice yesterday when preparations for the new season began in earnest with the call-up of the capped players and the senior Colts. It is also indicative of the County Cricket Club Committee's determination that last season's lost reputation should be recovered that the call-up should be made earlier than usual.
>
> Throughout his long illness Appleyard, whose 200 wickets in his first and so far only season for Yorkshire was a major achievement, was steadfastly determined he would play again. Yesterday, looking remarkably fit, he had a goodish spell at the nets and was none the worse for it at the end. But it will be a case of making haste slowly with him.
>
> The attack will be strengthened by the return of Trueman after National Service, Close and maybe Appleyard for some games.

'Maybe Appleyard for some games.' How his summer would confound their caution!

"People always talk about the year I took 200 wickets," he says, "but really that summer I came back was the greater achievement."

Bob practising in the pre-season nets, 1954
The Yorkshire coaches Bill Bowes and Maurice Leyland can be seen beyond the net

April became warm and dry but, when the season started on Saturday the first of May, the rains returned. Yorkshire were at Lord's, playing an MCC side. 'The rain was heavy enough to delay the first over for forty minutes,' Jim Kilburn wrote, 'and there was another brief downpour before lunch, leaving conditions more favourable to MCC, who were batting, than to Yorkshire. The ball was wet, and the pitch was placid, useless to any man or beast of bowling burden.'

Trueman, back from his controversial tour of the Caribbean, ran in from the pavilion end, and Norman Yardley himself took the Nursery end for two overs before summoning up his eager returner. Eighteen months earlier Yardley had stood by Bob's tilted hospital bed, looking with alarm at the tubes attached to his chest, the pumps running noisily as they spoke. Was it really possible to achieve full fitness again?

After lunch, the sun came out, the pitch began to take turn, and the attack was once more Wardle and Appleyard, as it had been for so much of the summer of 1951.

"Bowling in tandem is so important," Bob says. "If the batsmen play the other guy easily, you know it's going to be harder for you to get at them. With Johnny, I was turning it in, and he was turning it away. That was a perfect combination. But we don't get that anymore in English cricket, do we?"

Bill Edrich, coming in at number three, was on strike when Bob dropped in a short ball. 'He hooked with arms alone,' J.M. Kilburn reported, 'and was brilliantly caught ankle-high at square leg by Illingworth.'

Edrich, caught Illingworth, bowled Appleyard, 13.

"Well done," Norman Yardley called across. "Only 199 to go."

After all he had been through, perhaps that one wicket stays more in Bob's memory than any other in his career.

He bowled 19 overs and finished with two wickets for 45 runs – "That wasn't a bad start, was it?" he says now – before further rain washed away the match, as it did the first day of their next fixture at Oxford.

Conscious of the need to rest him when possible, Yorkshire stood him down from the Oxford match, though as twelfth man he took the field from the outset of the university's reply. In the first over of the innings, with Fred Trueman determined to assert the superiority of his mining background over those of the students, Bob stood at short leg and off the sixth ball he caught the young Colin Cowdrey to reduce Oxford to a score of no runs for three wickets.

"I liked fielding close in," Bob reflects, "but I didn't often get the chance. In fact, the best catch I ever caught was at short leg, at Hove. Don Smith was batting against Ray Illingworth. I dived down to my left, and I caught the ball inches from the ground. But there was no great praise, certainly no kissing and hugging. 'Bad luck,' Vic Wilson said to Don Smith. 'He's never caught one like that before.' That was the kind of support you got."

The weather at Oxford was miserable, with 'an unfriendly north-west wind strong enough to blow down a marquee and a sight screen and cold enough to demand all available sweaters for the fielding side and overcoats and scarves for the spectators.'

It was no weather for the athletes who assembled that evening at Iffley Road on the other side of town. Once more their aim was to break the magical figure of four minutes for a mile but, with the cross-wind measured at fifteen miles per hour, 'The conditions are stupid,' Roger Bannister declared. Fortunately, as the race drew near, the wind dropped, and history was made.

"Frank Lowson and I sat in the car with the radio on," Bob recalls. "We heard the commentary."

From Oxford the cricketers drove on to Bristol, where Bob took his season's tally to four wickets and Fred Trueman hit his first fifty. 'He swung the bat and hit boundaries in unlikely directions, and he swung the bat and missed the ball by considerable margins, but he also played down the line when discretion compelled, and he knew where he was and what he was doing, or trying to do, all the time.'

"Maurice Leyland had said to him on one occasion, 'If you get fifty, I'll give you a stone of mint humbugs.' Maurice turned up with them at the next home game."

It was during this match that the great George Hirst died and on the final day, with the flag at half-mast, the two teams stood in silent tribute. Jim Kilburn wrote the tribute in the *Yorkshire Post*:

> Always he played cricket true to himself, happy, earnest and unselfconscious. In the noontide he was ready to bat, bowl or field; in the evening he enjoyed a pipe and a pint and talk of cricket.

"He wrote to me when I was in the sanatorium," Bob recalls, and there is real irritation that he cannot find the letter among his belongings. "I've looked everywhere for it. It must have been one of the last letters he ever wrote."

From Bristol they drove south-west to Taunton. "It was a momentous match for me. Taunton was where I was taken ill."

On the Wednesday the Yorkshire batsmen made runs. 'The outfield was smooth as a college lawn, the pitch gleaming an invitation, and the scoreboard figures waited to revolve at the slightest provocation.' Lowson, 115. Wilson, 91. Watson, 78. The runs flowed, 350 in all, and there was time for Trueman and Appleyard to take the new ball in the evening.

"Norman Yardley said to Fred, 'Don't hold yourself back. There's only half an hour to go.' And Fred bowled faster than I'd ever seen him."

Harold Gimblett, the troubled Somerset opener, felt compelled to take on the challenge, playing 'an indeterminate hook' and being caught for a duck. "He's too fast for me," he muttered as he returned to the pavilion. "I've had it." He packed his bag and told the secretary he had finished with cricket, though a meeting the next morning persuaded him to see out the match. Meanwhile his partner Roy Smith made only four, and the Guyanese newcomer Peter Wight was hit in the ribs and retired from the fray. At the other end, Bob had Tremlett caught behind by Roy Booth, who had taken over the gloves from Don Brennan that summer.

Somerset were a poor team, in the middle of a sequence of four summers in last place in the championship, and the next day Bob struck four more times in their first innings. "That was a bit of a milestone, the first time I'd taken five wickets since I'd come back." Then, after quick Yorkshire runs, Somerset's openers were batting again before close of play and once more Fred Trueman was at his fastest. Gimblett was lbw for five, the final sad innings of a long career that had burned so brightly in its earlier, more carefree days. 'Gimblett asked the committee to release him from his contract in order that he may regain his health completely,' the *Yorkshire Post* reported.

Peter Wight appeared at number three. "He didn't like quick bowling. He played at this ball from Fred, he must have been six inches away from it, but it came off something. Fred stifled an appeal, and he set off walking straightaway." Shortly afterwards, bad light and rain ended the day's play.

If Bob had established a hold on Harold Gimblett back in 1951, then Fred certainly did the same to Peter Wight in 1954. Only on one occasion did the prolific Somerset batsman come good against Yorkshire, and that was on the famous occasion in 1962 when Fred was late to the ground from his hotel room. Vic Wilson, by then the captain, sent him home, and the wristy Guyanese stroke-maker celebrated his absence with a double-century.

Bob chuckles. He had left the world of county cricket by then, but he knows the stories. "I don't think we need to go into what caused Fred's lateness that day."

Yorkshire's bowlers needed only fifty-five minutes on that Friday morning in 1954, as Somerset collapsed from 22 for two to 48 all out, with Bob Appleyard their principal destroyer.

> Although the rain on the previous evening had left no notable evil in the pitch, the morning air was heavy with moisture and Appleyard took the opportunity to float the ball bewilderingly through feeble batting defences. Lomax pulled Appleyard hard and high to long-on, where Wardle ran twenty yards and created a splendid right-handed catch. There was no murmur of protest from the remaining batsmen. They came, they looked – or failed to look – and they were conquered.

In 9½ overs Bob had taken seven wickets for 16 runs. "One of my best performances ever," he says, "and extra special because it was at Taunton, where I was taken ill."

The next day they were back in Bradford to play Hampshire, Bob's first home appearance since 1951. Hutton and Lowson put on 108 runs for the first wicket, but a batting collapse meant that Bob was stepping out from the pavilion at 174 for nine.

It was Saturday afternoon, the crowd had swollen to 12,000, and they rose as one to applaud their fellow Bradfordian. 'One of the nicest things I have seen on any field of sport for a long time,' Eric Stanger called it in the *Yorkshire Post.* 'It was a welcome back to warm the heart.'

On the balcony of the Victorian pavilion were several of the great pre-war players: Arthur Mitchell, Maurice Leyland, Percy Holmes, Wilf Barber, Abe Waddington, Brian Sellers. "Our heroes, really," Bob says. "We used to sit and pick their brains." They, too, joined the applause.

Bob's ten runs were watched appreciatively, but the clapping was nothing compared with what followed when he took the ball. Running in as if he had never been away, he bowled Hampshire's Walker with his third delivery, and a great roar went up all round the ground. With Trueman at his hostile best at the other end, the visitors managed only 72 all out.

Bob took three for 19 in that innings, then on Monday he added another seven for 35. Back in 1951 he had played three times at Park Avenue, taking 29 wickets. Now he was raising that total to 39 in four games. Bowling from the pavilion end in Hampshire's second innings, 'he flighted his off-breaks with rare skill, and no batsman met him confidently.' Hampshire, set 318 for victory, subsided to 89 all out and 'by six o'clock, the ground was empty.'

Bob had taken 22 wickets for 142 runs in less than a week and, with no play necessary on the Tuesday, there was space in Wednesday's *Yorkshire Post* for Eric Stanger to pen a tribute to the returning bowler:

> Bob Appleyard has not only made a wonderful recovery to full health but an astounding return to cricket. I know when the doctors were expressing the opinion that there was every probability that Appleyard would be able to play cricket again there was a strong view in official circles that he might be able to play in a few championship games this season after a cautious run-out in two-day games. Again there was always the fear that he might be a long time recapturing his old form after a two-year lay-off. I remember Maurice Leyland saying to me last winter, "If he can do only half as well when he comes back as he did in 1951, we will be satisfied."
>
> Yet here is Appleyard not only fully and happily restored to health but taking wickets like clockwork again. Everyone, I think, admires him for his fight back from illness. He is a likeable, modest fellow who takes his cricket very seriously, ever seeking to improve his bowling and his knowledge of batsmen.
>
> Appleyard and Trueman have transformed the Yorkshire team beyond recognition from last year. The championship is still a long way off but, as the old member said, Yorkshire are "looking summat like."

"I was trying to start again from where I'd left off," Bob says. "Looking at the batsmen and working out their strengths and weaknesses. I wasn't too worried about my fitness, but I was practising the yoga relaxation a great deal.

"It was quite an emotional time. The reception at Bradford was a bit special. At Taunton, too, if I remember rightly. The team was much the same as in 1951, and that helped. Norman Yardley was still there, and Leonard – and Johnny. Fred had become a much better bowler in the two years. I seemed to be able to fit in fairly comfortably."

The next week was less productive. He rested from the fixture at Cambridge University, then spent most of the Warwickshire match at Headingley in the pavilion in weather that was so cold and wet that, according to Jim Kilburn, 'the dressing room fire would have been allowed as a necessary expense by the sternest of tax inspectors.'

In the championship race Warwickshire and Middlesex had made the early running but, as May drew to a close, Yorkshire's cause was advanced with a sequence of three emphatic victories, their bowling attack sweeping away Gloucestershire, Warwickshire and Sussex in quick succession.

On the fifth of June, when *The Times* printed the leading first-class averages, there were three Yorkshiremen among the first five bowlers, and pride of place went to the man whom they had expected to be having 'a cautious run-out in two-day games':

	Overs	*Maidens*	*Runs*	*Wickets*	*Average*
R. Appleyard	274.5	75	561	43	13.04
J.B. Statham	130.2	42	292	22	13.27
F.S. Trueman	257	69	585	44	13.29
B. Dooland	349.1	114	804	60	13.40
J.H. Wardle	321	129	619	44	14.06

Further down the list there also appeared the name of D.B. Close, with 23 wickets at 18.91. He did not probe the batsmen with relentless accuracy as Bob did, but somehow he possessed the knack of taking wickets.

Young of Gloucestershire, caught Trueman, bowled Appleyard

"Brian turned the ball quite a lot. Maybe because he was trying to spin it so much, he wasn't so accurate. He'd get wickets with long hops and full-tosses. You do get bowlers like that. If he'd bowled a lot more, he might have been more accurate. I played against him in the Bradford League, when he was about 17, playing for Yeadon. He bowled quick in those days, and he never lacked confidence. He was a very talented player."

With Brian Close there is always a 'but', and Bob pauses before delivering it. "He had tremendous talent but, with all that talent, he should have done better. Trevor Bailey had far more limited ability, but he got the most out of it. He had the application. But then you rarely get both in one person, do you?"

His memory runs back to the Old Trafford Test of 1961, when Close went out to bat against Benaud. The series hung in the balance, England needed 256 for victory and Benaud, bowling into Trueman's footmarks, had just removed Dexter and May with the score on 150. A Yorkshireman like Bob, or Norman Yardley who was in the commentary box at the time, would have sold his wicket at a high price, but Close was looking to counter-attack. For seven pages of his autobiography he justifies his strategy. 'My whole upbringing in all sport,' he wrote, 'had been that if you had any chance to win, you pursued that chance to your utmost until it had gone.'

"He tried to lap Benaud," Bob says. "He had about five goes. Everybody on the ground knew that, if he kept doing it, he'd hole out. And it was such a crucial time in the game."

O'Neill held a finger tip catch to remove him for eight, Australia won the Test, and Norman Yardley on *Test Match Special* said that, after such a shot, Close should never again be picked to play for England.

"Brian was always trying to beat the system," Bob says, a naturally more conservative man. "He went out to Australia when he was only 19, and he was telling everybody what he was going to do to the Australians. Well, they might do that today, but they didn't do it in those days. A youngster coming into the dressing room, they spoke when they were spoken to. That's how we were all brought up. It's how Len was brought up."

Close, the unfulfilled talent. It is a harsh judgment, and Bob softens it. "He was a superb player. That summer I came back, he hit 60-odd on a turning pitch at Bradford, against Dooland and Goonesena, and it was one of the most brilliant innings I've ever seen. Leonard got some runs with orthodox batting, but Brian was hitting shots all round the wicket. It was a Gilchrist kind of innings.

"He might have been immature early on, but there's no harm in Brian. He's never been vindictive. And he did mature. He became a very fine captain. Yorkshire's decision to sack him was completely stupid."

By the summer of 1954 Close was out of the minds of the selectors, not having played for England since his ill-fated tour of Australia in 1950/51, and it now seemed that his county team-mate Freddie Trueman was to suffer the same fate as a result of incidents in the Caribbean the previous winter.

It had been a hard tour, with controversy on and off the field, and Trueman was not the only man whom the selectors jettisoned. Tony Lock was also absent during the summer Tests, and neither was selected for the winter tour of Australia. More significantly for Bob, neither was Jim Laker. Though he had not been implicated in any of the incidents in the Caribbean, there lingered the feeling in some quarters that the Surrey off-spinner was not a man to count on for hard graft when the pitches were unresponsive.

Tom Graveney remembers an evening in the bar at the end of the West Indies tour, when he sat around a table with Jim Laker, Brian Statham and their captain Len Hutton. "Len turned to Brian. 'Well, how do you feel about spending next winter in Australia?' he asked him, and Brian said he'd love to go. 'And you, Tom?' I told him the same. Then he turned to Jim. 'Now then, Jim, what will you have to drink?' We all knew what he was saying."

The team for the first Test against Pakistan at Lord's was selected on Saturday the fifth of June and, though Laker survived, the main shock among the pressmen was the omission of Trueman. 'Statham played an important part in the West Indies last winter,' Jim Kilburn acknowledged, 'and he can sustain the burden of a hard day in the field. Yet most batsmen would probably agree that there is more alarm in Trueman. There need be no quarrel with his omission this time, but it will be surprising indeed if he has made his last appearance for England.'

Meanwhile at Headingley 29,000 spectators gathered for the start of another Roses match and among them, as he had promised, was the surgeon Geoffrey Wooler. Yorkshire batted first so he had no opportunity to see his former patient in action. But he was entertained by the Yorkshire committee, and at lunchtime Bob took him into the team's dressing room.

Bob with Geoffrey Wooler

"I always remember Len Hutton and a few others were there. They all started telling me about the pains in their legs and their backs. A great mass of muscular bodies groaning away. I said, 'I think I'm fitter than you are.'"

"Whenever I went to Headingley," Mary Dobson the medical social worker says, "I used to send a message up to him, and he always came down."

On the Monday of the Roses match 20,000 waited till mid-afternoon in the rain, and the cricketers did not play again till Friday at Park Avenue, Bradford, where in a single innings match Bob took three Somerset wickets for 32 runs.

If ever a bowler enjoyed a ground, it was Bob at Bradford Park Avenue. This was his home, the place where he had sat as a schoolboy with his bottle of pop, where Stanley Douglas had demonstrated to him the off-break, where in May 1951 he had won his first headlines with six South African wickets. Beyond the stone terraces and the old football stand, he could see the mill chimneys and the distant hills. He was a Bradfordian. This was where he belonged, where so much of Yorkshire's great cricketing tradition belonged.

Park Avenue was not a ground of easy comfort for the spectators, as Yorkshire's historian, the late Tony Woodhouse, lovingly recalled:

> The drainage system always seemed to be spilling over in the region of the members' entrance, and the lavatories were dusty and had grimy pink soap that had been untouched since the previous summer. You could eat the pork pies they sold in one mouthful. And in dry weather the seating had an uncanny knack

of covering one's jacket with white paint; in wet weather, with a slimy green.

'The seats left such a distinctive mark,' Peter Snape of the *Dewsbury Reporter* added, 'that you could easily spot, at 7 pm in the city centre, those who had spent the day at the Avenue.'

'In spite of it all,' Tony Woodhouse added, a cricket spectator all his life, 'it was my favourite ground for watching cricket anywhere in the country.'

The 18-year-old Ken Taylor was in the Yorkshire team for that match against Somerset, the first time he had represented the county at Park Avenue. "It was my favourite ground in Yorkshire," he says. "It was spoilt a bit by the football stand, but it had an intimate feeling. It was small enough for the crowd to feel part of the action – not like at Headingley or Bramall Lane, where you felt very isolated from the spectators."

"It was the best watching ground in England," Ray Illingworth reckons. "It had a hell of an atmosphere."

"The atmosphere was tremendous," Fred Trueman agrees. "You were down there, and the spectators were on top of you, looking down. I knocked Alan Revill's off stump out one morning there. It cartwheeled backwards, and the roar was unbelievable. He said to me, 'Now you know what it must be like to score a goal in a Cup Final at Wembley.'"

With stepped terracing, some visiting batsmen found the walk out to the middle intimidating. "It was like a bull ring," Sussex's Jim Parks says. "The old gate would clang behind you. You'd drop down. And invariably Fred would be running in at you."

For the spectators there was a good view, wherever they sat. The pavilion was an eccentric structure, with a half-timbered upper storey. The grass was as green and smooth as anywhere in England, and the square tended to produce interesting cricket: runs when it was dry, challenging bowling when – as so often – dampness descended from the clouds that made their way over the surrounding hills.

"It was a good place to play cricket," Ray Illingworth says. "When the weather stayed fine, it was a good pitch and, if it was a bit damp, it did a bit. You never felt the game was going to sleep there." Or, as Fred puts it, "It was a sporting wicket. It proved two things as far as I was concerned. If you could bowl, you could take wickets. And if you could bat, you could score runs. There's nothing so wrong with a wicket that gives both departments in the game a chance."

This truncated match against Somerset in 1954 was the fifth of Bob's Yorkshire career to be played at Park Avenue, and in 176.5 overs there he had taken 42 wickets for 315 runs. Yorkshire's first innings lead in a one-day game was enough to lift them to the top of the table. Once more, with their bowlers all in form, they were 'looking summat like'.

Against Derbyshire at Chesterfield they only managed a draw, and that was largely thanks to two uncharacteristically defensive innings by Ted Lester. "An unsung hero," Bob calls his team-mate. "He was a strokemaker, unorthodox but very effective. He used to get on with it, and cricket is all about creating winning time. It's a very important aspect of the game. If a bowler's taking 15 overs to get a wicket, or a batsman's messing about, he's using up winning time. That's why I wouldn't rate Boycott amongst the greatest players. He was a fine batsman, he could bat all day, but great players not only score runs, they create winning time for the bowlers."

Their next match at Huddersfield against Leicestershire went to the final ball. Terry Spencer had startled Yorkshire with nine second innings wickets, and the visitors needed only 137 runs for victory, though time was short. Fred Trueman struck early, Bob bowled a long accurate spell, wickets fell, and there was a break for rain that did not help the bowlers. When the last over began, nine wickets were down and Leicestershire still needed nine runs for victory. It fell to Johnny Wardle to bowl it from the churchyard end, and Terry Spencer himself took strike.

'No match could have had a more fictional finish in its facts,' Jim Kilburn proclaimed. The first two deliveries were each worked away for singles, then Wardle, with three men behind him on the boundary, tempted the batsman by tossing the ball higher in the air.

"He was the ideal bowler for that final over," Terry Spencer reckons. "You were never certain what was going to come down. The first one he pitches up, I thought, I'm going to have a whack."

Spencer swung his bat, and the ball sailed into the air, high above the distant fielders, and landed among the gravestones. Now there was just one run required for victory, and the bowler reverted to bowling fast and flat. Spencer tried to push the ball to leg, but the final delivery was reached with that one final run still unscored.

"He pushed the last ball into short mid-wicket," Bob recalls, "and set off for the run. He probably thought he wasn't running to the danger end, but Johnny leapt across, picked the ball up and threw down the wicket at the bowler's end." According to John Bapty in the *Yorkshire Evening Post*, the batsman was 'only an inch or two from the crease to which he galloped so gallantly.'

The umpire's finger was up. The crowd was in uproar. The game had gone to the last ball of the last possible over, and a run out of inches had brought about the first tie in the long history of Yorkshire cricket.

Kilburn's pen ran lyrical:

> The breathlessness of it will demand days of recovery for those who saw, and they are never likely to see the like again.

There was a fighting spirit in this Yorkshire team, just as there had been when Bob last played in 1951, and nobody in the side was as exhilarated as Bob himself. Few of his team-mates knew the full extent of his operation or his demanding programme of rehabilitation. He preferred not to reveal too much, in case people started to think he needed careful treatment.

From Huddersfield he travelled to Lord's and to Romford. After eight weeks of the season he had played in 14 three-day matches, bowled 450 overs and taken 67 wickets.

Bob spoke with satisfaction to the *Yorkshire Post*:

> During those two years when illness kept me idle and threatened to end my cricket career, the skill of the surgeon and my own will to recover did much to restore me to fitness. I feel better than I dared to expect, though, naturally, after such a long lay-off from the game, I am tired occasionally after a strenuous day in the field.
>
> Anyway I feel every bit as fit as I did in 1951, and a month ago, when I had a thorough check, I was told by a specialist that not a trace of the disease remains. So I hope now to go on playing cricket without any further interruptions.

Yorkshire rested him from the match against the Pakistani tourists at Bramall Lane, Sheffield, but on the Sunday, his thirtieth birthday, he received the best present any county cricketer could hope to receive. He was in the England team for the second Test at Trent Bridge, replacing Jim Laker.

Twelve months earlier he had been sitting on the sidelines, studying the batsmen in the hope that he might one day bowl at them again. The year before that, he had been lying in bed at Gateforth Sanatorium, coping with the devastation of his life and fingering his cricket ball under the bedclothes, determined to retain the hard skin on his spinning finger.

It was a fairy tale for the press to report, and the letters poured in to the Yorkshire club, letters that he still cherishes.

'Remember,' a man in Acton wrote, 'every wicket you take, every catch, every run on the scoreboard makes dozens of people now in hospital think: 'Well, if he can do it, so can I!' If you take 20 wickets in the next Test, forget about the glory for English cricket. Think about the hopes you are giving people ... better than drugs or an operation.'

'I am now working in the hospital where I was treated for tuberculosis,' a nurse in Birmingham told him. 'When you play, you are in the minds and prayers of all of us. Your example is going to help many who feel that everything for them is at an end. Good Luck to You. God Bless You. Yours is a great achievement.'

'Watching you running about the field,' a boy from Huddersfield wrote, 'has inspired us in the hope that my father will soon be up and about. If he does as well as you, we will be terribly thrilled.'

'May England always be represented,' an elderly Yorkshireman declared, 'by men who will never acknowledge defeat, men like Bob Appleyard.'

The letters strengthened his will to succeed. "I felt I was representing everybody who had had tuberculosis. I was carrying a torch for them. That gave me a great determination to do well."

CHAPTER 8

ANOTHER PAGE OF ROMANCE

July – September 1954

The English summer of 1954 was the worst of the twentieth century. According to meteorological statistics, it was the coldest, the gloomiest and the third wettest. The touring Pakistanis had not long been elevated to Test match status, and at Lord's they did not start their first Test against England till the afternoon of the fourth day. In three hours on a damp surface they crawled to 50 for three, the opener Hanif Mohammad unbeaten at the close on 11. The English spinners – Wardle, Laker and Tattersall – 'sent down a succession of maidens,' *Wisden* reported, 'but only occasionally beat the bat.'

England pressed for victory the next day, bowling Pakistan out for 87 and scoring a rapid 117 for nine, but too little time remained and the sparse crowd had to watch Hanif once more in defensive mode. In almost six hours of batting in the match, he scored only 59 runs.

There were four changes in the England team for the second Test. Len Hutton the captain had withdrawn with neuritis in the shoulder, the travails of his winter in the Caribbean catching up with him, and he was replaced by David Sheppard. Key figures at Lord's viewed with unease the prospect of the professional Hutton captaining MCC in Australia, and they persuaded the young amateur to arrange an extended leave from his theological college.

Graveney and Bedser, who had been unfit for the previous game, returned in place of Edrich and Tattersall. These were logical alterations, but the fourth switch – Appleyard for Laker – marked a shift in the selectors' thinking, and E.W. Swanton celebrated it in the *Daily Telegraph*:

> The last change is that which will catch everyone's fancy, for Appleyard's career is so wholly unusual. Having taken 200 wickets in his first county season, he went down with tuberculosis and was thought to be a sad and permanent loss.
>
> Now, after two years of illness and recuperation, he is back more or less where he left off, and it is the best of all compliments to him that the selectors have chosen the Trent Bridge wicket to try him out on.
>
> If he can look a high-class Test bowler on that, there can be hopes for him, even at Adelaide, and he will have become appreciably nearer getting there.

Bob had been selected ahead of his fellow Bradfordian, Surrey's Jim Laker, and this was not a surprise to Tom Graveney, who remembered Len Hutton at the end of the Caribbean tour: "Now then, Jim, what will you have to drink?" Laker did not know it at the time but he, like Lock and Trueman, would have to wait for the captaincy to pass from Hutton to May before he received another call from the selectors. To underline further Laker's slip from favour, the selectors' twelfth man for Trent Bridge was the 21-year-old Middlesex off-spinner Fred Titmus.

From their encounter at Hove in 1951 the incoming captain, David Sheppard, already knew the high quality of the Yorkshire newcomer's bowling, and the passing of time has only reinforced his admiration: 'I rated Appleyard very highly indeed,' he wrote in *Parson's Pitch* in 1964. 'I think I would make a place for him if I had to select a post-war England team.' Does this sentence mean that he would have picked him ahcad of Jim Laker, who for many was the finest off-spinner in the history of the game? "Jim was a very different sort of bowler," he says now. "When he came back, he was absolutely terrific. I don't think I'd want to say no to Jim, but it would be very, very difficult between the two of them."

The greatest of Jim Laker's bowling feats were still two years away – the 19 Australian wickets at Old Trafford, the 46 wickets in the series – and David Sheppard delights in asking an even more tantalising question. "Had Bob Appleyard stayed fit, would Jim ever have got back into the England side? Work that out."

The new captain may only have played once against the newcomer in his England team, but Bob recalls another time when they had met in 1951. David Sheppard had sat with him in the old Fenner's pavilion, and they had discussed Christianity. "At that time, before I was ill, I wasn't going to church as much as I should have done, and he made quite an impression on me. I was very struck by his sense of mission."

News of Bob's selection came on the Sunday that fell between the first two days of Yorkshire's match against the Pakistanis at Bramall Lane, a match in which Bob was being rested, and on the Monday he sat attentively as Wardle, Close and Illingworth worked their way through the tourists' first-choice batting line-up. Together they inflicted on the Pakistanis their first defeat of the summer, and Bob noted every hint of weakness in the batting. Eighteen months earlier he had lain in hospital, studying the statistical charts that Lorna Smart had sent him. Now he could use his own eyes.

"As Wilfred Rhodes once said, 'There's more to bowling than just turning your arm over. There's such a thing as observation.' No man could take over 4,000 wickets like Wilfred did without having a deep knowledge of human nature and its inevitable frailties. He was also wary of coaching. 'You can't teach pluck nor judgment nor concentration' – although I beg to differ a little with him on that. I think you can teach concentration, actually."

Bob had returned to cricket with only three-quarters of the breathing power of an average person, and he was practising ways to compensate for his physical shortcoming.

"I'd developed an interest in yoga when I'd been in hospital. I had a book, and in it there was this expression which you had to repeat to help you concentrate. SIM-LA. When I was walking back to my mark, I used to say it to myself. SIM-LA. SIM-LA. It helps you to focus, to concentrate."

His mind runs forward to the cricket he watches now. "I don't know how I'd have coped with Nasser Hussain, coming up and talking to the bowler between balls. I wanted to get myself into my own cocoon, with no outside interruptions. Walking back to my mark and turning around."

He was not a gregarious man, sharing such unusual techniques with his team-mates – "They might have thought I was stupid" – but he was quick to learn and apply all he could about the mental side of sport. "I read somewhere that the average intense concentration period is about three seconds, though they reckon top sportsmen like Len Hutton and the golfer Jack Nicklaus had five seconds. So, if you are going to get your concentration to bear on your delivery stride, you've not to be concentrating too intensely at the start of your run-up. If you're coming in 16 yards, it will be gone by the time you deliver the ball. So that's what I'd do, I'd run up and I'd start concentrating intensely as I approached my delivery stride, and it did help me.

"Then, if I came off the field after bowling a spell of 20 or 30 overs, I used to lie down on a bench in the dressing-room. I'd put a pair of pads under my head, and I'd do some yoga relaxation for half an hour. I found that very beneficial. Winston Churchill used to have similar periods of yoga relaxation in the war when he was working so hard. But you have to follow the correct procedures to enjoy the full benefits. You have to work at it.

"The only time I didn't do it was if we'd bowled a side out by mid-afternoon and Leonard was going out to bat. I used to think, 'I'll never see the like of this again.' He was the best, and I knew he was getting close to the end of his career. I had to watch him play. It was compulsory as far as I was concerned. I remember Brian Close telling me how he'd been sitting with Norman Yardley, watching Leonard and admiring his stroke-play. And Norman said, 'You should have seen him before the war.'

"I've seen different players – exciting ones, interesting ones. I saw Bradman score 200 in a day, though I was only watching through the eyes of a boy. But somehow for me Leonard was perfection. His cover drives, his defence, the time he had to play the ball. There have been other good players – Peter May still stands out in the memory – but for me Leonard was on his own. He was the one."

In twelve months, almost to the day, Hutton would be playing his last innings for Yorkshire – though, before that melancholy match, the two of them would be key participants in one of English cricket's most exhilarating adventures, winning the Ashes in Australia. But to book his passage on the trip, Bob had to meet the challenge of his first Test – and, as on every other occasion when he stepped up a level of cricket, he did so beyond all expectations.

'Meet at 3 p.m. at Trent Bridge on the day before the Test match,' were the instructions from Lord's. 'The professionals will be allowed 10 shillings per day for the actual duration of the match for incidental expenses, £75 in total for match fee.'

Bob getting a lift to Trent Bridge from his neighbour Martin Vallance

There was a total eclipse of the sun at lunchtime on the Wednesday, and the players assembled for practice soon after the light returned. Then the following day, it was the Pakistanis, choosing to bat first, who were, according to *The Times*, 'eclipsed by England, a phenomenon arranged mainly by Appleyard of Yorkshire.'

The sun was hidden by clouds when play began, but the pitch was true and the Pakistani openers Hanif and Alim-ud-din soon settled. 'So far had either opening batsman been from making a false or hasty shot,' Denys Rowbotham wrote in the *Manchester Guardian*, 'that it was almost surprising when, after 35 minutes, Statham knocked Alim-ud-Din's off-stump out of the ground with the speed and immaculate length of a ball to which the batsman unwisely played back.' It was not a major setback. The score progressed to 37, with Waqar and the obdurate Hanif playing comfortably. 'Of imminent collapse there was not a hint.'

The radio commentators on the Light Programme had been on air for fifteen minutes at the start and were not due back till one o'clock. The BBC television coverage would begin at one before giving way to the women's semi-finals at Wimbledon. There was no other television channel, though the bill to create an Independent Authority was passing contentiously through the House of Lords. Earl de la Warr, the Postmaster General, extolled the virtues of free choice – "Those who do not want to see the new programmes need not even have a second knob." – but Lord Reith was more concerned with the potential of commercialism to do harm: "If this bill is passed," he thundered, "you will find that it will introduce a maggot into the body politic of Britain."

There was only the Nottingham crowd able to see or hear the action at half past twelve, when David Sheppard summoned Bob from third man to bowl his first over in Test cricket. He was given 'a heartening reception' by the spectators as he marked his run-up and prepared to bowl to Hanif, who was setting himself to play another long innings. 'Not for nothing, it seemed, had Appleyard watched and studied his opponents from the stands at Bramall Lane. The Pakistanis were in trouble at once.'

'His second ball – the sort of which schoolboys dream – appeared to move away from Hanif, and Hanif moved across his stumps to play it. Before his shot was half-completed, the ball had whipped wickedly into his pads. He was lbw as comprehensively and piteously as a man could be.' It was 37 for two.

"An early wicket gives you confidence," Bob says, and he did not have to wait long to add three more. 'In his third over Appleyard had Maqsood caught at the wicket with a ball that moved beautifully away off the seam.' 'The bat was drawn like steel to a magnet,' Jim Kilburn added, and the score became 43 for three.

'In his fourth over he confounded and bowled Waqar with a fast yorker which undoubtedly was conceived at Bramall Lane.' "Godfrey was standing up," Bob remembers, "and the middle stump was out of the ground." 50 for four. Then, with his bowling spell barely half an hour old, 'in his fifth over he deceived Imtiaz with a similar quickening of pace, this time combined with sharp off-spin.'

Imtiaz, bowled Appleyard, 11

Thirty-seven for one had become 55 for five. There was no rapturous celebration, no hugging and kissing, but, according to *The Times* correspondent, 'a group of English players gathered, filled like Appleyard with delight but with admiration as well.'

'His mixture of in-swingers, off-spinners and leg-cutters, his variation of pace and flight,' *Wisden* thought, 'bore the stamp of a high-skilled craftsman.'

With his first 27 balls in Test cricket, on a pitch that was firm and true, he had ripped out four front-line Pakistani batsmen. 'Appleyard's career,' the *Times* correspondent wrote, 'has been something of a romance built round the conquest of a serious illness, and now another page to rank with the best has been added.'

'A bowler taking four wickets for six runs in his first five Test overs must have a place in cricket's story,' Jim Kilburn enthused in the *Yorkshire Post*, 'but there should be many more pages awaiting the adornment of Appleyard's name. His dramatic beginning has virtually assured him of further invitations.'

With a fifth wicket late in the innings, he was the hero of the first day and, thanks to elegant evening batting by Nottingham's own Reg Simpson, England were only 36 behind Pakistan's final total of 157 at close of play with eight wickets remaining, one of them Denis Compton who was 'content to survive' after Peter May had dragged a long hop onto his stumps.

Leading off the team with five for 51

The next day there was no such joy for the bowlers as Denis Compton – 'the Compton of old' – took his score from 5 to 278 in little more than 4½ hours. 'He sent the bowling to all parts of the field with a torrent of strokes, orthodox and improvised, crashing and delicate, against which Kardar could not set a field and the bowlers knew not where to pitch.' In the morning Tom Graveney matched, even bettered his stroke-play – 'Some of Graveney's punishing drives left the bat with the sound of a pistol shot' – but, when in the afternoon Compton added 192 in 1¾ hours with Trevor Bailey, 165 of the runs were his own.

"We had quite a problem in the dressing-room," David Sheppard reveals. "We'd had a television set installed so that we could watch the men's final at Wimbledon, but no cricketer could fail to watch the kind of innings Compton was playing." By way of compromise, when Compton was on strike, they looked out to the middle; when it was Bailey, they turned back to the tennis.

It was thought to be the last chance of the Wimbledon title for the popular Egyptian Jaroslav Drobny, 32 years old, carrying a bad knee and in his third final. His opponent was the young Australian Ken Rosewall, and the match ran to 58 games, the longest final in the history of the tournament. With no tie-break to hurry the match on, the first set reached 11-all before Drobny clinched it. Then Rosewall levelled the match 6-4 in the second, Drobny won the third, and in a topsy-turvy fourth set Rosewall was just two points away from making it two sets all before Drobny eventually triumphed 9-7. 'The best and bravest final seen for very many years,' *The Times* reckoned.

At close of play Jim Swanton told the BBC viewers how he had spotted the England captain signalling to Compton from the balcony, presumably – he suggested – to stay in and make as great a score as he could. The truth, in fact, had nothing to do with the state of the Test match. The England players were simply sticking up fingers to relay news of the end of the third set. Drobny 2, Rosewall 1.

On a Saturday shortened by several rain breaks, the Pakistani batsmen made better progress than in their first innings, Bob's bowling figures suffering when Maqsood launched a counter-attack against him. He should have perished in Bob's first over, 'Statham seeming to lose the ball in the sun at mid-wicket', and it was only after Maqsood's spirit of adventure lost all caution that the Yorkshireman gained his recompense. 'He pulled successive balls from Appleyard far and high to the leg boundary. May caught the first at deep square leg before discovering that he was 'out of bounds' as it were and over the white boundary line, and Statham held the second towering hit as he almost kicked up the chalk of the line at his feet.'

After heavy weekend rain, the match ended shortly before lunch on the Monday, when David Sheppard held a catch off Bob to complete an emphatic innings victory. The opposition was not the strongest, nevertheless it was the first time England had won on Trent Bridge's easy batting pitch since 1930.

"Bob's first spell won us the match," David Sheppard reckons. "It was a beautiful batting wicket, and someone was bound to score heavily."

"It was a very comfortable match as far as I was concerned," is all Bob will say.

At home after the Test match

In his absence Yorkshire had completed victories at Bradford and The Oval, and he returned to play a crucial part in a third win, this one at Northampton where he had match figures of eight wickets for 71 runs off 53.5 overs. The season had passed the half-way mark, Yorkshire – the only unbeaten county – had opened a 14-point lead over Warwickshire in the championship table, and Bob was second in the national averages, wedged between Statham and Trueman. He had 82 wickets, he had won his first England cap and there was even the prospect of a winter in Australia.

'I'm proud – and life is wonderful,' he told the *Daily Express* as even more letters arrived..

'Appleyard is my very favrit bowler,' said a seven-year-old from Leicester, his teacher forwarding his writing along with the boy's crayon drawing of Bob. 'He is a very big man. I saw him on television but I caden't see his fase very well. Wen I grow up I will bowl leg brakes like him.'

Geoffrey Wooler received a letter from the Yorkshire secretary John Nash, asking on behalf of MCC whether in his opinion his patient would stand up to the demands of an Australian tour with 6½ months of travelling.

"It was certainly a little soon after his operation," the surgeon says now, "but I always liked to help people to do things. I didn't like to restrain them. We'd removed the disease, there was no sign of any recurrence, and I think it did his morale a lot of good to go – which is important. If he'd sat at home moping, I think he wouldn't have done so well."

Perhaps today, with doctors frightened away from risk by the fear of litigation, the decision might be different. But Geoffrey Wooler's instinct was always to treat the whole person. "It probably was a bit of a risk, but I think it was worth taking. The pleasure of being able to get back into his stride outweighed any other risk, and that helped him to overcome the disease."

Fifty years on, his patient is still in fair health. "Bob's a great fellow, a charming man. He's had a remarkable life, and he's done a lot of good in the world. I wish there were more like him playing cricket today."

The surgeon's opinion was sent to the Yorkshire secretary, and the name of Appleyard was added to the list of those under consideration for the winter tour. It was a turn of events that had certainly not been foreseen by the Yorkshire committee member who three months earlier had suggested to the *Yorkshire Post* that the returning bowler might build up gently to a few championship games later in the summer.

He played for the Players against the Gentlemen at Lord's where, in the opinions of C.B. Fry and Sir Pelham Warner, the fast bowling of his team-mates Brian Statham and Peter Loader 'had never been surpassed in this historic fixture.' Despite this, there was opportunity for Bob to make his own mark by capturing five wickets, the most memorable of which was his county captain.

'Appleyard certainly showed intelligence,' Jim Kilburn reported. 'He kept Yardley playing forward to two overs of off-breaks. Suddenly he introduced his faster ball and Yardley, much too late with his stroke, was clean bowled.'

"I remember Bill Bowes telling me in my first season how Hedley Verity used to bowl a quicker ball every two or three overs, putting the batsman on pins, waiting for it. So I started to do the same. Then I noticed that every time I ran in to bowl it, Len at slip would move back a yard or so. I was intrigued to know how he could guess my intention. 'I can tell from the way you hold the ball,' he said. So I had to cut out the flick of the wrist, just use the middle finger to impart the spin. I'm sure by the time I came back in 1954, I could disguise my quicker ball pretty well."

Ted Lester supports this. "What he used to do was to get the batsmen playing back to the off-spinner, then he'd come up without any altering of his action and bowl a quickie. They used to be on the back foot, and it was through them before they realised. He just bowled it straight. His accuracy was amazing."

Yardley, bowled Appleyard, 18.

The selectors had seen enough. For the third Test at Old Trafford, they decided to take a look at Glamorgan's Jim McConnon. "They did indicate to me that it wouldn't affect my selection for Australia."

McConnon had spun his way into this surprise selection by taking seven Surrey wickets for 23 on a spiteful Oval pitch earlier in the month, and his first spell in Test cricket was almost as dramatic as Bob's, with three wickets in six overs. But, where Bob had taken his wickets on an easy Trent Bridge surface, Jim McConnon had the advantage of bowling on treacherous turf, only fit for play because the groundsman had gone out to dry it under hurricane lamps at one o'clock in the night.

On such moments of fortune can cricket selections hinge. Within hours of McConnon's spell, the selectors were at work on their tour party. They had already announced Hutton as captain, their fleeting interest in David Sheppard having passed. "I feel we've been unfair to Len," an apologetic Walter Robins had told the stand-in captain one evening during the Trent Bridge Test. "He was in a very difficult position in the West Indies."

McConnon was picked along with Hutton's county team-mates, Wardle and Appleyard, though none of them heard of their fate till Tuesday evening, a delay that did not impress Eric Stanger in the *Yorkshire Post*. 'There is a tendency of modern selection committees – and others – to sit on their decisions like a clutch of eggs,' he wrote. ' Sometimes there is good reason for delay, but mostly there is a lot of making mystery for mystery's sake. Probably the habit is an inheritance from the war.'

Only that month had the government announced the end of all rationing, with meat freely available for the first time for fourteen years. It was a time of national recovery, with new technology creating the hope of a better life: an Atomic Energy Authority, the Boeing 707 jet aircraft, Eurovision on British TV screens and IBM's electronic calculating machine.

'Fly me to the moon,' Frank Sinatra crooned. 'Let me sing among those stars. Let me see what spring is like on Jupiter and Mars.'

For Yorkshire cricket, too, there was the joy of a championship table with the White Rose county once more at the head. Then at the Bank Holiday weekend came the trip to Old Trafford to play Lancashire.

The Yorkshire keeper Roy Booth recalls the crowds that gathered in those days for this match. "The next year I was batting overnight, and Vic Wilson picked me up on the Monday morning. Before we got to Old Trafford, I had to get out of the car and run into the ground. The traffic was so packed, and there were thousands pouring out of the station. All the Lancashire members with red roses in their button holes, the Yorkshire members with white ones."

This contest in August 1954 was the 19th time the two counties had met since the war, and such was the determination of both teams not to be bettered that all but one of their previous 18 encounters had ended in a draw. The exception was at Bramall Lane in May 1950 when Yorkshire, on a wet wicket, chased 182 for victory and were bowled out for 167. Brian Close, on National Service, was making his only appearance of the summer, and his partnership on the last afternoon with his captain Norman Yardley seemed to be taking them to victory. Then, setting off for a sharp single, he slipped in mid-pitch, and his departure precipitated a collapse. There was disbelief in the dressing-room when it was discovered that he had gone out to bat without spikes in his boots.

Lancashire's Geoff Edrich recalls that match at Bramall Lane in 1950. "Harry Makepeace, the coach at Old Trafford, always said, 'If a Lancashire player during his career beats Yorkshire twice, he's done well.' And that was my first. The Brian Close run out was a real turning-point."

Yorkshire's Ted Lester remembers the reaction of Norman Yardley. "Instead of taking Brian to one side and giving him a rollocking, he wrote him a letter. That was Norman all over. He wouldn't fall out with anybody. He was such a nice bloke, but he'd let people commit murder rather than tell them off."

That is the orthodox view of Yorkshire during those years – a great team with a leader too gentlemanly to impose the necessary discipline over some awkward individuals: "Too nice a chap to stand up to the hard men," Ray Illingworth has written of him – but Bob Appleyard does not share it.

"I saw Norman as a leader whom everybody respected. He had a huge knowledge of the game. Leonard and he together had the best pair of cricket brains you could imagine. And he didn't ask anybody to do anything he wasn't prepared to do himself. We're all different as individuals. Some need a carrot, some a big stick. Norman offered the carrot in front, and that suited me. I would have rebelled against anybody with a big stick behind."

Yardley was a good enough cricketer to have played for England as an all-rounder, and at Old Trafford in the 1954 Roses match he made his way to the middle with the scoreboard showing 34 for four. "He was one of those players who, if he went out to bat and you were struggling, you'd expect him to do well. One of the most unselfish players I ever met, he did what had to be done. He could score quickly, or he could prop and cop to save a situation."

That Saturday Yardley propped and copped for a long time, adding 170 runs with Vic Wilson who, according to Jim Kilburn, was playing 'the innings of his life':

> It was the apotheosis of cricketing character. He began in bewilderment and never lost heart; he continued in the staunchest spirit and never lost concentration; he ended in fierce attack and utter confidence.

Yorkshire's final total of 248 contained 67 from Yardley and 130 not out from Wilson.

On Monday, when the pitch started to dry out after morning rain, Johnny Wardle was unplayable, taking nine wickets for only 25 runs. 'A performance to be remembered all his days,' Jim Kilburn called it, 'and losing no sweetness in this particular setting.' Lancashire were dismissed for 73 and ended the shortened day on 17 for no wicket, following on in their second innings.

The next morning the effects of the roller soon wore off:

> Wardle and Appleyard could scarcely have devised more encouraging bowling circumstances for themselves. For Wardle the slips, for Appleyard the leg trap crept to the bat edge and had promise of reward almost every ball.

By ten minutes after lunch, with thickening drizzle settling into the Manchester air, it was all over. Lancashire, 137 all out, had lost by an innings, and Bob was returning to the pavilion with figures of 23 overs, seven wickets for 33 runs.

For the first time since 1939, since the golden days of Verity and Bowes, Yorkshire had inflicted defeat on their neighbours. "That meant more to me than beating Pakistan in the Test match," Bob admits.

The season was reaching its final stages, Yorkshire were 18 points clear of Derbyshire in the championship table and, when Compton's unreliable knee required an extra batsman to tour Australia, the selectors looked no further than the evidence of the Roses match and opted for the genial Vic Wilson.

Trevor Bailey's verdict on this last selection is unequivocal. "Oh dear, oh dear," he sighs, ascribing the responsibility directly to the tour captain. "Len had some strange ones. To take McConnon ahead of Jim Laker was extraordinary, but Vic was an even more ridiculous choice. He was a good player of medium-paced county bowling on good wickets, and he had a good pair of hands in the field. A nice, easy-going farmer. But they selected him ahead of Willie Watson, and that made no sense at all. He was just a good county player. Willie was class."

"I don't agree," Bob says. "On the firm Australian pitches, Vic's selection made sense. Just look at the runs he'd scored that summer."

For Bob, there was much to be done: an England tour blazer to be fitted, inoculations to be received and all the attention that stemmed from the *Daily Express* articles. His last day of cricket would be on September the seventh at Scarborough, and on the fifteenth he would be boarding the SS Orsova at Tilbury.

The season drew to its close. In Yorkshire's last five matches he took 41 wickets, at an average of 10.41 each, but alas it did not bring the championship north – with the dismal weather playing a crucial part.

In their match at Hove, they had Sussex five second innings wickets down and only 16 runs ahead at the end of the second day. Heavy rain then fell, and there was no further play. With Surrey already having won in two days at Kettering, the gap between them narrowed perceptibly.

"They called the match at Hove off at one o'clock," Bob says. "But the sun came out, and it dried brilliantly. I think we could have played, but the Sussex team were all on their way home."

Rain also brought Yorkshire's last championship match at Dover to a premature end, and that deprived them of further points. It was a game that had started so well, too, with Fred Trueman dismissing Kent for just 76 on the first morning. His figures of eight wickets for 28 runs would be the best of his long career, but he did not leave the field in happy mood.

At one stage, with the first six wickets to his name, it looked as if Fred was going to win the £100 award for the best bowling figures of the summer, but that would not have been good news to all his team-mates as Johnny Wardle, with nine for 25 at Old Trafford, was at that point in line for the prize. When Wardle then dropped a straightforward bat-pad chance at short leg and promptly took two wickets himself, sparks inevitably flew. In another team such an altercation would soon have blown away but not with powerful characters like this. "There have been one or two accusations over the years," Bob admits. "I find them very hard to believe."

Later in the day Frank Lowson set them up for victory with a fine 150, but on the second evening the young Colin Cowdrey – destined, like Bob, for Australia – stood between the Yorkshire bowlers and an easy win. "I had a real battle with him," Bob says. "He kept pushing forward. In the end I bowled a ball that ran down his bat, trickled underneath it, hit the stump and dislodged a bail. I think, if I could have got him out earlier, we would have won in two days."

As news arrived that Surrey had already won at Lord's, the deteriorating weather at Dover presaged further disappointment for Yorkshire. 'There was sunshine in the morning, a cloudy sky in the afternoon and drizzle after tea, and the wind from the north-west had sharpness in it.' Just as at Hove, there would be no play on the final day.

Yorkshire's championship programme was over, but Surrey had two remaining games at The Oval, and they won them both to finish champions for the third year running. Bob took the field for the Scarborough Festival just as he had done in 1951, part of a Yorkshire side that had finished runners-up.

They had a bowling attack that included Trueman, Wardle and himself. They had Hutton, Lowson and Watson as batsmen and Close as an all-rounder. Yet they could not win the championship. It has been easy for historians to point to internal difficulties in the side, but Bob is adamant that the explanation lies elsewhere.

"The reason we didn't win the championship," Bob counters, "is that Surrey were so predominant."

On the boat to Australia, he sat one evening with Len Hutton. "We were chatting after dinner, and he came out with this statement. It flabbergasted me. He'd been thinking, and he felt that the present Surrey side would have beaten the pre-war Yorkshire one. You see, they had one international bowler more than any other side had ever had. They had Bedser, Loader, Lock and Laker. Four. And all different styles for different wickets. I doubt if any county side in the whole history of the game has had four like they had. And they were playing at The Oval, which was a result wicket at that time, where we had to go all round the county, taking the pitches we were given."

Bob had rounded off his annus mirabilis of 1951 with eleven MCC wickets at Scarborough. This time he took twelve – 'They tumbled into his analysis as quickly as they could get themselves caught in long field or leg-trap' – and it was enough to put him in second place in the final national averages.

	Overs	*Maidens*	*Runs*	*Wickets*	*Average*
J.B. Statham	615.3	194	1300	92	14.13
R. Appleyard	1027.3	315	2221	154	14.42
P.J. Loader	699.2	167	1589	109	14.57
L. Jackson	939.4	296	1851	125	14.80
A.V. Bedser	957.4	299	1828	121	15.10
J.C. Laker	966.2	315	2048	135	15.17

He had bowled more than a thousand overs. It was not a bad summer's work for a man missing half his left lung.

But this time there was no winter to rest and recuperate.

Australia beckoned. The greatest cricketing challenge of all.

BOWLING FIGURES 1954

(Test match in bold type)

			First innings				Second innings			
May 1,3,4	Lord's	M.C.C.	19	1	45	2				
May 8,10,11	Bristol	Gloucestershire	24	7	47	2	8	4	13	0
May 12,13, 14	Taunton	Somerset	29.2	7	72	5	9.3	3	16	7
May 15,17	Bradford	Hampshire	12.2	5	19	3	15	3	35	7
May 22,24,25	Headingley	Warwickshire	25	7	61	1				
May 26,27	Sheffield	Gloucestershire	22	6	40	3	22	11	45	3
May 29,31	Coventry	Warwickshire	21.4	5	44	3	20	7	32	6
June 2,3,4	Hull	Sussex	15	5	33	0	32	4	59	1
June 5,7,8	Headingley	Lancashire								
June 9,10,11	Bradford	Somerset	21	8	32	3				
June 12,14,15	Chesterfield	Derbyshire	32.5	9	71	6	26.1	11	55	3
June 16,17,18	Huddersfield	Leicestershire	31	11	62	2	20	8	38	1
June 19,21,22	Lord's	Middlesex	45	9	95	1				
June 23,24,25	Romford	Essex	17	1	58	3	25	7	51	5
July 1,2,3,5	**Trent Bridge**	**Eng v Pakistan**	**17**	**5**	**51**	**5**	**30.4**	**8**	**72**	**2**
July 7,8,9	Northampton	Northamptonshire	16.3	8	24	5	37.2	23	47	3
July 10,12,13	Sheffield	Surrey	14	4	42	3	20	3	67	2
July 14,15, 16	Lord's	Players v Gents	11	7	14	1	7.5	1	24	4
July 17,19,20	Trent Bridge	Nottinghamshire	36	16	83	1				
July 24,26,27	Sheffield	Worcestershire	26	10	53	5				
July 28,29,30	Headingley	Derbyshire	29	5	99	3	8	1	16	1
July 31, Aug 2,3	Old Trafford	Lancashire	16	7	27	1	23	8	33	7
Aug 4,5,6	Hove	Sussex	12	2	21	0	29	8	56	2
Aug 7,9,10	Bradford	Nottinghamshire								
Aug 11,12	Scarborough	Essex	11	3	36	6	21	5	47	3
Aug 14,16	Headingley	Middlesex	37	13	62	6	16	5	41	4
Aug 18,19,20	Bournemouth	Yorkshire	16.1	9	12	6	17	4	45	1
Aug 21,23,24	Dover	Kent	4	1	12	0	19	8	48	3
Sept 1,2,3	Scarborough	M.C.C.	18.1	5	44	7	20	1	80	5
Sept 4,6,7	Scarborough	Players v Gents	18	5	31	1	4	1	11	0

Matches	*Overs*	*Maidens*	*Runs*	*Wickets*	*Average*
30	1027.3	315	2221	154	14.42

CHAPTER 9

LEARNING TO BOWL IN AUSTRALIA

September 1954 – January 1955

From Bradford to Adelaide. From mill chimneys and biting Yorkshire winds to the spires of St Peter's Cathedral and the brilliant blue of a cloudless Southern hemisphere sky. After just two summers of English county cricket – one as a spectacularly successful apprentice; the next, adapting with extraordinary resilience to the loss of half a lung – Bob Appleyard was facing a new challenge. And the prize this time was the most coveted in English cricket: victory in Australia.

Not for 22 years, not since Douglas Jardine and his men hatched their Bodyline theory, had an English side returned from a trip to Australia with the Ashes, and at Forster Square railway station, Bradford, one of the heroes of that campaign, Herbert Sutcliffe, was on hand to wish Bob and his captain Len Hutton good luck as they started out on their six-and-a-half month adventure.

Bob, Len Hutton and Herbert Sutcliffe
Jim Kilburn is the figure at the back, between Bob and Len Hutton
"We don't go down to see Gough off to Australia.
There's not the same relationship now between past and present."

For Bob, whose previous experience at sea was as a petty officer sleeping forty to a cabin, the luxuries of the *SS Orsova* marked how far cricket had brought him. "After I married Connie in 1951, we were living on the premises of her mother's sweet-and-tobacco business. Now I was travelling first-class on an ocean liner, dressing for dinner each night, coming into contact with people higher up the social scale." But, he is quick to point out, it was not a world of instant wealth and celebrity such as today's footballers enjoy. "Look at this lad Rooney. Seventeen years old and signing for Everton for a million pounds. We were never pushed into the limelight like that."

The first port-of-call was the Bay of Naples, and there the Yorkshiremen of the party – Hutton, Wilson, and Bob, though not Johnny Wardle, along with Bill Bowes and Jim Kilburn, and accompanied by Bill Edrich and the Bedsers – made pilgrimage to the war grave of Captain Hedley Verity of the Green Howards. Two cab-drivers raced them to the military cemetery – "That was a hair-raising journey. They seemed to be trying to knock Fangio off his perch as world champion." – and there, after following several paths through immaculately kept lawns, they found the simple gravestone. On it Hutton placed a spray of white roses fastened together by a Yorkshire County Cricket Club tie. 'He said nothing,' Kilburn wrote. 'Nothing needed to be said.'

Hutton had played alongside Verity for Yorkshire and for England, as had Bill Bowes. Bob was younger, but he was old enough to have idolised him, wearing for years a pair of his cricket trousers. Eleven years after Verity's death, there was no need for words as they stood together before the grave.

Geoffrey Howard, the efficient and charming tour manager, sensed immediately the strength of this Yorkshire contingent. "There was a heavy emphasis from the word go on Yorkshire. A lot of players, a lot of journalists. The leadership of the party was in the hands of the Northerners."

Through the Suez Canal they sailed, incurring extra fuel costs as they increased their speed to reach Colombo in time for a one-day match on September the 30th. For Bob it was a return to the city where he had spent three months in the dockyards in early 1946, and he took delight in telling his hosts, the Colombo Cricket Club, that his naval rank had then precluded him from appearing in their first eleven.

Unfortunately the match did not mark a happy return. At the game's conclusion, a large crowd spilled exuberantly onto the playing area, and one lad collided at full pelt with Bob. He felt the blow to his ribs, on the left side where he had had the operation, and back at sea the pain did not recede.

"I couldn't breathe properly. It's not like it is today with all the medical back-up. We had Harold Dalton as our masseur. He gave out salt tablets, that's all he ever seemed to do. I really didn't have a lot of confidence in him. So I went to the ship's doctor. He had a small x-ray machine, and he couldn't find anything. But it persisted. We were at sea for five days, and there was no improvement. So I insisted on having an x-ray at hospital when we landed."

He still has the letter Geoffrey Howard wrote to him, courteously admonishing him for bypassing Dalton.

'Appleyard was anxious,' E.M. Wellings of the *Evening News* wrote. 'Without consulting anyone he had x-ray examinations on the ship and was still not satisfied. So there was more trouble about examinations in Perth. The results were all the same, but Appleyard was difficult to persuade and it seemed that he was worrying himself into a mental state that was anything but conducive to good cricket.'

'Worrying himself into a mental state'? It is a harsh judgement to make on a man who had had a mark on his lung in 1946 and been cleared by the Navy, who had been told by a whisky-smelling locum in 1951 that he had 'a touch of pleurisy' and should get back to cricket as soon as possible, and who had then spent almost a year in hospital, wondering if he would ever be fit enough to play cricket again.

Bob persisted in his quest for a diagnosis.

"When I was x-rayed on a proper machine, they did find a crack in one of my ribs where it joined the breastbone. But it was just a matter of waiting for it to heal up. So it set me back quite a bit. I lost time, and time was important. It was necessary to adjust my style of bowling for Australian conditions, and I was late getting into training. I missed the first matches."

At the hospital his x-rays created great interest. "The radiographers were more interested in my lung than my ribs. They couldn't believe I was playing. And some medical journal in Australia had publicised the *Daily Express* articles so everybody else wanted to see my x-rays as well."

He bowled just 71 overs in the first two months in Australia, and several of the pressmen were writing him off as a potential member of the Test side. He was trying to bowl too fast, he was concentrating too much on leg stump, he was not attacking sufficiently with flight and spin. 'Oh for Tony Lock,' the London-based Wellings exclaimed, 'now that Appleyard has disappointed.'

"There was an eruption of North-South rivalry. Johnny and I had been preferred to Jim Laker and Tony Lock, and that hadn't been well received by the writers on the London evening papers."

The first important matches of the tour were at Perth, against Western Australia and a Combined XI, and MCC won both by large margins. Then they travelled to Adelaide where against a weak South Australian side they stood on the verge of a demoralising defeat. The home team, needing 174 for victory, seemed in control at 142 for five, and Bob's first eight-over spell had gone for 40 runs. 'He bowled too much at the leg stump,' was Alan Ross's verdict, 'with not enough variation of pace.'

Hutton, however, trusted him with a second spell, and in it he began the process of adapting to Australian conditions, 'slowing down and flighting the ball'. As a result, he struck four times in three overs to clinch an unlikely and, to many eyes, an 'undeserved' victory: 'Every batsman except the last threw his wicket away with wild indiscretion,' Alan Ross wrote. 'Not one was beaten by anything the ball did off the pitch.'

"I was bowling eight-ball overs in temperatures of 100 degrees. The ground was very hard, and coming in to bowl was like running on concrete, which I found very difficult. The ball didn't turn as much as it did in England, and it didn't swing, either. So I had to rely on change of pace and on flight, especially flight. And flight was something that nobody had ever really taught me. I'm not sure that there are that many people who know how to flight a ball. I can hardly remember discussing it with anyone – except Wilfred Rhodes."

His brief success at Adelaide was not enough to secure him selection for the first Test, scheduled for the end of November at Brisbane. None of the three slow bowlers had made an unarguable case for inclusion and, with Hutton resolved to win the series with raw pace, the decision was taken to play four quick bowlers: Tyson, Statham, Bailey and Bedser, the last of whom was still recovering from a debilitating attack of shingles. If spin was required, they would turn to Denis Compton's occasional chinamen. Even this last variant was lost, alas, when Compton impaled his hand on a picket fence on the first morning and departed the field.

Two months of preparation had built up to Hutton's strategy of a four-man pace attack at Brisbane, and it was quickly clear that it was a disaster. Hutton, without a spinner, had no choice but to ask Australia to bat first, and they responded with 601 for eight, declared. The four fast bowlers wilted in the heat, catches a-plenty were spilled and, when it was England's turn to bat, they could muster only 190 in reply. By the second innings, the pitch was rewarding Benaud and Johnson with turn, and Hutton's men went down to defeat by an innings and 154 runs. "We should never have lost that Test," Trevor Bailey reckons. "It was a crazy piece of selection if ever there was one."

'What a nightmare that Brisbane Test was to English eyes!' Jim Swanton wrote later. 'Here surely were the fruits of the captain's obsession with speed. In brutal truth the game had been bungled by England from start to finish.'

But Bob, a spinner who might have been the one to benefit from the picking of an orthodox bowling attack, is quick to defend his fellow Yorkshireman. "I could understand Leonard's reasoning. The pitch was hard and fast, it was going to be covered against the rain, and he thought the surface would help his fast bowlers. There was no hint that it would take any turn. Unfortunately whatever luck that was going went Australia's way."

In the gloomy aftermath, Hutton took Jim McConnon and Bob to the nets and looked once more at their relative merits. "I bowled quick at him," Bob remembers. "I made him jump about a bit. I think he realised then that I had it coming together. Fortunately."

Geoffrey Howard the manager remembered it differently. Although Bob took nine wickets in a light-hearted two-day match at Rockhampton, it was not Bob but McConnon who was chosen to play the only first-class match before the second Test and it was McConnon whom Hutton initially advocated when the selection party sat on the overnight train from Melbourne to Sydney.

Jim McConnon was a quiet Catholic, not comfortable with having been plucked from the familiarity of Glamorgan county cricket. "He was homesick by the time we got to Aden," Geoffrey Howard reckoned. "Len was for selecting him, but I said, 'Let's put it this way. If Jim learns he's playing, he'll pull a muscle. And if Bob learns he isn't, he'll come and cut your throat.'"

The tour's baggage man and scorer was the old Lancashire wicket-keeper George Duckworth. A player on three Ashes tours before the war, he was a valued member of the selection committee, and he supported the manager's view. So the second Test at Sydney would see a better-balanced bowling attack, with Wardle and Appleyard replacing Alec Bedser, who had not fully recovered. "I felt very sorry for Alec," Bob says. "He went out as England's number one bowler. He got shingles on the boat, and he tried to come back too soon. Then he was rested, and he couldn't get back into the team."

E.M. Wellings, now advocating a late call-up for Tony Lock, was dismayed at the inclusion of Wardle and Appleyard ahead of Bedser. 'Three cheers were called for and joyously given in the Australian dressing room.'

Meanwhile Bob recorded Christmas greetings for his family back home in Thornton onto a vinyl disc, to be played at 78 revolutions per minute. It remains a prized possession almost half a century on, though somehow the first quarter of an inch has grown distorted and hard to hear.

'Hallo, Connie. Hallo, Rosemarie and Elizabeth. What a thrill this gives me!' The crackles take over, then the voice becomes clear once more, its Bradford vowels still winning through his attempt to speak the Queen's English.

'Out here the temperature can reach over a hundred degrees Fahrenheit, and in this heat it is difficult to feel the spirit of Christmas. Thinking of you and the children in our own home gives me the nearest image of the festive season. I feel so happy that my voice is amongst you now. I can see you all very clearly in my mind as you are listening to these words. On so many occasions I think of you and the children, wondering where you are, what you're doing. It's a very full life we lead here, but it could not quite make up for moments such as these. It makes me very happy to think you're all waiting for me. April will soon be here.'

"I would say that Bob was quite a lonely individual in Australia," Trevor Bailey says. "I can't remember anybody in the side who was particularly close to him. Who did he share a room with?"

Vic Wilson.

"Yes, well, Vic was a nice, easy-going farmer; he got on well with everybody."

Trevor was one who was happy to make up a group for shooting wild animals, but that was not Bob's idea of a good time. "I felt sorry for the animals," he admits, and he recalls the nickname he acquired on the tour. "Whenever I met anyone who offered to show me round their company, I would go along and take anyone who was interested with me. So they started calling me 'the Factory Inspector'."

Was he lonely, or self-sufficient? In Bob's view he was a mature 30-year-old, one who had served in the Navy and who was well-equipped to cope with the strains of such a long tour. He was not a party-goer, not a hard-drinking fun-lover like some of his team-mates, but then nor was his captain.

"I remember the eve of one of the Tests. Len and I were drinking coffee in the hotel, and Denis Compton, Bill Edrich and Godfrey Evans came down, all dressed up for a night on the town. 'Look at those three,' Len said to me. 'They're going out in their glad rags. They think that they've got to forget about tomorrow and enjoy themselves. But this is the time to be thinking about the match.' Len would already have been thinking about going out to face Lindwall, his field placings, the atmosphere."

Here were the two poles of English cricket: the trio heading out of the hotel, fun-loving Southerners who lived life to the full and took their cricket as it came, and the pair at the coffee table, hard-working Northerners who said little and looked inwards for their mental strength.

"Len wasn't really criticising them so much as telling me what he thought. Denis was an instinctive player. He played on the seat of his pants. He was brilliant. A natural at whatever he turned his hand to. But Len had learnt his trade as a joiner. I don't think Yorkshire people like charisma. Denis was a glamour boy, and glamour boys in Yorkshire were treated with suspicion."

Bob might not be at the hub of the tour's social life, but he had a captain who understood him.

"The War had a great effect on Leonard's career. He was at his peak in 1939, and he had eleven months in hospital after he broke his arm in a gymnasium. He talked to me once about the accident, how he'd had his arm reset three times and how he felt he owed a lot to his surgeon, Reg Broomhead, just as I did to Geoffrey Wooler. His arm used to ache after a long innings, and of course he'd had to cut out certain shots. I think perhaps he and I had a kind of affinity. He understood what I'd gone through. Maybe that's why I didn't do more bowling on the Australian tour. He was giving me a chance to get acclimatised."

On side two of the treasured vinyl, delivered to Connie on Christmas morning by their friends the Vallances who lived across the road, was a recording of a church service in Adelaide on the Sunday of the South Australia match. The service was broadcast by the local radio station, and during it Bob read once more the words of the 23rd Psalm, being followed to the lectern by the young Colin Cowdrey, who read the verses from Saint Luke's gospel in which 'Our Lord taught his disciples how to pray.'

The early lines of the psalm are lost to the crackling and distortion, but Bob's voice rings out clear as the conclusion is reached.

> *Thou preparest a table before me in the presence of mine enemies: thou anointest my head with oil, my cup runneth over.*
>
> *Surely goodness and mercy shall follow me all the days of my life: and I will dwell in the house of the Lord for ever.*

Christmas approached, as did the Sydney Test. It was scheduled from December the 17th to the 23rd, its outcome bound to set the mood of their festivities. Would they be celebrating the levelling of the series, or would they be two-nil down and almost beyond recovery?

First morning at Sydney. Lindwall appeals in vain for a catch off Hutton

There were two spinners in the side where there had been none at Brisbane, but curiously the two Yorkshiremen made their most telling contributions with the bat. Wardle's came on the first afternoon when England had slumped to 99 for eight, and fresh disaster seemed upon them. At first he could hardly lay bat on ball – 'cavorting,' according to Alan Ross, 'as though wearing someone else's glasses' – but he suddenly found his focal length, advancing down the wicket and hitting 17 off one over from Bill Johnston. 'He moved forward,' A.G. Moyes wrote, 'like a pirate about to board a victim ship, waving his bat like a cutlass, not caring much where the ball went.' By the time he was caught on the long-on boundary, the England total had leapt to a half-respectable 154 all out.

It was batting that Bob had often seen at Yorkshire, from both Wardle and Trueman. "If a tail-ender goes in and messes around for an hour for a few runs, you've lost an hour of winning time. And that's terribly important, especially when there's bad weather. Johnny and Fred, when they were batting, you'd as soon watch them as anybody."

Six-day Test cricket did require a different approach but, their spirits lifted by Wardle's carefree hitting, the England team were left time to test the Australian openers with four overs of pace bowling. In the last of them Bailey had Morris caught at leg-slip.

That was Friday evening. On Saturday Australia built a first innings lead of 74. On Monday Peter May scored a fine century. But, when Bob and Brian

Statham came together on Tuesday afternoon, the England total was still only 250 for nine, a lead of just 176. They were facing the prospect of a despondent Christmas.

"I said to Brian, 'We'll get this up to 300' and we nearly did."

In the words of Bruce Harris of the *London Evening Standard*, 'They batted with the sang-froid, if not the skill and polish, of a Hobbs and Sutcliffe.' 296 all out left Australia 223 for victory.

Earlier in the England second innings Ray Lindwall had struck Frank Tyson on the head with a bumper, sending his fellow fast bowler to hospital for an x-ray. It was an electrifying moment, not at all what fast bowlers were supposed to do to each other, and the next day the Australian batsmen felt the consequences. 72 for two overnight, they were soon 77 for four, with Burke and Hole beaten for pace by Tyson yorkers.

"That was some of the fastest bowling I've ever seen," Bob says. "Graeme Hole was still at the top of his back-swing when Frank hit his wicket."

Harvey and Benaud survived an hour of 'grim cricket' before relief came with a bowling change.

"Leonard knew quick bowling won games," Bob says. "That was his tactic. He was accused of slowing down the game, which he did, but he also used Trevor, Johnny and me to rest Frank and Brian. We were just the support bowlers. Then, if one of us took a wicket, he'd whip us off. The incoming batsman would come out of the dark pavilion, and immediately he'd be facing Tyson or Statham in the full glare of the sun.

"A lot of these pavilions have their backs to the sun. They cast a shadow over the members, and the players can't sit out in the sun. They say that Don Bradman used to get used to the light by walking in a big arc on his way to the wicket."

With lunch approaching, Bob bowled to Benaud. It was only 102 for four, and perhaps the young Australian sensed an opportunity to move the score forward. There were still another 121 runs required for victory.

Alan Ross takes up the story:

> Appleyard is not a safe bowler to drive indiscriminately, for he varies his pace and makes the ball hold up at the last second, before dipping into the batsman. Just such a ball Benaud, fancying a half-volley, attempted to sweep to mid-wicket. He swung early and sent the ball swerving high to square leg. Tyson stood under it, gazing upward and weaving anxiously from side to side. Palpably it drifted and equally obviously Tyson misjudged it. At the last moment he lunged forward on bended knee, extending his hands as for the sacrament. The ball found them, miraculously.

For the rest of the Australian innings it was all Tyson and Statham and, despite a valiant 92 not out from Neil Harvey – "One of the best innings I've ever seen," Bob reckons – it was the tourists who left for Christmas in jubilant spirits. Victory by 38 runs had levelled the series.

Bob had contributed only one wicket but, as he says, "If you win a Test match like that, you don't bother about personal performances." In any case, as he likes to point out, his last wicket partnership of 46 with Brian Statham exceeded by eight runs the winning margin.

A chaotic Christmas Day followed. "A lunch-time turkey arrived about four o'clock, most of the waiters had gone home, and we finished the day on the beach in the hot sun." For some of the freer spirits in the side, it was all tremendous fun – but not for the quiet Bradfordian. "It was the worst Christmas Day I've ever had."

Then, after a minor match in Newcastle, they reconvened at Melbourne to start the third Test on New Year's Eve. Compton, having recovered from his hand injury at Brisbane, took the place of Graveney, but the bowling attack was the same as at Sydney.

There followed another contest in which the fortunes of the two teams ebbed and flowed repeatedly, with a final day as thrilling as at Sydney.

On the first morning the English batting collapsed again, this time against Miller and Lindwall, only to be rescued by a maiden Test century by the young Colin Cowdrey.

Ron Archer is beaten by Bob

Their final total of 191 looked better by the end of Saturday's play, by which time Australia had been reduced to 188 for eight with Bob claiming the two vital wickets of Neil Harvey and Richie Benaud.

Benaud pushed the ball lamely into the great hands of the substitute fielder Vic Wilson, hovering at short leg, but the dismissal of Harvey, Australia's premier batsman, required a ball of the highest quality.

'In his first over,' Jim Swanton wrote in the *Daily Telegraph*, 'Appleyard hit Harvey's off stump with a real beauty that had pitched on the leg. From this moment England were on top.'

Gradually it was being realised in the press box that the Appleyard who was bowling for England on New Year's Day was not the bowler who had caused them to shake their heads back in early November. Even E.M. Wellings – though he still thought him 'extremely lucky' to have got into the team for the previous Test, when 'his bowling did not in the slightest degree entitle him to selection' – joined in the praise:

> It is pleasant to record the measure of success achieved by Appleyard, for it had previously seemed that he was not going to adapt himself to Australian conditions and would eke out the tour as a hopeless failure.

"Australia was a real learning curve," Bob reflects. "I had a setback at the start with the rib injury, but by Melbourne I was starting to sort out how to bowl in those conditions. And I do remember that Saturday at Melbourne. It was intensely hot, and I came off feeling absolutely whacked. I slumped into a corner of the dressing room, and I sat there in a pool of perspiration. I felt I simply wasn't fit enough to play at that level. Then I looked around, and everybody else was struggling just the same. It was a long time before any of us could summon up the energy to shower, dress and leave for the hotel."

Whatever worries had lurked deep in his psyche about his fragile health were dispelled in that revelation. "From then on I had no worries. I was rehabilitated. My fears were unfounded. It was a load off my mind."

On the Sunday he was driven out to the home of a couple who had emigrated from Bradford, and he recalls the stifling heat. "We got into this car with leather seats, and it was burning hot. So we opened the windows, and the air outside was even hotter. We sat there dripping with perspiration. It was impossible to get out of the heat."

As Margaret Hughes wrote in her book *The Long Hop*, 'It was as if the steam in a laundry had been turned on the city and left on all day.'

They had left the pitch on Saturday evening looking, in Bob's words, "like crazy paving". Cracks were everywhere, and Ron Archer was bowled by a ball from Wardle that barely left the ground. With such intense heat, there seemed little hope for the batsmen when they returned on Monday morning.

Yet, when they took the field, the cracks were mysteriously gone, and there was moisture in the soil.

The controversy over the illegal watering of the pitch lasted for days, but fortunately for the assistant curator who had been responsible it was the tourists who gained the main advantage from his actions. On the easier surface the Australian tail added a further 43 runs, but in the England second innings Peter May was able to provide an exhibition of driving that led Alan Ross to compare his innings to 'the kind the best amateur number threes used to display on seaside grounds in the 'twenties and 'thirties.' His 91, followed the next day by further effective 'clouting' by Wardle, left Australia wanting 240 to regain the lead in the series. In the evening session they lost Morris, but Favell and Benaud were scoring freely till 'Favell, moving out to drive Appleyard, was beaten by the late in-dip and bowled.'

"Dip," Trevor Bailey repeats. "That was what was most remarkable about Bob's bowling. I'd never come across a bowler of his pace with dip before, and I've never seen it since. I liked practising in the nets, and he did, too. Not everybody took them seriously – Denis didn't – and there were bowlers you didn't want to face in the nets. I wouldn't have Tyson anywhere near me; he didn't know where the ball was going. But Bob was perfect. He kept on and on, and of course he was always so accurate. He never gave you anything to hit. And I just couldn't work out the dip. I thought I had plenty of time, and I'd think, 'This is a half-volley,' and it wasn't.

"With a slow bowler, you could charge down the wicket and hit him on the full-toss. But not Bob. I've never come across another bowler quite like him."

Favell, bowled Appleyard, 30. The pitch was taking turn, Australia ended the day on 75 for two, and the view in the pressbox was shared. 'It has been a match of extraordinary fluctuations,' Alan Ross wrote, 'and much will depend on Appleyard.'

But it was not to be. On the final morning, in little more than an hour of fiery pace, Australia's 75 for two became 111 all out as, in the words of *Wisden*, 'Tyson blazed through them like a bush fire.' Bob had been tipped to be the key bowler on a pitch that was once more cracking, and he did not bowl a ball.

The pace of Tyson and Statham had established a crucial psychological advantage, but the series only stood at two games to one and, when the teams reconvened three weeks later at Adelaide, everything was still at stake.

"If we'd won it, we'd have won the Ashes. If we'd lost, we'd have been back to square one."

For Bob, it turned out to be the greatest match of his short career.

CHAPTER 10

TRIUMPH AT ADELAIDE

January – April 1955

"I was really at the peak of my game by Adelaide," Bob says. "Everything had come together."

The city of Adelaide had spent January sweltering in a heat-wave and, with the first three Tests all won by the side batting first, it was clear that the toss for the fourth Test was of vital importance. 'The best one of all to win,' Jim Swanton reckoned. Under a clear blue sky, the largest crowd to fill the ground since the Bodyline tour watched as the coin spun into the air. Then they breathed a collective sigh of Australian relief as Hutton turned forlornly towards his team-mates in the dressing-room and signalled that they would be bowling.

'England trooped out to field in a temperature of 90 with a high degree of humidity,' Swanton related. 'This was back to Brisbane, save that the two slower men, Appleyard and Wardle, were available now while Bedser, with mixed feelings one may suppose, watched from the stand.'

Hutton restricted his bowlers to spells of no more than three overs in the morning, and Australia crawled laboriously to a lunchtime score of 51. 'It was just about as stodgy as introductions to Test matches generally are,' Swanton wrote, but there were no wickets down and Morris and McDonald looked intent on laying the foundations of a formidable total.

"I'd visited a couple of sanatoria for tubercular patients," Bob recalls. "Some of the lads were ready for coming out, and they'd got tickets for the Test. They were all sitting at a certain place on the ground. And, when I was fielding down there, they all cheered. 'Come on, Lofty.'"

They cheered enthusiastically half an hour after the start when Bob replaced Statham, and they cheered with even greater vigour when, after lunch, he returned to the attack, his slower ball drawing McDonald too early into his shot and giving May a catch at short leg. With Hutton permutating his quick and slow bowlers, and a coolness in the air replacing the recent stifling heat, there was a sense of calm control among the fielders, and the close of play score of 161 for four contrasted favourably with the 208 for two Australia had reached on the first day of the Brisbane Test. 'Today belonged to England,' the *Times* correspondent began his report.

That evening Colin Cowdrey and Bob travelled out to Don Bradman's house, two young cricketers whom the Don wanted to meet. "It was such an honour to have been invited. It was a simple family meal, cooked by Jessie, and we just listened in awe, like a pair of apprentices with their master."

Years later, when Bob was a Living Legend himself at Australia's Bicentennial Celebrations, he had the confidence to quiz the master more closely. "By then I was doing a bit of work with young cricketers in Yorkshire, not coaching them as such but showing them how I bowled and what the different options were. And I was keen to find out as much as I could about Wilfred Rhodes and Hedley Verity. The night before I flew out for that Bicentennial Test I stayed with Len Hutton. We sat up late, drinking some of Paul Getty's special brandy, and I asked him about Wilfred and Hedley.

"Then when I was at Sydney Don invited me into this room in the pavilion. It was a special room, for the holy of the holies, and we sat together for the whole afternoon. I asked him too, and he gave exactly the same answer that Leonard had given. Hedley bowled it a little bit quicker whereas Wilfred flighted it. Wilfred was the master of flight, probably in the whole history of the game. He bowled with his wrist under the ball; Hedley's was more vertical."

Bob recalls no such details from the evening meal in Adelaide, only that he left with a great sense of inspiration, inspiration that was still with him the next day when, for the third time in the series, his 'hanging flight and changes of pace' secured the wicket of Benaud.

Margaret Hughes caught the probing quality of Bob's bowling in her description of this dismissal:

> It seemed as if the batsman might have been more successful, had he used his feet to meet the spin, for he was being shunted farther back with every ball and in the dying moments of his innings was beaten twice before he fell into what appeared an openly laid trap. It can't be easy to know just how to play a spinner of this type when he is bowling on the spot all the time.

That was 175 for five, and only Keith Miller of the front-line batsmen remained. Halfway through Bob's next over he seemed to be setting himself to play a major innings, summoning a cap from the dressing room, but, before it could be delivered, he too was a victim of the bowler's hard-to-read flight. At the start of the day the elaborate Adelaide scoreboard had displayed Appleyard, 11 overs, one wicket for 31 runs. Now it recorded 18 overs, three wickets for 42. 'He bowled the best of the English bowlers on the first day,' Margaret Hughes reckoned, 'and his performance on the second morning was even better.'

"By the time of the Adelaide Test, I'd got used to the eight-ball overs and, because it was so warm all the time, I could bowl short spells and I didn't stiffen up so much afterwards. That made a huge difference. At the start of the tour my bowling relied on spin and bounce and, because the Australian pitches didn't take much spin and weren't that quick or bouncy, I had to work hard to perfect my control of flight, my changes of pace and direction. And by Adelaide I really felt in control. In fact, in my whole career, it was the closest I came to 100% control when I was bowling. When you bowl on pitches that help you, you can experiment a bit. But if everything's in the batsman's favour, you have to concentrate on your control. You have to concentrate on your stock ball, just bowl one, maybe two, an over that are a little different."

What was it Emmott Robinson told him? 'If tha's to be a bowler, tha knows tha hasta bowl five good balls an over, and the sixth hasn't to be a bad 'un.' In Australia it was a case of 'seven good balls an over, and the eighth hasn't to be a bad 'un.'

Archer and Davidson fell to the new ball and, at 229 for eight, 'Australia were almost at the last ditch.' Or, as the *Times* correspondent wrote, 'It looked as if England could not be beaten.'

Maddocks and Johnson soon changed that with a partnership of 92 that owed most of its runs to a calamitous piece of fielding.

"Oh no," Bob groans. "I hoped you weren't going to bring that up."

Len Maddocks pushed the ball towards Bob at mid-wicket and set off for a sharp single that his partner refused. The two were stranded for an age in mid-pitch as the tall fielder gathered the ball and sent it towards Godfrey Evans. It was a simple run out and, with only Bill Johnston to come, the Australian innings was effectively over.

'Appleyard almost had time to carry the ball to the wicket and still run out Maddocks,' E.M. Wellings wrote. 'He took slow, deliberate aim and amazingly threw the ball gently over the head of Evans, so high that he could do nothing about it.'

"I lobbed it to Godfrey, and somehow it just kept going for ever, high above his head. It's something I try to forget."

Australia reached 323 all out, and there was time for England to make 57 for no wicket before the close on Saturday. The game was in the balance.

Monday the 31st of January was Australia Day, and the celebrations were in full swing when Edrich and May fell early. But 80 from Hutton, his highest innings of the series, and a late partnership by Cowdrey and Compton lifted England to 230 for three. 'England could lead Australia by such a margin,' *The Times* suggested, 'as would give a chance of victory.' And, as everybody knew, with victory would come the winning of the Ashes.

Alas, Tuesday morning brought a quick reverse in England's fortunes, both overnight batsmen dismissed immediately, and only Evans – 'his innings more than a cheerful wallop' – and Bailey – 'as watchful as Cerberus at the other end' – prevented the Australians from taking the first innings lead for the fourth time in the series. By half past three, however, they were all out for 341, a lead of just 18: 'not, by any means, what had once been hoped for,' Alan Ross thought, 'but acceptable as a small, unexpected remittance from an aunt to a man whose capital has been lost overnight.'

Now all was at stake. McDonald and Morris cleared the arrears, and tea approached with a result a seeming certainty on a wicket that was taking increasing turn. Could Australia post a large enough total, one that the English batsmen would struggle to reach on the final day? Or would the English bowlers once more cut through their opponents' increasingly hesitant batting?

There was no initial breakthrough by Tyson and Statham, and the last over before tea was delivered by Bob. He hit the seam outside the off-stump, Morris stepped back and middled his cut, and the ball bounced in front of Colin Cowdrey in the gully, climbing to crack the bridge of his nose a painful blow. For eight minutes the game was suspended, as fielders – Bob among them – carried him away into the pavilion. The nose was broken, and Bruce Harris of the *London Evening Standard* claimed afterwards that the incident turned the course of the match.

It was 24 for no wicket. Bob's first ball after the delay was a slower one, dipping late, and Morris, his concentration unsettled, pushed too hard, sending it back in a gentle loop waist-high to the bowler. Now it was 24 for one, and the smiles were on the English faces at tea.

Through the evening session the Yorkshireman continued to bowl from the Cathedral end while Tyson, Statham, Bailey and Wardle shared the supporting duties. Margaret Hughes tells the story:

> Burke stayed stubborn for 27 minutes, made five runs, and then delivered his soul to Appleyard at 40 for two. Unfortunately for Australia, Harvey showed no form at all. After 20 minutes'

silent, almost underground, resistance, he suddenly seemed teased beyond endurance by Appleyard and, throwing up his head as if in anger, he wildly thrashed over a ball, missed it completely and found his wicket shattered.

That was 54 for three, and the Australians were grateful to reach the close on 69 with no further loss.

Harvey, bowled Appleyard, 7

'Come on, Lofty,' the sanatorium patients cheered, inspired by the sporting glory of one of their own, and such was his mastery that he finished the day with figures of ten overs, five maidens, three wickets for 13 runs.

Jim Swanton was full of praise for the performance of the Yorkshireman:

> I can scarcely remember an English bowler in Australia who picked up so well the art of pace-change. He let go from his full height at speeds ranging from slow to medium, and bowled a wonderfully good line, with always the hint of turn from the off.

'APPLEYARD IN HIS ELEMENT,' ran the *Times* headline. 'This was Appleyard's day,' cheered Bruce Harris in the *Evening Standard*. 'Australian wickets probably do not suit him as well as those of his native Yorkshire, but what the pitch did not do for him his own brains achieved.'

'England's chances of victory,' Alan Ross suggested, echoing his words at Melbourne, 'seem to rest with Appleyard.'

"That was the peak of my career," Bob reflects. "Everything I'd worked for came to fruition in that match."

The parallel with Melbourne was uncanny. There Australia went into the fifth day on 75 for two. Here at Adelaide they were 69 for three. In both matches overnight opinion had labelled Appleyard as the danger man, yet both times he stood in the outfield in his sweater as the young pacemen took the ball at mid-day and wreaked destruction. And both times Australia were reduced to 111 all out.

On that final morning at Adelaide Tyson bowled nine overs and took three for 25, Statham seven overs, three for 12. Bob Appleyard's contribution was two maidens in the last moments of the innings, and we can only speculate what figures he might have returned if Hutton had thrown him the ball at twelve o'clock as everybody expected.

But at Melbourne Australia had been batting last. Here at Adelaide the match was not yet won. England had to bat again, and they needed 94 runs for victory, 94 runs to win the series, to win the Ashes.

Jim Kilburn was at his most feverish:

> In cool contemplation 94 to win might have seemed a formality. All cricketing reason said it was a formality, but where was reason, where was contemplation on that blazing Adelaide afternoon? Not on the Adelaide Oval.

In thirty minutes Edrich, Hutton and the broken-nosed Cowdrey were all unbuckling their pads, swept away in a counter-burst of pace by the veteran Keith Miller. Then, just as nerves were steadying, Miller swooped in the covers to claim a catch from the bat of Peter May. It was 49 for four, and the whole England party watched intently from the pavilion as Denis Compton – 'a Cavalier turned Puritan for the cause' – and Trevor Bailey – 'his batting tempered to his own traditional habits' – inched the score slowly forward.

Alas, with only four runs required, 'Bailey, like General Wolfe, fell in the moment of victory,' and it was left to the jaunty Evans to crack the winning boundary.

In no time the England dressing-room was awash with champagne.

"We'd beaten Australia in Australia," Bob says. "Not many people had done that."

The *Yorkshire Post* editorial was delirious with excitement:

> This is a time for exulting and complacency – rare indulgences in these days. There is a wealth of proven talent which will return to England – the seething Tyson, the implacable Cowdrey, May and Statham, and that thoughtful bowler Appleyard.
>
> The future is fair to look upon. Sir Pelham Warner foresees the beginning of a great new era in English cricket. There will be grumblers who will say that this is because cricket is at its lowest level. Tyson, Statham, Cowdrey, May, Appleyard? This is a renaissance, not a funeral.

A letter arrived in Australia.

Dear Bob
I wish to congratulate you on your recent successes and tell you how very proud I am of your achievements. I know very well how hard you have worked and it is a great credit to you that you have been able to stand up to so much strain. When you have a moment let me know how you feel.
Yours ever
Geoffrey Wooler

*

Hutton was England's first professional captain, and he had succeeded where Freddie Brown, Wally Hammond and Gubby Allen had all failed before him. In just two months Peter May and Colin Cowdrey had grown into mature Test cricketers while the new fast bowling sensation 'Typhoon' Tyson had taken a staggering 25 wickets in England's three victories.

Statham, Bailey, Evans, Compton, Edrich, Graveney. Here was a team stacked with the great names of English post-war cricket and, in time, their Ashes-winning triumph after such an inauspicious start at Brisbane would come to be viewed as one of the high peaks of English cricketing history.

Rain ruined the final Test at Sydney, though even in that match there was time for England to establish its superiority. Tom Graveney hit a century, and on the damp track Johnny Wardle created problems with his chinamen.

The series was over, 3-1 to England. It was a triumph for the young fast bowlers, with Tyson capturing all the headlines, but the final averages underlined the part played by those in support, especially the man whose name comes least freely to the tongue when that historic team is recalled:

	Overs	*Maidens*	*Runs*	*Wickets*	*Average*
R. Appleyard	79	22	224	11	20.36
F.H. Tyson	151	16	583	28	20.82
J.H. Wardle	70.6	15	229	10	22.90
J.B. Statham	143.3	16	499	18	27.72
T.E. Bailey	73.4	8	306	10	30.60

Bob was the most economical bowler in the side, the hardest to hit away, and for most of the Tests his role was to provide rest for Tyson and Statham. "He was such a key member of that side," David Sheppard reckons. "Len relied enormously on Tyson and Statham, but Bob's part in it was vital. The Australian batsmen found they couldn't get at him."

But Bob also took wickets – and important ones, too, as he will point out. "All my eleven wickets in that series," he says, "were top six batsmen."

The England party bristled with self-confidence as they flew on to New Zealand for a final four weeks. Twenty-five years had passed since the New Zealanders had been admitted to the Test-playing fraternity, and they were still awaiting their first victory. If Australia's batsmen could not withstand the pace of Tyson and Statham, there was little expectation that the New Zealanders would be able to do so, either.

In the first Test at Dunedin the hosts crawled to 125 all out in a full first day, Bert Sutcliffe – 'standing out like a lighthouse on this black day' – making 74. Then second time around they managed 132 as Tyson ran amok. 'His was blistering pace,' the young John Reid recalls. 'He was through us before we had our bats half up.'

In the second Test at Auckland, matters got worse. Reid (73) and Sutcliffe (49) batted well, but there was little support and, when Bob claimed three late wickets, stumps were drawn at 199 for eight. Bob was preciously poised on a hat-trick when play resumed, but it was Statham who concluded proceedings. A total of 200 all out might have seemed disappointing, but it was riches compared with their second effort.

On a pitch that was taking turn, Hutton dropped himself into the middle order and hit a laboured 53. He was eighth man out at 201, and he stopped for a word with his partner Tyson. "If you can get a few, Frank," he said wearily, "we won't have to bat again." In the end they managed a lead of just 46, but it was enough to fulfil his prophecy.

At three o'clock on a gloriously sunny day New Zealand began again. 'The pitch was dry and not particularly fast, though there was some unevenness of bounce. Before double figures had been reached, Tyson and Statham had three men back in the pavilion. Then after tea Wardle, floating up a chinaman, tempted Sutcliffe into a wild heave which missed the ball.

'Bad batting, of course,' Bert Sutcliffe later wrote of their efforts. 'Good bowling, undoubtedly. Lack of resolution, almost certainly. And perhaps the intensity of the struggle earlier had taken something out of our rather inexperienced and diffident batsmen. I was fourth out, at 14. I went back, had a quick shower, and as I emerged from the dressing-room the last of our batsmen were coming in.'

By that stage Bob had taken over, and he relished conditions that were closer to England than any he had experienced in Australia. "It was the only real turner I'd bowled on all winter. I had two short legs, Peter May and Tom Graveney, and they both took catches. It was over so quickly."

'Once a landslide starts,' John Reid wrote, 'it is difficult to arrest.' And so it proved. McGregor was caught by May, and that was 14 for five. The score inched forward to 22, then Bob – according to the *Yorkshire Post* – 'coaxed wizardry out of the wicket.' In one over Cave was caught by Graveney, MacGibbon was lbw second ball, and Colquhoun, as in the first innings, lasted only one ball, this time caught 'splendidly' by Graveney off a hard hit. Suddenly it was 22 for eight.

Wicket, dot, wicket, wicket. Bob was on a hat-trick for the second time in the match. "There's nothing like getting two or three wickets in an over," he says. "You can imagine the panic in the opponents' dressing room, and of course your best chance of getting a batsman out is with the first ball he faces, before he's had a sight of the ball."

As in the first innings it was the leg-spinner Alex Moir who came to the crease to prevent the hat-trick, and his tentative prod at Bob's well-pitched off-break landed tantalisingly short of Graveney. But, before the Yorkshireman could do any more damage, Len Hutton turned back to his quick bowlers, and Statham finished the innings.

"Len was asked by the press afterwards why he took me off. I might have taken five or six wickets. And he said how he wanted to end the tour as we'd started, with Tyson and Statham bowling."

In 27 overs, the home batsmen had managed a new record low Test score of just 26. 'It was the nadir of New Zealand Test performances,' John Reid wrote. 'We had been pretty low on occasions in the past, but this time we really scraped the bottom of the barrel.'

'It was incredible,' Bert Sutcliffe wrote, 'but, as one of our well-wishers said, at least all the 26 runs came from the bat!'

With four wickets for seven runs in six overs, Bob completed his tour. From a cracked rib in Colombo through tentative early weeks of adjustment, he had become a pivotal part of an England bowling attack that was now the best in the world. He had only bowled the equivalent of 429 six-ball overs in six months, but he was top of the averages for the seven Tests and he was top of the averages for all first-class matches on the tour.

A trip to a Maori settlement
(left to right) Brian Statham, Frank Tyson, Bill Edrich, George Duckworth, Godfrey & Jean Evans, Bob Appleyard, Peter Loader, the Maori hostess, Len & Dorothy Hutton, Vic Wilson, Peter May (hidden), Keith Andrew, Geoffrey Howard

'This side of Hutton's was a particularly happy one,' Bruce Harris wrote, 'and Appleyard fitted into the pattern perfectly. It was good to notice that hard work under an Australian sun served only to show how thoroughly he had recovered from the serious illness which threatened to end his cricket career.'

Four years earlier Bob's 20-year-old Yorkshire team-mate Brian Close had returned from Australia distraught. A gauche Northerner, he had not found the young amateurs of the party easy company, and his outspoken assertiveness went down badly with senior players like Len Hutton. "But then," Bob says, "Len wouldn't have wanted to be associated with a youngster who told everybody what he was going to do. That wasn't his style. In some respects Brian was more like Denis."

The 1954/55 tour had no such fault lines. The youngest member of the party, Colin Cowdrey, was nurtured by Hutton, the oldest, and the distinction between professional and amateur was lessened by the appointment of Hutton and his forward-looking manager Geoffrey Howard.

"There were occasions when the amateurs were invited to functions," Bob recalls, "but, as far as the players were concerned, people like Peter May, Colin Cowdrey, Trevor Bailey, they were players like the rest of us. At one time they'd have been poles apart, but the gap was narrowing. I think that's why we all got on so well. And Geoffrey Howard was so good. He was one of those people you don't notice, so meticulous. And he and Len got on very well together.

"It was a very good tour to be on. There was no difficulty being part of it. You couldn't be left out. There was nobody left out. The atmosphere was tremendous."

We listen once more to the 78 rpm record.

> I know it must be very hard for you, Connie, staying at home, but try to think only of when our normal family life begins again. I look forward to it so very much. We seem to have so much to do yet in our home and with our children's future. It's a lovely thought and very Christmassy. Bye, bye for now, Connie. Rosemarie and Elizabeth, give them a big kiss for me. God bless you.

BOWLING FIGURES 1954/55

First-class fixtures
(Test matches in bold type)

Eight ball overs in Australia, six ball overs in New Zealand

			First innings				*Second innings*			
Oct 22,23,25	Perth	Combined XI	10	5	19	0	17	4	36	3
Oct 29,30 Nov 1,2	Adelaide	South Australia	9	2	31	0	11	1	46	5
Nov 12,13,15,16	Sydney	New South Wales	21	3	58	1	3	1	7	0
Dec 17,18,20,21,22	**Sydney**	**Australia**	**7**	**1**	**32**	**0**	**6**	**1**	**12**	**1**
Dec 31, Jan 1,3,4,5	**Melbourne**	**Australia**	**11**	**3**	**38**	**2**	**4**	**1**	**17**	**1**
Jan 13,14,15	Launceston	Tasmania	6	0	15	1	4	2	6	0
Jan 21,22,24	Adelaide	South Australia	17	6	50	2	4	2	13	0
Jan 28,29,31 Feb 1,2	**Adelaide**	**Australia**	**23**	**7**	**58**	**3**	**12**	**7**	**13**	**3**
Feb 11,12,14,15	Melbourne	Victoria	6.1	2	14	3				
Feb 25,26,28 Mar 1,2,3	**Sydney**	**Australia**	**16**	**2**	**54**	**1**				
Mar 11,12,14,15,16	**Dunedin**	**New Zealand**	**7**	**3**	**16**	**0**	**7**	**2**	**19**	**2**
Mar 19,21,22	Wellington	Wellington	20	7	36	3	21.4	13	21	6
Mar 25,26,28	**Auckland**	**New Zealand**	**16**	**4**	**38**	**3**	**6**	**3**	**7**	**4**

Matches	*Balls*	*Maidens*	*Runs*	*Wickets*	*Average*
13	1963	82	656	44	14.90

Non-first-class fixtures

			First innings				*Second innings*			
Dec 4,6	Rockhampton	Queensland Country	11	4	18	2	14.7	4	51	7
Dec 27,28,29	Newcastle	Northern NSW	12	2	44	1	19.2	2	59	5
Jan 18,19	Mount Gambier	South Australian Country	12.2	4	26	6	7	4	8	0

Matches	*Balls*	*Maidens*	*Runs*	*Wickets*	*Average*
3	611	20	206	21	9.80

All Matches	*Balls*	*Maidens*	*Runs*	*Wickets*	*Average*
16	2574	102	862	65	13.26

CHAPTER 11

WE'LL NEVER SEE THE LIKE OF HIM AGAIN

The Summer of 1955

The plane journey home from New Zealand lasted several days. They flew by night, catching what sleep they could, and during the days they were welcomed and entertained so royally that they became utterly exhausted. At Fiji there was dinner with the local cricket board. At Hawaii they were garlanded as they stepped off the plane. In San Francisco there was a coach trip to the zoo and lunch with the British Consul. In New York, a tour of the Empire State Building and a celebratory lunch with Henry Sayen, their American admirer. And in the evening during the night flights their attempts at rest were broken by refuelling stops.

"We flew in a DC6, with petrol engines. I remember stopping to refuel on the Canton Islands in the Pacific. It was just a coral reef about a mile long and not very wide."

Early on the morning of Tuesday the fifth of April they landed in Scotland, and from there they were flown to London. "That was a bit traumatic. I just wanted to get home by then, and I had to sit and watch the plane flying south over Yorkshire. And, when we landed at Heathrow, they wanted us to go to a press conference in Central London. 'That's all right for you Londoners,' I said. 'But I'm going home to Yorkshire.' Vic Wilson and I went off and caught the train."

They were without their captain Len Hutton, who was travelling back at leisure on the *SS Orsova*. They were without Denis Compton, who had gone to South Africa. But they were met on arrival by Tom Graveney and Colin Cowdrey, who had returned a week earlier. Cowdrey was on his way to his National Service interview the next day. The rising star of English cricket, he was to be rejected by the RAF – on the grounds that he had stiff, rigid toes.

Tuesday the fifth of April, 1955. As they landed, the Prime Minister Winston Churchill was making his way to Buckingham Palace, tendering his resignation in favour of his long-time deputy Anthony Eden.

In the seven months in which they had been away, so many changes had been set in motion: a network of motorways to be built, the railways to be electrified, a smokeless zone in London, equal pay for women civil servants, a switch to nuclear power. The first wave of rock'n'roll was sweeping across from the States, and a commercial television channel was soon to be on air.

At the airport Johnny Wardle was met by his wife Edna and their two boys, and they headed off for a London hotel where a *Yorkshire Post* reporter caught up with them. "There's never been a finer team spirit than that which we had this time," Wardle said. "I suppose you could put it down to great leadership." Meanwhile the boys played with their new presents, Gerald waving two cowboy-style six-shooters and John setting to work on a construction kit. Australian boomerangs would arrive later by boat.

The *Yorkshire Post* was also present at York railway station when Vic Wilson was reunited with his family, but the ever-private Bob alighted at Forster Square, Bradford, and caught a taxi unnoticed.

"I'd bought two very nice little matching dresses at Macy's in New York, for Rosemarie and Elizabeth. That was very popular, I remember."

Already their county team-mates had reported back to Headingley from their less exciting winters. Frank Lowson had been working in the accounts office of the Yorkshire Electricity Board, Norman Yardley selling wines and spirits for a Sheffield firm, Ray Illingworth helping his father's cabinet-making business, Ted Lester with a firm of accountants in Scarborough, and Roy Booth making gears for David Brown's tractors.

All this was set out by Derrick Boothroyd in the *Yorkshire Post*. 'The only player in the dressing room who was not very communicative about his winter activities,' Boothroyd continued, 'was the 24-year-old Brian Close. 'Well,' he said guardedly, 'I don't do anything full-time in the winter, but I ...' 'He plays golf full-time,' Norman Yardley said, and one or two others prompted, 'Eight days a week, isn't it, Brian?' Brian seized his cricket tackle with great dignity and made his exit.'

"Brian got to be a very hard worker," Bob says. "There was one winter when he was selling paints. He rushed around getting so many orders that the business failed. His back-up staff couldn't keep up with the deliveries and collecting the money."

Before the month of April was out, the Yorkshire players would be travelling down to Lord's, starting out on their summer round of 34 matches in 18 weeks. Each of them was issued with a schedule detailing the train times for their various journeys:

> May 10. Leave Bradford at 6.03 p.m. Change at Birmingham. Arrive in Oxford at 12.55 a.m.
> June 28. Leave Nottingham at 6 p.m. Change at Birmingham. Arrive in Bournemouth at 12.14 a.m.
> August 26. Leave Southend at 6 p.m. Alight at Fenchurch Street and travel to Euston. Arrive at Leeds at 1.30 a.m. "And then I'd got to get to Bradford."

"The worst one of all was the year we played Scotland at Paisley. We got in to the station at about two o'clock, then when we got to the hotel we found it had closed down."

In the event, Yorkshire's schedule of railway journeys was redundant. Anthony Eden called a general election in May, and no sooner had he won it than the country was brought to a standstill by a lengthy rail strike. It was back to a summer of negotiating the roads of a pre-motorway Britain.

Twelve months earlier the Yorkshire committee had speculated how Bob might make a gentle return to cricket, 'a few championship games after a cautious run-out in two-day games', yet now he was preparing for a second full summer. By the end of August he would have played continuously for sixteen months.

It was a demanding schedule, but Bob was brimming with confidence and by the time May was out he had taken another 59 wickets.

At Bradford, on a damp pitch, Yorkshire began their championship programme against Northamptonshire. The visitors included the Australian left-arm spinner George Tribe, whose back-of-the-hand bowling created such confusion among the home batsmen that he took thirteen wickets on an extraordinary first day.

Tribe finished the match with figures of fifteen wickets for 75 runs, the best bowling return ever achieved at the Park Avenue ground, yet such was the character of the pitch and the quality of Yorkshire's own spin attack that Northants had lost by 78 runs after less than two hours' play on the second day. 'It was the sort of pitch,' Jim Kilburn wrote, 'Appleyard and Wardle would choose for themselves were they required to challenge the whole world of batting.' On his favourite ground Bob's final figures were 25 overs, eleven wickets for 48 runs.

"Can you imagine it?" Don Wilson says, a 17-year-old boy from Settle who was growing up with the romance of Yorkshire cricket and who in time would inherit Wardle's role as the county's slow left-armer. "George Tribe took fifteen wickets, and he finished on the losing side. But there were so many wonderful games at Bradford. It was a memory ground. The cricket was never dull there."

Fred Trueman bowling on the first morning of the Roses match at Old Trafford

Bob's eleven wickets at Bradford were followed by ten at Bristol, nine at Headingley against Somerset and ten at Chesterfield. That gave him forty in four games. Warwickshire were beaten at Sheffield, Lancashire at Old Trafford, and the month ended with Yorkshire on top of the championship table, with six emphatic victories out of six.

This was competitive county cricket of the highest order, but unfortunately for Yorkshire it was matched in the south by the reigning champions Surrey. They too had six victories out of six, and they too had a deadly spin attack.

Cricket history gives pride of place to Surrey's Laker and Lock, but not everybody in the North shares this perspective.

"As far as I'm concerned," Fred Trueman says, "Wardle was the best left-arm spinner on all wickets that I saw. He could bowl it out of the back of the hand as well and, with Bob Appleyard at the other end, it was a magnificent partnership. Locky wasn't as good a bowler as Johnny Wardle, and also he had a very doubtful action."

And Bob, compared with Jim Laker?

"Bob was one of the all-time greats. I don't like to say it about Jim Laker, because he was a very fine bowler, but he had only half the heart of an Appleyard. Bob would bowl on anything and never know when he was beaten. He'd keep coming back at you. He bowled from a great height, sideways on, close to the stumps, and he was so accurate. He bowled with the new ball, and he bowled off-spin, and he never gave away anything. He was something different, Bob Appleyard. If you were picking an all-time England side, you'd have to consider him very seriously. And if it came down to a choice between him and Jim Laker, on all wickets, well for me it would be R. Appleyard."

"I agree with Fred," Ray Illingworth says. "Bob would be in my side ahead of Jim. He was a big man. His arm came right over the top, and he got tremendous bounce. He had a wonderful change of pace. He bowled a loop ball, a slower ball that went up and bounced a bit, and he also bowled a magnificent quick leg-stump yorker."

"Big Bob," says Ken Taylor, a youngster breaking into the Yorkshire team in the mid-to-late '50s. "He was tall, and he had this tremendous jump in his delivery stride. His arm was at full height so he delivered from a long way up and, of course, that meant that he could get extra bounce from further up than most bowlers. He had great hands, and you could hear the ball spinning f-f-z-z-z-z as it came down the pitch. He was a fantastic bowler."

"He could still get something out of a dry pitch," Ray Illingworth says, "as he did in Australia."

It is hard to find another bowler in living memory with whom to compare him. Perhaps the left-handed Derek Underwood of Kent, who toured Australia under Illingworth's captaincy in 1970/71?

"Bob was a bit quicker than Derek," Ray says, "and, because Derek had a low action, he'd skid it through more. So he had to pitch it on a fuller length than Bob did. Bob, because of his height and his extra pace, he could catch the end of where the seamers had been knocking the pitch about. A normal spinner wouldn't do that. It would be too short for him. There's no doubt that Bob was a good all-round bowler on any pitch."

Comparisons. All cricket enthusiasts love them. Let us turn to Trevor Bailey for a more neutral assessment. How would he compare the two left-armers? "Tony Lock was throwing whereas Johnny Wardle was bowling. And we all knew it. Surrey were the people to blame for that. Originally Tony had a lovely action, but he never got any wickets." And Wardle, compared with other slow left-armers since the war? "As a wrist-spin bowler he was the best in the world for three or four years. But in his orthodox style he wasn't nearly so deadly. He was better than Tufnell, better than Edmonds, but not as good as Underwood. But then he was a different type of bowler from Underwood."

Bob's pace, compared with Derek Underwood? "Oh, Derek's pace was much less. When Bob bowled seam, he was a genuine medium-pacer; he had his wicket-keeper standing back. But Derek, when he started as a seamer, his keeper stood up.

Trevor Bailey recalls again the first two times he faced Bob. At Brentwood he was bowling in-swing: "He was good, but there were plenty of bowlers like that at the time. And some of them, like Cliff Gladwin of Derbyshire, were better." Then on a drying pitch at Bradford Bob was bowling fast off-breaks, and "he came as close to being unplayable as any bowler I have ever faced."

He looks up the Bradford scorecard. "17 overs, six for 17. Then 23.4 overs, six for 26. OK, it was a turning wicket, but those are terrific figures."

So has any bowler in the history of cricket done so much with the ball at such pace as Bob Appleyard? He pauses for thought before producing an answer. "I should think probably Sydney Barnes."

So how does Trevor rate Bob against Jim Laker?

"Oh, Laker was easily the best off-spinner in the world. He had a classic bowling action, he had wonderful control, and he *was* an off-spinner. To my mind Bob wasn't really an off-spinner, he was an off-cutter."

Spin or cut, where is the dividing line? Trevor thinks for a long time. "If you're going to spin it," he replies eventually, "you probably use all your fingers more than you do when you cut it."

This was the conversation Bob had had with Jim Swanton on the *SS Orsova*. Bob did not bowl text book off-spin, and among cricketing purists he was destined to be labelled an oddity. Curiously the only bowler in his playing career who ever asked him to demonstrate his grips was Glamorgan's Don Shepherd, and he too suffered the tag of being an off-cutter, not a proper off-spinner. Don took 2,218 wickets in his career, at an average lower than contemporaries like Fred Titmus and David Allen, but he never played a Test. No bowler in the history of the game has taken more wickets without winning a cap.

"Why do you have to be in a category?" Bob asks again. "Surely what matters is what the ball does. By bowling as I did, I could spin the ball at pace, and I could get bounce. And that gave the batsman less time to play."

"Bob Appleyard was something special," Fred Trueman says. "Bowling like that, he must be the best ever at what he did. If I ever speak at a dinner and Bob is there, I always say, 'We've got Bob Appleyard here tonight. Don't any of you go away without knowing that he is one of the great bowlers of all time.' And I mean it. He's somebody we'll never see the like of again."

*

Surrey and Yorkshire. Without doubt they were the two most formidable teams in these years, and their meetings did much to determine the destination of the championship title.

On Saturday the fourth of June 1955 Yorkshire travelled to The Oval, and on a saturated pitch Norman Yardley asked the home side to bat first. 'Trueman, charging like a buffalo from the pavilion end, bowled fast and unluckily for half an hour,' the *Times* correspondent reported. 'Appleyard was the gentler schemer in contrast.'

By lunch Surrey were 53 for seven, and Bob had taken six of them. 'Three short legs, all brilliant fieldsmen, were hovering over the bat, and Appleyard, with his clever, evasive flight, was turning the ball enough, and not too much.'

Laker, caught Wilson, bowled Appleyard, 0
The other short legs are Sutcliffe, Lowson and Trueman (half in picture)

"I always enjoyed bowling at The Oval," Bob says, perhaps a little envious of the Surrey spinners who had a home pitch to their suiting, where he and Wardle had to adapt to the variety of Yorkshire's seven home grounds. "I did well there on my debut, and I seemed to do well there quite often afterwards."

Surrey managed only 85, Bob finishing with figures of 18 overs, seven wickets for 29 runs. But the advantage was not decisive, as Loader, Laker and Lock struck back in the evening.

Len Hutton had not arrived back in England on the *SS Orsova* till the 10th of May, being greeted by the MCC secretary Ronnie Aird, who had gone down to his cabin to present him with honorary membership of the MCC. On the 18th at Headingley he had batted for the first time, but he was still exhausted from the strains of two long winter tours as captain and his lumbago quickly flared up in the damp weather.

By the time Hutton reached The Oval two weeks later, well-wishers were bombarding him with suggested remedies: "A popular one was to place a nutmeg in my pocket," he wrote. "I was sent enough nutmegs to start a business." On this occasion he tried out wearing an 'awkward appliance' that had him grow hotter and hotter as the day progressed. "Mercifully, as it was becoming intolerable, Appleyard began taking wickets, and I was relieved of the torment."

It was the benefit match of Surrey's Arthur McIntyre and, with the ground full, the gate receipts were £200 and a collection for the popular wicket-keeper raised £535, a larger sum than several counties paid their players for a full summer's work. But his first action in the Yorkshire innings brought a groan from the visitors:

> By ten minutes to three Hutton was fingering his cap on the way to the wicket. His first ball he left, the second he stunned with a dead bat, and off the third he was caught at the wicket, feeling for an out-swinger. He seems to be temporarily dispossessed of his mastery and assurance. It is sad to see, but touch is an elusive thing that comes as quickly as it goes.

Hutton, caught McIntyre, bowled Loader, 0.

Back in the pavilion the England captain penned a letter to the selectors, withdrawing from Thursday's Test match against South Africa at Trent Bridge. 'On my return home from Australia I felt fit and well, but after a few days' cricket in this climate my pains returned.'

Later batsmen struggled to 108 for seven, a disappointing score but not enough to muffle the jubilation at the Café Royal that evening where the Society of Yorkshiremen held their dinner. A *Yorkshire Post* reporter described the arrival of the players and the excited enquiries about the state of the Oval pitch.

> Along came Mr Appleyard. Mr Appleyard had taken seven Surrey wickets for 29 runs. Here was the authority on the Oval wicket. He would have the last word. Well, Mr Appleyard, what was peculiar about the wicket today?
>
> Mr Appleyard beamed. It was a beam that made the lighting in the room look dim. It promised a full and fascinating account of

> why Surrey had scraped together only 85 runs. We balanced ourselves comfortably and waited upon his account.
>
> Then Mr Appleyard spoke. 'It was wet,' he said. He beamed again, and it suddenly became clear that there was nothing more to tell. Mr Appleyard nodded genially and moved on down the room.

The laconic Len Hutton could not have bettered his brevity. "Leonard was quite a private person," Bob says with approval. "He didn't say anything unless there was something worth saying. I mean, why use two words when one will do?" The distrust of unnecessary words has stayed with him all his life. "Tony Blair, he uses twenty words where one will do. Mind you, Neil Kinnock was worse. He used forty."

The weather was not kind to Yorkshire when they returned to The Oval on Monday. Weekend sunshine had made the pitch dry and easy, 'one that the batsmen could now enjoy', and Surrey were able to score 261 for seven. Then on early Tuesday morning heavy rain returned, and Yorkshire 'were snared on a spiteful pitch.' Chasing 216 for victory, Hutton was bowled by Loader for just one run, Frank Lowson followed within minutes and, as the pitch deteriorated further, Alec Bedser became almost unplayable. A match that had started in triumph on Saturday morning ended in defeat by 41 runs late on Tuesday afternoon. 'One's last feeling,' the *Times* correspondent wrote, 'was of regret that the weather should have had an appreciable say in the final result.'

Surrey had opened a 20-point lead in the championship and, for all Yorkshire's later triumphs, it was an advantage that the Southern county would never surrender.

On the Saturday of that Surrey match at The Oval, Bob had sat with Stanley Barnett of 'Edward Sommerfield, Personal Management', and they had discussed the terms of a contract in which Barnett would act as his agent, to secure a suitable fee for the book he was being urged to write and to arrange interviews with the newspapers and on television.

'Dear Mr Sommerfield,' he was asked to sign, 'I am desirous of obtaining the benefit of your expert advice, assistance and co-operation as my Business Manager in my career as a television performer and author and particularly in the exploitation and management of my professional activities and talents otherwise than solely as a professional cricketer associated with the Yorkshire County Cricket Club and as an employee of Short's Lifts, Ltd.'

Denis Compton – the Brylcreem Boy – had been the first cricketer to make such an arrangement, in his case with the agent Bagenal Harvey, but Bob did not follow suit. He was a Northerner, from stock not comfortable with such fancies, and he preferred to let his cricket do the talking. By August the correspondence had come to an unproductive conclusion.

The first Test followed on Thursday at Trent Bridge. Bob took two first innings wickets, but in the process he acquired a niggling pain in his shoulder, and his roller-coaster career took another turn. A bowler renowned for his relentless accuracy, his efforts in the South African second innings drew harsh comment even from Jim Kilburn in the *Yorkshire Post*:

> The disappointment was Appleyard, who not only failed to take a wicket when wickets were reasonably expected of him but descended to uncharacteristic inaccuracy.

"I began to get an ache in my upper arm after bowling, and I was sent to see various specialists. At first nobody could find a reason for the problem. The orthopaedic surgeon was at a loss, and the blood tests didn't reveal anything."

At the start of that Trent Bridge Test he had taken 71 wickets in 5½ weeks at an average of under 11 runs each. He had played only 2¼ English summers and one Australian tour, and his career record stood at 481 wickets at an average of only 13.91 runs each. Averages can never tell the whole story, but they must be an indicator of some sort. At this point he had a career average of 13.91, and no bowler in first-class cricket since the First World War – neither before Bob nor since – has finished with a career average below 14.

He had come into county cricket at a relatively great age, immediately changing his bowling style. He had recuperated from major surgery and altered his action a second time. He had had to adapt to the Australian pitches with their lack of turn. Yet here he was with the best bowling figures in the history of the modern game.

But the pain in his arm and shoulder did not go away, and it set off a sequence of further injuries. Perhaps, like Hutton, he had played too much cricket, driven his body beyond its natural endurance. But Hutton was nearly 39 years old, he had achieved the highest honours in a twenty-year career, and Bob was only approaching 31. He had played less than three full English summers, and he was still learning, still hungry for new peaks of success.

The shoulder injury kept him out of the next match at Hull, but he was back on the Saturday for Surrey's visit to Headingley. Here was the second head-to-head showdown of the championship's two leading sides, and 35,000 spectators 'watched the play, or tried to watch it, in varying degrees of comfort or discomfort.'

"As far as I was concerned," Bob says, "the Surrey game was another Test match."

The Headingley game was one of the most dramatic of Bob's career but it was not, alas, one in which the names of either Hutton or Appleyard stood out. Bob took three good wickets when Surrey batted first, helping to reduce the visitors to 119 for eight on a good batting pitch, but after that he 'struggled with a strained leg muscle' and the Surrey tail, inspired by the unlikely belligerence of Loader, lifted the score to a healthy 268.

On Monday morning a gentle drizzle delayed the start, the pitch became damp and Yorkshire were soon in trouble. Len Hutton was lbw to Alec Bedser for six, and only a resolute 48 by Vic Wilson steered the home team past the ignominy of following on. There was gloom among the 8,000 spectators as

Surrey went out to bat a second time, 102 runs ahead and with 80 minutes remaining of the second day.

There was also gloom in the air. The sky had darkened and, according to Jim Kilburn, 'Above the scoreboard the illuminated figure denoting the fieldsman shone like a lighthouse. How narrow must have been the margin between play and no play.'

"Peter May always told me that he never played in light so bad. I remember somebody lighting a cigarette at the other side of the ground, and it was like a beacon. The only time I've ever seen anything to compare with it was in the Test a year or two ago, when Ganguly and Tendulkar stayed out with five lights showing on the scoreboard. The English bowlers were tired, and they milked them. Headingley is more built up now, less open, but the darkness in that game against Surrey was similar."

Bob was off the field, resting his injured leg, and he watched "with some amazement and amusement" as Mike Cowan – "a good bowler, pretty quick" – and Fred Trueman tore into the Surrey batsmen with 'pace bowling of real hostility and venom'. Fletcher, Clark, May and Constable all fell in the half-light, to reduce the visitors to 21 for four. Bedser and Surridge did not survive as night-watchmen, and the final ball before play was called off saw Barrington, coming in at number eight, yorked by Trueman for nought. As they returned to the pavilion, the scoreboard read 27 for seven.

One member suggested that the light was improving and perhaps they might go back out. 'Eh,' Barrington replied in an exaggerated Yorkshire accent, ''T'moon's coomin' oop.'

By lunchtime the next day Yorkshire were 28 for one, needing 150 more in 140 minutes, and the crowds flocked through the turnstiles. It was a working day in Leeds, but somehow 17,500 people managed to find the time to be there. Hutton had gone, bowled by Bedser for one, his tally in the two Surrey matches eight runs in four innings, but 'Lowson and Wilson, first slowly, then with growing mastery, gained the upper hand.'

With the score on 99 both fell, and the scoring rate dropped as Billy Sutcliffe and Willie Watson 'played stolidly for quarter of an hour.' Meanwhile, 'the crowd consulted their watches with agonised intensity, made their calculations with mathematical precision – and changed their opinion every few minutes.'

The Surrey fielders were suspected of slowing down the game, according to the *Yorkshire Post*.

> The fair-haired Tony Lock, Wardle's rival for a place in the Test team and a man of somewhat lethargic movement, was considered to waste a lot of time, and there were repeated cries of 'Gerr-on-wi-it', 'Come on, lightning' and 'Give 'im a bicycle' as he dawdled back to his mark to bowl.

Yet even this was fast work compared with the men who were supposed to be building the pavilion extension. 'Their hammers banged merrily between overs in the morning, but in the afternoon there was not even a token hammering. The stillness and concentration were complete. "'Appen they'll work overtime tonight," someone suggested.'

Aided by the steady Sutcliffe, Watson reached a fifty 'that contained many boundaries of grace, beauty and power', and with ten minutes remaining he pushed the single 'that not only keeps the current championship alive but wins a place among the most memorable of cricketing occasions.'

It was a day of joy for the folk of Leeds, for all Yorkshire, but Jim Kilburn perceptively noticed a harbinger of events about to unfold:

> There was only one thing to tarnish the glory. Len Hutton was clean bowled for one and, as he came rather dejectedly back to the pavilion, a sadness seemed to creep over the crowd, like the mist on an autumn day.

Yorkshire had beaten Surrey and, in the process, they had brought to an end the Southern county's unparalleled sequence of victories. Surrey had stolen the championship from Yorkshire's grasp the previous August, winning their last six matches, and they had started the new summer with nine straight victories. With county games lasting only three days and the weather often unsettled, their record of fifteen successive victories – eighteen, if non-championship matches are included – is one of the most remarkable in cricketing history. However well Yorkshire played in those years, it seemed that they were always chasing Surrey. And, for most of the rest of the summer, they would be chasing them without either Hutton or Appleyard.

While Bob rested his leg, Hutton went to Trent Bridge where, on a perfect batting surface, he made the 129th and last century of his career, racing from 100 to 194 in little more than an hour. 'Len Hutton is himself again,' Eric Stanger celebrated in the *Yorkshire Post*, but the strain of the innings, coupled with the long journey to Bournemouth – by car now, with no trains running – sapped his strength. 'When I woke the next morning,' he wrote, 'I could not move. I was virtually a prisoner in my own bed.' He made scores of nought and two and retired for ever from Yorkshire cricket.

Bob also played at Bournemouth but, 'after eight rather inaccurate overs, he had to leave the field with a recurrence of his leg trouble.' When the team for the second Test was announced, neither he nor Hutton was considered. Then, for the third Test, Tyson and Lock replaced Trueman and Wardle, and for the first time for twenty years an England side took the field without a Yorkshireman.

Bob tried once more in mid-July at Lord's, but here he ran into Compton at his most dashing. "It was the only time I saw him take a thrashing," Fred Trueman says. "Yorkshire had taken a couple of early wickets, and Denis came out. I said, 'Morning.' He replied, 'It will be when I've finished with these spinners.'"

In quick time Compton made 84. 'All he knew or cared,' Jim Kilburn wrote, 'was that a beautiful day made batting an entertaining occupation. The choice of bowler and the bowler's choice of length was a matter of indifference.'

In the second innings Bob managed six wickets, but it marked no revival in his season's fortunes. They travelled next to Taunton where they were kept all day in the field by the bottom-of-the-table Somerset. Bob had not shaken off his bad shoulder, his leg muscle was causing concern, and now the big toe of his right foot was aching. It was a hot day, and Jim Kilburn was quick to observe his difficulties:

> With one exception Yorkshire bowled tight and with unflagging persistence. The exception was Appleyard, who could seldom strike length and often varied remarkably in direction. For the time being, his injuries appear to have upset his rhythm completely.

It was the middle of July, but Bob had completed his last bowling spell of the summer: 18 overs, no wicket for 75. He had conceded his runs at the unaccustomed rate of more than four an over. "And giving runs away," Ray Illingworth says, "was all against Bob's nature."

Eventually a neurologist, Hugh Garland, identified the problem in his shoulder. "He stuck pins all round the affected area and measured the nerve reactions, and from that he deduced that a nerve was trapped in a small orifice in the shoulder blade and it was interfering with the blood supply to an important muscle in my bowling action. And the muscle had become wasted. I had to report for a course of physiotherapy in Leeds. 'We can try to clear it up,' they said, 'but it may never be right again.'"

Bob had overcome tuberculosis, but the trapped nerve in his shoulder would prove a more intransigent problem. For three years he would battle on, determined to overcome adversity as he had always done before. What were those words of Kipling that he read at Sunday morning service on board HMS Ganges?

If you can force your heart and nerve and sinew
To serve your turn long after they are gone,
And so hold on where there is nothing in you
Except the Will which says to them: 'Hold on!'

"I didn't want to make a fuss about my injury. I had so much to be thankful for, and I'd been held up as an example of how to recover from illness. When I was in hospital, I'd said to myself that I would play another five years. I'd become a torch-bearer for fellow-sufferers. I didn't want people thinking that my previous problems had come back. So I was determined to struggle back to form and fitness."

In his first full summer, 1951, he had finished top of the national bowling averages. On return in 1954 he was second to Brian Statham. In Australia he was top of both the Test and tour averages. Now at the end of the summer of 1955 his 85 wickets put him once more at the head of the list. His average of

13.01 was the lowest achieved by a bowler for nine years, and below him lay Lock (14.39), Wardle (16.14) and Laker (17.90).

'No replacement for Appleyard could be found,' Jim Kilburn said in his end-of-season summary in the *Yorkshire Post*, 'and off-spin duties had to be divided between Close and Illingworth, both of whom enjoyed days of success without ever suggesting approach to great bowling.'

The following summer Bob was still struggling with his shoulder. He battled through 26 matches, but he was no longer the same bowler. His 112 wickets cost 17.25 runs each, and his name appeared as low as 16th in the final averages. He was 32 years old now, and above him lay not only Laker, Lock and Wardle but also his Yorkshire team-mate and fellow off-spinner, the 24-year-old Ray Illingworth.

*

In that summer of 1955, when Bob's shoulder injury started, Yorkshire won 21 matches out of 28. Their proportion of matches won, 75%, was exceeded only once in the years between 1924 and 1994. Unfortunately for Yorkshire the team that bettered that record was Surrey in the same summer of 1955. The champions won 23 out of 28 and condemned Yorkshire – for the fourth time in five years, the third in Bob's three-year career – to second place.

To Bob, they were simply beaten by a better team, a team who Len Hutton thought would have beaten the great Yorkshire side of the 1930s, but Ray Illingworth takes a different view. "We should have won the championship in both 1954 and 1955, but there were too many arguments in the side, too many jealousies."

He tells the story of a day at Bramall Lane when he was asked to take over the bowling at Bob's end.

"'Pavilion end, next over, Ray,' Norman Yardley said. I got there, took my sweater off, and there was Applecart. 'What you doing here?' 'Skipper's told me to bowl.' 'Well, bugger off.' And, when I went back to Norman Yardley, he said, 'Oh leave it for an over or two, then.' Norman was a very nice man and a good captain technically, but Bob was an awkward bugger, and he wasn't the only one. Wardle was as bad. They'd argue about ends and all sorts, and then you'd get Fred who'd throw a bit of wood on the fire as well. And Norman wasn't strong enough to handle them."

"I can well believe Ray's story," says Bryan Stott, another youngster who was breaking into the team at this time. "Bob just wanted to bowl. He thought he was going to get somebody out every ball. He really did. And if he felt he was going to get somebody out, he *was* going to get them out. And that was it. I remember myself one instance when Norman Yardley was wanting him off. And Bob was saying, 'Just one more, I know exactly what I can do.'"

"Norman Yardley wasn't too nice," Bob insists. "He had all the knowledge in the world, and he'd talk it all through with Leonard. There were times he wanted to take me off, but sometimes I think he was only threatening it just to gee me up."

We shall never know who is right. All we can be sure of is that Bob always wanted the ball in his hands. "I've never understood," he says, "why the laws prevent you from bowling at both ends."

Bob Platt, another youngster at that time, laughs at the thought of Bob bowling in tandem with himself. "Mind you, he was good enough to do it."

Peter May told a similar story of trying to take off Johnny Wardle in South Africa. The bowler had just been hit for three boundaries in an over, yet he protested. "No, I've worked him out now, skipper. I've seen all his shots. I know how I can get him."

"Unfortunately," Ray Illingworth says, "the man who could have altered things at Yorkshire was Leonard Hutton. I admired him throughout my career, he was my boyhood hero, but he didn't do anything about it. If we hadn't had that sort of attitude, I'm sure we would have won those two championships."

Without doubt they were argumentative among themselves, but was this their Achilles heel or was it part of the way in which they motivated each other? "They were always arguing," the late Maurice Hallam of Leicestershire used to say, "but, when you tried to argue against them, you came up against a brick wall. They were one clan, Yorkshire for Yorkshiremen."

A new generation was starting to appear by 1955 – Illingworth, Doug Padgett, Mike Cowan, Bryan Stott, Ken Taylor – and they were not as comfortable with the hard, hierarchical world of the Yorkshire team as their elders had been. This was a post-war generation, reaching manhood in a world with motor cars and television sets, not air raid sirens and ration books. Rock'n'roll was in the air and, though there was still respect for their elders, it was not uncritical respect.

"Johnny looked after himself," Ken Taylor says of Wardle. "He was a bit of a loner in that way. He would come on to bowl, and he wouldn't try to spin the ball for two or three overs. He'd bowl some maidens, get a good length and line, then when he'd got everything under control he'd start.

"He was always counting his wickets. Down at Hove one year ten and eleven were in, and I was fielding at mid-wicket. They pushed one to me, nice and slow, and set off for a run. I picked the ball up and looked at the running end for Johnny to be there. I just had to throw it gently to him, but he wasn't there. So I had to aim at the wicket, and I missed. 'Christ, Johnny,' I said, 'you should have been behind the wickets.' And he said to me, 'You don't run nine, ten, jack out.' And he got him out next over."

In the same match Bryan Stott at short leg dropped the Reverend David Sheppard and, according to Ken, Wardle in frustration sank down onto his knees in a praying position. "I didn't see that," Bryan says, "but I don't think I'd have been looking in his direction. He certainly got a lot of us on edge in the field."

"Bob could be just as bad," Ray says. "In one of my first matches I dropped a catch off him. I was a bit late picking it up, but I ran a bloody long way for it, from mid-on to wide mid-wicket and I got my hands to it. But Bob gave me a rollocking like I'd never had in my life before.

"I had an out-and-out go at Johnny one day. Youngsters were frightened to death to go for catches. 'Look,' I said, 'when I came into this side, I was a bloody good fielder, and I'm still a good fielder. But buggers like you have destroyed all the confidence in everybody.' After that, he was fine with me. But it was very unpleasant at the time, I can tell you."

"I suppose there was a bit of a generation gap," Bob says, 15 years old at the start of a war that ended when Ray Illingworth was still only 13. "The war affected the lives of so many people. Connie's cousin had been a prisoner-of-war in Japan, and my solicitor Jack Mewies in Skipton was one, too. He came back, and only 28 out of 280 of them survived. Their lives were never quite the same again."

Bob had seen enough tragedy all around him and in his own life to harden the gentlest spirit, and he had worked in the war as an engineer in the dockyards, repairing ships with tough working men from all over Britain. "They were all different ages, from Bristol, London, Tyneside and the Clyde, and they were pretty rough, some of them. There was a lot of mickey-taking, because people had nothing better to do, and some of it was quite harsh. If you didn't stand up for yourself, you could have a miserable time.

"Ray Illingworth was a nice lad, and he was a very good young cricketer. In fact, he's got one of the best cricketing brains alive in the country today, but people like him and Doug Padgett, they weren't coming out of the same world as I'd come from. I'd had to learn to be hard to survive."

What a thin line there is between the compliment – "Bob would bowl on anything and never know when he was beaten. He'd keep coming back at you." – and the criticism – "He was an awkward bugger; he really was. He wanted to bowl all the time."

What a thin line there is between the instilling of discipline – "In the Navy they didn't tell you twice to do things. And if you didn't do them right, you expected a rollocking" – and the undermining of the personality – "Buggers like you have destroyed all the confidence in everybody."

"Some people could dish it out," Bob says, "but they couldn't take it. Johnny Wardle was one." He pauses to reflect. "Perhaps I was too harsh at times. Perhaps I did take the mickey too much. It's just how I'd learnt to be when I was a young man."

Yorkshire had had a great side in the 1930s, a team blessed with exceptional talent but a team moulded in the harshness of pre-war Yorkshire life. They tell how Ellis Robinson once held a spectacular slip catch, diving full stretch, only for Arthur Mitchell alongside him to growl, 'Gerrup. Thar't makin' an exhibition of thissen.' What would Mitchell have made of all the hugging and kissing that now accompanies the fall of a wicket? Len Hutton once asked Mitchell's son, only to get the reply, "He didn't even kiss my mother."

Hutton also told how in his first Roses match he was batting with Mitchell and tried to get off the mark with a square cut. Filled with nerves he missed it, and a voice thundered down from the non-striker's end, "That's nae bluddy good." It was not an environment in which youngsters could expect tender loving care.

The young Hedley Verity took seven wickets for 26 one day early in his career but, leaving the field, he was immediately sat down by his seniors. There was no celebration, only an inquisition into a solitary long hop that had been cracked away for four.

The captain of that side, Brian Sellers, played till the end of the 1947 season, an autocratic figure who continued in the same vein as chairman of the cricket committee till the beginning of the 1970s. Never under his leadership did a fielder sit down when a wicket fell: "Don't let them think you're tired." And it was every man's job to glance in his direction between balls.

"He'd make discreet signals," Willie Watson remembers, "and, if you didn't see them, he'd roar at you. I remember chasing a ball to the boundary once, and I noticed a team-mate running alongside me. He was still there as I picked up the ball. 'Keep your eyes on the skipper, Willie,' he said. 'He's been signalling to you.'"

Norman Yardley was a gentler character, not one to crack a whip like that, and perhaps he did let the aggression of his bowlers cross the line from good-natured rivalry – "There's nothing like a bit of healthy competition in the team," Bob says – to morale-sapping disputation – "Man for man," Ken Taylor says, "they were better players than our side in the '60s, but they didn't have the team spirit we had."

It is hard for Bob to look back on those early years of his career, the years of his greatest achievements, as ones in which he played for unsuccessful teams. At the end of 1955 he had appeared in 94 first-class matches, of which 54 had been won and only seven ended in defeat.

Yorkshire were not a failing team in 1954 or 1955. In both summers they came second to the all-conquering Surrey, and no team could win 21 out of 28 matches without functioning well.

But it was not the same story in the next three summers.

BOWLING FIGURES 1955

			First innings				Second innings			
Apr 30, May 2,3	Lord's	M.C.C.	20.2	6	32	3	20	9	28	3
May 4,5,6	Cambridge	Cambridge Univ	23.4	12	35	1	12	3	36	0
May 7,9	Bradford	Northamptonshire	11.5	4	25	6	13.1	4	23	5
May 11,12	Oxford	Oxford Univ	15	7	30	1	11	2	34	2
May 14,16	Bristol	Gloucestershire	13	3	19	4	31	6	91	6
May 18,19,20	Headingley	Somerset	22.2	13	21	5	16.5	9	26	4
May 21,23,24	Chesterfield	Derbyshire	37	17	51	5	13.4	4	29	5
May 25,26,27	Sheffield	Warwickshire	17	6	35	1	23	7	38	3
May 28,30,31	Old Trafford	Lancashire	26	5	41	3	24	9	38	2
June 1,2,3	Hove	Sussex	22.2	9	45	5	13	7	18	0
June 4,6,7	The Oval	Surrey	18	6	29	7	30	9	66	0
June 9,10,11,13	**Trent Bridge**	**Eng v S Africa**	**28**	**9**	**46**	**2**	**19**	**4**	**32**	**0**
June 18,20,21	Headingley	Surrey	19	7	36	3				
June 29,30	Bournemouth	Hampshire	8	1	35	1				
July 16,18,19	Lord's	Middlesex	14	3	51	2	17.5	2	51	6
July 20,21,22	Taunton	Somerset	18	2	75	0				

Matches	*Overs*	*Maidens*	*Runs*	*Wickets*	*Average*
16	558	185	1106	85	13.01

CHAPTER 12

THE YEARS OF DECLINE

1956–58

"If Leonard had been given the captaincy of Yorkshire," Bob says. "he'd have continued to play. I've always thought that. Other people disagree. But I know how much Yorkshire cricket meant to him."

"Norman Yardley wanted to pack up earlier than he did," Ted Lester says. "'If they'd give it to Len,' he used to say, 'I'd pack up tomorrow.' But they wouldn't."

Hutton was a professional, and that still counted against his appointment though Ted Lester thinks that there was more to it than that. "I remember one of the committee saying one time, 'I wish lumbago came out in spots.' They felt that Len was swinging the lead quite a lot of the time."

In the end Hutton retired at the age of 39 and Norman Yardley, a year older, followed at the end of that same summer of 1955. They had been the last survivors of the great 1930s side, and the county now had to find a leader from the ranks of the post-war players.

"My own choice," Brian Close has written, "would have been Wardle. He was the most knowledgeable cricketer in the side, and he had a strong character too."

This was the poacher-turned-gamekeeper scenario, and Ted Lester is not so certain that it would have worked. "He probably would have made a good captain, but he had so many enemies in the camp, it would have been extremely difficult for him to do it."

Bob agrees with Brian Close. "Johnny would have been a good captain. He read the game very well, but I think I would have appointed Willie Watson. He was a very good captain at Leicestershire after Yorkshire let him go, and he would have done well with the younger players. He would have passed on to Vic Wilson, and the whole of Yorkshire's post-war history would have been different. A proper line of succession could have been established."

Ted Lester disagrees with this. "Willie would have been much too quiet. Sometimes you'd say 'Good morning', and he'd walk straight past you. He was in a world of his own."

"He didn't say a lot," Bob admits, "but he was very astute. People had tremendous respect for him. He was a real professional, he'd played football for England, and he was a fighter, too. That stand with Trevor Bailey against the Australians, that showed his character."

In fact, neither Watson nor Wardle was seriously considered by the committee. They wanted an amateur and, with Norman Yardley retiring, they appointed the only one remaining in the first eleven: Billy Sutcliffe, son of the great Herbert.

"Billy was a nice lad," Bob says, "but he wasn't what a Yorkshire captain should have been. They were clinging to the idea of the amateur captain, which was totally wrong. It was time for a change. After all, England had had a professional by then – and a very successful one, too. To win in Australia is the height of any England captain's ambition.

"To me, the most sensible thing would have been for the committee to get together two or three senior players and say, 'What do you think of playing under Billy?' But that was the last thing they'd have done at the time, especially somebody like Brian Sellers who was such a powerful chap. So they appointed Billy, and it wasn't the best decision."

Here was the irony. Billy Sutcliffe's father had been a model professional. Immaculately dressed and taking elocution lessons, he acquired the bearing of a gentleman. "He was a cut above the other professionals. He had something special about him, and he had this charisma as well. He did for the professional cricketer what Henry Cotton did for the professional golfer." In fact, so respected was Herbert Sutcliffe as a man and as a cricketer that in the autumn of 1927 he was offered the Yorkshire captaincy, an offer which ensuing controversy forced him to decline. But his aspirations, thwarted by the social conventions of the 1920s, were then transferred to his baby boy.

"Horace Kippax told me," Bob says, "that, when Billy was born, his father said, 'There's a future Yorkshire captain.'"

The young William Herbert Hobbs Sutcliffe was sent to public school at Rydal. He was brought up to be a cricketer, and he progressed easily from school to club to Yorkshire Colts cricket. His father installed him as manager of their sports retail business in Leeds, and this meant that Billy could play his cricket as an amateur.

But he was not a batsman in the class of his father. "He was a good batsman," Bob says, "and he played some good knocks. His father had taught him how to play the forward defensive stroke and, if he was told to go in and defend, he could defend. But if he was told to go in and get quick runs, he could do that as well because he was a natural hitter. But he only seemed able to do one or the other. Unlike his father or Leonard, he was rarely able to build an innings and then take advantage of his natural ability."

Bob pulls out the Yorkshire yearbooks to inspect Sutcliffe's season-by-season batting averages: 31, 35, then 19 and 20 in his two years as captain. "By which time the crowds were on his back constantly. 'Tha'll niver be as good as thi father.'"

He was not an astute reader of a game, either. "He seemed to work on hunches. We played Surrey at Park Avenue. We didn't start till halfway through the second afternoon. Billy had won the toss the previous day, and he said to Johnny and me, 'What do you think?' Well, we went and looked at the pitch. It was so wet you couldn't run up to bowl; you had to bat. 'What a stupid question!' we thought. But, by the time we'd gone back, he'd decided to send them in. We were struggling to get to the wicket. Then, when we got to bat, the sun had come out, and Laker and Lock were turning the ball square. We almost lost by an innings. We had no faith in him at all."

And, alas, in the eyes of those who felt the team needed pulling together, he did not have the bearing necessary to impose discipline. "He hadn't a chance at all, what with his father," Ted Lester says. "He was one of the lads, was Billy. There was no way he could instil the discipline." Or, as Brian Close has written, "He was happier having a pint and a natter when the day's work was over than he was cracking the whip on the field. We had some outstanding bowlers with minds of their own, and he could not stand up to them."

"He wasn't considered a success," Bob sums up and, after two summers in which Yorkshire had finished seventh and third, his father Herbert instructed him to resign.

*

The month of May was normally a good one for Bob, with the pitches often damp, but in May 1956 he struggled for wickets. He had some success at Bradford against the Australians, but he was doing more service as a seamer than he had done in the previous two summers and, as Peter West wrote, 'it was rumoured in Yorkshire that he was not turning the ball as much.'

'He was not in peak physical condition,' Alan Ross suggested. 'He was not bowling at his best, and he puffed and blew from ball to ball.'

Nevertheless, he was a regular once more in the Yorkshire side and such was his reputation that he was in the England team for the first Test at Trent Bridge, pitting his wits against the Australians.

England at Trent Bridge 1956: Standing (left to right): Jim Parks (12th man), Peter Richardson, Colin Cowdrey, Alan Moss, Bob Appleyard, Tom Graveney, Tony Lock Sitting: Willie Watson, Trevor Bailey, Peter May, Jim Laker, Godfrey Evans

The other bowlers in the side were two seamers, Trevor Bailey and Middlesex's Alan Moss, and two spinners, Laker and Lock, but the balance was altered on the third day when Moss tore a stomach muscle while fielding.

Rain ruined the game, but at lunchtime on the final day Peter May tried to bring it to life by declaring the England second innings. That left Australia 258 to win in four hours. The pitch was damp and, in the absence of Alan Moss, it fell to Bob to share the new ball with Trevor Bailey.

"I tried a spinner after a while, and I found some response. Had it been a county match, with Norman Yardley in charge, I'd have turned to spin immediately and reset the field. But, when I mentioned it to Peter May, he took me off and gave the ball to Jim Laker."

Laker had already taken all ten Australian wickets for Surrey at The Oval so May, his county colleague, knew his potency against the frail Australian batting. Here at Trent Bridge Laker had McDonald caught in the leg trap with the total only 13, Tony Lock forced Harvey to play on at 18, then Miller was lbw to Laker to make it 41 for three. Davidson had sustained a chipped ankle bone and was unlikely to bat so, with more than two hours remaining, there were brief hopes of a remarkable English victory.

It was not to be. Jim Burke played resolutely, the well-prepared Trent Bridge pitch soon lost its dampness, and Bob was unable to match the earlier breakthroughs of his Surrey counterparts.

"It was one of those pitches where the moisture dries out under the sun, and the spinner only has an hour or two to get maximum advantage. And by the time I came back, it wasn't so responsive."

'May's final gesture was the taking of the new ball at six o'clock,' Rex Alston wrote, 'and Bailey and Appleyard bowled Australia into the draw with ten innocuous but steady overs.'

"I could see Peter's point of view," Bob says now. "Jim was the leading off-spinner, but of course the episode did have a significant impact on my career."

So the summer that might have belonged to Appleyard and Wardle, even Appleyard and Lock, belonged instead to Laker and Lock. At Old Trafford in late July Jim Laker wrote himself into cricketing immortality by taking first nine, then ten wickets in the two Australian innings.

"I've often wondered how successful I'd have been if I'd played in that Test. Who knows? I certainly don't think Jim would have taken 19 wickets if he'd had Johnny Wardle, rather than Tony Lock, as his partner."

What was it Sydney Barnes once said? "No bugger ever got all ten when I was bowling at the other end."

In the event Johnny Wardle regained the slow left-armer's position from Tony Lock in South Africa that winter, but Bob never played another Test.

"I played in three Test matches in England, and they were all at Trent Bridge. And that was the best batting pitch in the country at that time."

In nine Tests for England he had taken 31 wickets at an average of 17.87. They were not sensational figures, but then he was not a sensational bowler –

unlike Tyson and Statham in Australia. Yet, if you look up the records, you will find no English Test bowler since the First World War with 30 wickets at a lower average. In fact, only one overseas bowler has a better average: Mike Procter, whose South African side was banned from Test cricket after he had played only seven Tests.

"More importantly," Bob says, "I played in nine Test matches, and I was never on the losing side."

Of his nine games, seven were won, and the other two – at Sydney and here at Trent Bridge – were rain-affected draws where England had the upper hand.

From the disappointment of that Tuesday afternoon at Trent Bridge he returned to Bramall Lane, and on Thursday he finally achieved the first and only hat-trick of his career.

Twice in the Test in Auckland he had bowled to Moir in the hope of one; twice in his career he had gone to bed with the prospect of completing one with the first ball of the next morning. "I must have had two in two at least eight times." But never had he managed the third, never until he bowled that afternoon at the Gloucestershire tail.

'At that time,' Jim Laker wrote years later, 'it was rare in county sides to find anyone after number eight having any great pretensions as a batsman; in fact, they were little more than rabbits. Gloucester, for example, could guarantee half a dozen cheap wickets in a match by courtesy of McHugh, Cook and Wells.'

And so it was at Bramall Lane:

> Cook pushed back the gentlest of catches, Wells missed a yorker, and McHugh played no stroke to be leg before.

"Wells, Cook, McHugh," Fred laughed. "That must be the easiest hat-trick there's ever been."

"You've still got to bowl the balls," Bob insists, determined to cherish his achievement.

From there they moved down to The Oval, and again he showed his liking for Jim Laker's home turf. Last year, seven for 29. This year, six for 31. But again the last word was with the relentless Surrey bowlers: chasing 124 to revive their lacklustre summer, Yorkshire reached 60 for one, only for 'reckless and foolish mistakes' to reduce them to 100 for seven with 25 minutes left.

Then came the painful finale:

> Padgett edged a slip catch for which May dived triumphantly to the right. Ten minutes were spent with the scoreboard still motionless on 100, and the total was still 100 when Laker's off-break jumped from Binks's bat into the leg trap where Lock seized it with the speed of a lizard's tongue. Still at 100 Appleyard mishit to cover, and the match was complete. Yorkshire were hanging their heads.

Bob was still an effective bowler, but his health and fitness were taking their toll. Influenza kept him out of the next match at Bristol. Then at Kidderminster he bowled all day at Don Kenyon with an infected big toe. "Before the match I went to a local hospital. There was all this pus under the nail so they gave me an injection, then they got out one of those hand drills and drilled a hole through the middle of the nail. It was agony once the injection had worn off."

Worcestershire, continuing to bat on the second day, made 440 for six. Kenyon's 259 the highest innings played against Yorkshire in the twentieth century. "I bowled 34 overs in that innings, and I certainly didn't take my boots off at lunchtime."

Bob was absent at Bramall Lane the next week when Surrey completed the double over their great rivals, for the first time since 1921. On a pitch that *Wisden* described as 'not too difficult', Yorkshire needed 97 for victory, and they slumped from 40 for two to 82 all out.

Was it the loss of Hutton and Yardley, the ineffectiveness of Sutcliffe's captaincy, the decline of Appleyard, or just the toll of too many years of being outpointed by Surrey? Somehow the county was losing its self-belief.

For Bob, the struggle was more private. He could overcome the influenza and the swollen toe, but the shoulder injury from the previous summer had not gone away and it was affecting his action.

"I'd bring my two arms up together as I went into the delivery stride but, when I brought down my bowling arm in the final swing, my wrist was catching my thigh. I was black and blue, the wrist and the thigh. I took to wearing a thigh pad to bowl. And I was finding it more and more difficult to retain any accuracy, however much I tried to alter my action. My rhythm was thrown out, and I was always trying to recorrect myself as my arm was coming up. I never really got back."

In all the circumstances, 112 wickets in 870 overs represented a triumph of spirit, but Yorkshire were down to seventh place in the table. The season's summary in *Wisden* cried out for 'a return to the old fighting spirit and determination of the Sellers era.'

*

The best of Bob's year came on its last day, December the 31st, when Connie gave birth to their third child – and this time it was a boy.

Who knows? Maybe young Ian would one day follow his father into the Yorkshire team.

"When I was in the Royal Navy I was stationed for a few weeks in a transit camp in Corsham. We had dances at the camp, and girls from the Admiralty in Bath used to come across. I became very friendly with one of them – one of my first girl friends, I suppose – and I used to hitch into Bath to see her. We went to dances in the Pump Rooms. It was a romantic time in my life.

"We kept in touch for a while after I moved, and she sent me a poem. I used to know it by heart, but I can only remember some of the lines now."

All these I wish my son.
The tan of health upon his face,
Smooth glades and tranquil paths to pace.
A zest for life and honest fun.
I hope he will grow straight and trim
With strength of limb
And hands that deftly catch and throw.

"Those were the important lines. 'With strength of limb, And hands that deftly catch and throw.' It was a romantic notion of a son, but I used to think of the words a lot after Ian was born. I suppose it's how every father feels."

*

The summer of 1957, Billy Sutcliffe's second in charge, brought some improvement, with a rise to third place, but Bob's decline continued, exacerbated by a major change in the playing regulations for county cricket.

A special committee of the MCC, under the chairmanship of Harry Altham, the influential Winchester schoolmaster, met five times between October and February, charged with reviewing the present conduct of the game. There were concerns that gates at county matches were in decline and that that was in part due to a decline in the tempo at which the game was being played.

Their first discussion centred around the lbw law that had been in operation since 1935. Before its introduction a batsman could not be adjudged lbw if the ball pitched outside the off stump and, although this gave the batsman greater freedom to play the cover drive, it also led to some like Herbert Sutcliffe endlessly padding away balls that turned in from the off. "I remember going to Park Avenue to see Herbert," Bob says, "and he'd go across with his bat in the air. He wasn't playing a shot. Anybody bowling wide, it would go on and on. It was a real stalemate."

The change, however, had created a great increase in off-spin and in-slant bowling, with packed leg-side fields, and this concentration on leg stump was thought to be harmful to the game's aesthetic spectacle. "The amateurs were always the ones with influence, and the off-side cover drive was an elegant shot but it wasn't natural like the agricultural shots. It was an amateur-taught shot, played on good pitches at public schools and universities."

The Wisden almanack of 1956 conducted a survey of great cricketers, and among those who argued that the revision in the lbw law had been bad for the game were Jack Hobbs, Bob Wyatt, Maurice Leyland, Learie Constantine and Herbert Sutcliffe himself.

The committee chose not to revert to the old law. Rather, they enforced a limit of five fielders on the leg side, with no more than two behind the popping crease. Gone immediately were the days when bowlers like Bob could pitch the ball on off or middle stump, turn it towards leg, get awkward bounce and have fielders gathered in close proximity for the edge. Gone, too, were the days when bowlers like Bob could bowl with just two men on the off. "There was even one occasion against Essex when I was bowling against Doug Insole and Trevor Bailey and, to take the mickey, I just had one man on the off."

"You just couldn't hit him through the off side," Trevor says. "He was so accurate, and it was always coming in to you."

"The change in law was momentous," Bob reflects. "Much of my success depended on the close-in fielders, and I couldn't bowl on the middle stump any more."

Ray Illingworth, an off-spinner who played most of his cricket under the new regulation, is quick to point out the advantage that Bob had. "I've always said to Bob that he wouldn't have been the same bowler if he'd had his career later on. He says, 'Well, I'd have bowled more at the off stump.' But, if he had, he wouldn't have been quite the same bowler – because he tucked people up, bowling into their ribs, many times with four short legs. Under the rules as they were, Bob was probably the best wet wicket bowler in the country, but he wouldn't have been after they changed the rules. And then, of course, they started covering the wickets."

Bob is adamant that he could have overcome these fresh obstacles to his success. "If I'd have been fit, I'd have bowled more leg-cutters, worked more on changes of pace. You can only bowl in the conditions you're given, and I showed in Australia that I could adapt my bowling."

The change in regulations led to a steady decline in the off-spinner's role in English cricket. Now, instead of committees worrying about his dominance, we fear his complete demise. "For my money," Ray says, "he's been the most penalised bowler in the game. He still is. I feel sorry for the present-day off-spinners, the rules they have to put up with. In one-day cricket they can pitch a ball on middle stump, it turns a bit, and it's a wide."

The summer of 1957 brought a further handicap to Bob's performance. During the winter Geoffrey Wooler had written to the committee, recommending that Bob would benefit from another pre-season break in Switzerland. This time they did not take up the idea. "They took it that I needed feather bedding. They told Billy Sutcliffe to bowl me in shorter spells. It was the worst thing that could have happened to me. I was bowling three or four overs, then getting taken off, and that was totally against my style. I had to work batsmen out, and you can't work anything out in that time."

The wickets came less and less frequently for Bob. In several matches he was asked to bowl with the new ball, leaving the main responsibility for spin to Wardle and Illingworth, and the decline in his bowling figures was obvious.

Fifteen times in 1954 he had left the field with five wickets in an innings. He did it nine times in his half-summer of 1955. By 1956 it was down to seven and in 1957 – despite playing in 22 matches – it was only three.

In little more than two years he had slipped from being an automatic choice in the England team, part of what the *Yorkshire Post* described as a renaissance in English cricket's fortunes, to one who was struggling to hold his place in the Yorkshire first team.

Several times that summer he was dropped down to the Colts, but each time he fought his way back. He was still good enough to top the Minor Counties bowling for the whole country – with an average of 7.74.

He was determined that he would overcome every adversity.

*

But the summer of 1958 brought his struggles to an end. It was a momentous year for Yorkshire – with the appointment of a captain who had never played first-class cricket and the midsummer sacking of Johnny Wardle – and perhaps Bob's own demise was overshadowed.

Not only did Yorkshire lose their captain Billy Sutcliffe at the end of 1957, they also lost their senior professional and most experienced batsman, Willie Watson. In mid-July he had been sitting in the pavilion at Hull, chatting after close of play with the Leicestershire captain Charles Palmer, and Palmer enquired whether he knew of anybody on the circuit who might be interested in taking over the Leicestershire captaincy. A five-year contract was on offer and Watson, now 37 and knowing that Yorkshire could dispense with his services any time they liked, was quick to reply, 'Yes, I might be interested.'

Away from the intensity of his home county's frustrated expectations, the quiet Yorkshireman enjoyed a glorious finale to his playing days. He was second in the national batting averages in his first two summers there, and he found himself recalled to the England team. He still looks back on his Leicester years as "probably the best of my career".

"We enjoyed the time he was here," Leicestershire's Terry Spencer says. "He was a very fine player. But he wasn't a demonstrative captain. I'm not sure how he'd have managed at Yorkshire. Everybody seemed to want to be captain in their side."

The new Yorkshire captain in 1958 was again an amateur, the 39-year-old Ronnie Burnet, a chemical engineer who had been bringing on the next generation as captain of the second team. Bob knew him of old from his days as captain of Baildon Cricket Club; they had clashed at the Bradford League meeting on illegal payments when Bob, fresh from his triumph of 200 wickets, had accused the meeting's organisers of hypocrisy. He was no more enamoured with the appointment of Burnet than he had been with that of Billy Sutcliffe before him.

"It was such a culture shock, having played under Len Hutton and Norman Yardley, to play under Ronnie Burnet with his lack of experience. He'd never played a first-class match, and there was such a wide gap. He simply wasn't a good enough player to command respect from the senior professionals. If only we'd have appointed a professional captain after Norman Yardley! The county wasted three years."

In the event Bob hardly took the field under Burnet's captaincy. During April he entered a Bradford hospital to have a stone removed from his bladder – "It probably formed during the months I spent lying in bed" – so he missed the final pre-season practice match when Burnet was struck a painful blow on the ankle by a Trueman yorker and departed to hospital. Then, when Bob rejoined the team at Fenner's, Burnet pulled a calf muscle almost as soon as they took the field, and Johnny Wardle took over the captaincy till early June.

Yorkshire at Lord's, 1958 – Bob's penultimate championship match
As well as his troublesome shoulder, Bob was having to cope with the softness of the ground where his feet were landing. Here he is carrying away handfuls of loose turf. "They didn't fill the holes like they do now. There was many a time you had to alter your delivery stride to avoid them."

The only championship game in which Bob played under the captaincy of Ronnie Burnet was at Bradford Park Avenue against Northamptonshire. Rain washed out the first and last days and, between showers on the second, Burnet asked the visitors to bat. It was the wrong decision in the opinion of the *Yorkshire Post*, but in his defence they thought that 'he could not have anticipated that his bowlers would bowl so badly.' Bob dismissed Dennis Brookes, 'slashing well outside his off-stump', but otherwise he and his fellow bowlers 'sent down more long hops and full tosses than they can reasonably be expected to do in an average week's cricket.'

Even on a helpful pitch at his beloved Park Avenue Bob could only manage figures of 14 overs, one wicket for 44 runs. When Fred Trueman returned from the Test, it was Bob and not the young David Pickles whose place he took. Bob had taken the field as a Yorkshire player for the last time.

In the second eleven, under the captaincy of Ted Lester, he struggled on till the end of July. Frank Lowson, his team-mate right back to Bowling Old Lane days, was also in difficulty, and he too dropped out of the first eleven. There were younger players emerging – Phil Sharpe, Bob Platt, Brian Bolus, Don Wilson, Mel Ryan. Burnet had captained them all in the second eleven, and now he was wanting to bring them through into the county side.

'YORKSHIRE TO RELEASE TWO TEST PLAYERS,' ran the *Yorkshire Post* story on Saturday the 19th of July, and it told how both Lowson and Appleyard were not to be retained beyond that summer. 'The county,' Jim Kilburn suggested, 'are thus giving themselves necessary elbow room for reconstruction of a side that has never realised highest hopes since 1946.'

Frank Lowson had opened the batting for Yorkshire since the start of 1949, playing seven times for England, and for much of Bob's career they were room-mates and travelling companions.

"We spent many a car journey, many an evening talking cricket, assessing the strengths and weaknesses of all our opponents. He was a fine batsman in the classical style, one of the best against spinners on a turning pitch, and he was brilliant in the leg trap. So much of my success as a bowler I owed to the close catching – and he, Vic and Fred were all exceptional."

"Frank was a superb batsman," Bryan Stott recalls. "Really beautiful. Balanced and flowing. Michael Vaughan plays with a similar stamp. In fact, when I first saw Michael, I thought, 'Gosh, that's Frank Lowson standing at the wicket.' Frank wasn't very strong, but he was a lovely batsman to watch. But, of course, he went in with Leonard, and there were times when the going was easy when Frank didn't see much of the bowling. And there were times when he saw too much of it."

According to Fred Trueman, Lowson complained once to the coach Arthur Mitchell that he always had 'to take the dirty end' when he was batting with Hutton. "Look, lad," Mitchell replied. "Before the War, Leonard had to do that for Herbert, and now you've got to do it for 'im."

Alas, with times changing and Lowson making way for the dynamic pair of Stott and Taylor, there would be nobody to 'do it for 'im' now that Leonard had gone. "It gave him a slight chip on his shoulder," Bryan Stott says, "so he wasn't the easiest for us youngsters to play with."

Jim Kilburn's valediction to the two departing players began with this tribute to Bob:

> Appleyard's first-class career has extended into the romantic. His first full season (1951) brought him the astonishing achievement of 200 wickets and was followed by a collapse in health that threatened any reappearance in county cricket. He did return, he recaptured his bowling skill, indeed he extended it. By 1954 he was touring Australia, an important member of a successful side. Since then his fortune in illness and injury has been poor, but his endeavour has been plain and praiseworthy.

"He was really struggling," Bryan Stott remembers. "He was wearing all these elastic supports and this great thigh pad to protect his leg from being hit by his hand in his bowling action. He very rarely changed in front of us. Once I remember seeing him, and he had this huge scar from where he'd had his operation. It was a great cut round his back and up to his front. And he was black and blue from hitting himself."

"We weren't aware of all his problems," Ken Taylor reflects. "He kept himself to himself. He never changed with us. He'd get in his car and drive home still in his cricket clothes."

"He was always a loner," Ted Lester says. "I never really got to know him. My interests weren't his interests. We'd follow racing and have a card school, but he never seemed to nip in at all."

"They used to play contract bridge," Bob remembers. "Wardle, Illingworth, Vic Wilson and Ted Lester. Sometimes Norman Yardley. I'd be standing at the window, putting my palm out to see if the rain had stopped, and they'd be playing their cards. And, if they had a good hand, they wouldn't want to put it down and get back out."

If you can force your heart and nerve and sinew

"He couldn't control the ball," Don Wilson says. "He was hitting his leg hard, and he lost his line and length. He was going through a terrible time and, of course, he got frustrated, blaming everybody for misfields."

"I wasn't blaming them for misfields," Bob retorts. "I was blaming them for fooling around. I remember the game. They weren't taking it seriously, and I felt it was my job as senior professional to say something. I mean, you don't beat Australia by fooling around, do you?"

"To me, as a very young player," Don goes on, "Bob Appleyard was a great, great man. I'd worshipped the ground he'd walked on. And here he was, playing in the second eleven, lost his action, lost everything. I couldn't believe it."

"It was very sad," Ted Lester remembers. "He'd been one of the most accurate bowlers of all time, and now he couldn't bowl line and length. He was straying down the leg side, and I wanted the short legs a bit closer. But they were in danger of their lives."

"I didn't say anything about my injuries," Bob admits. "I struggled on for a few years. I tried everything, but eventually I had to quit."

To serve your turn long after they are gone,

"In the second team," Ted continues, "your job as captain was to bring on youngsters. That was what Brian Sellers always insisted on. 'You're not there to win matches; you're there to bring the youngsters on for the first team.' It's difficult when you get the older players come down, and Bob, of course, was wanting to bowl all the time. All he wanted was to get back in the first team. He was a different kettle of fish from Frank Lowson. Frank let it be known that he didn't want to play in the second eleven.

"Apparently Bob went to see Ronnie Burnet," Ted continues. "'I ought to be back with you,' he said. 'I'm bowling well.' Then Brian Sellers came to see me. 'He says he's bowling well.' 'You can come and see for yourself,' I said. 'He can't bowl straight.' It was sad, really."

And so hold on where there is nothing in you

"He probably should have retired a bit earlier," Don Wilson suggests. "All good things come to an end – but you don't, do you? You think you're going to get back."

Late in Don Wilson's own career he suffered an attack of 'the yips', suddenly unable to pitch the ball and with no video camera to identify his technical fault. He had a reputation as a cheerful man but, he says, "I went to pieces completely. I wasn't a very nice person to be around, I can tell you straight." He makes the comparison with the great Bob Appleyard, struggling in the second eleven. "Bob terrified me. I remember thinking, 'Oh this fella, I can't be doing with him.' But now I can understand why."

"To be an all-time great like he was," Fred says, "and to finish up like that, it wasn't nice."

Except the Will which says to them: 'Hold on!'

The letter from John Nash, the Secretary, was dated 17 July 1958.

> Dear Appleyard
> I am asked by the Committee to inform you it has been decided that your services will not be required by the County Club after the present season. Your salary will, of course, be paid until 31st December 1958.
> I am also asked to convey to you the Committee's thanks for your loyal services during the past seven years and to wish you good health and every success in the future.
> Yours sincerely
> J.H. Nash
> Secretary

"You'd think after all those years," he says, "they could have written 'Dear Bob'. I was a bit upset. The fact that it had come like that. But on reflection it was time to go. I was struggling, really struggling. I'd tried everything. I'd even shortened my run. And they had a decent side of youngsters. I was ready to go, really."

The loss of Frank Lowson and Bob was overshadowed a week later by the sacking of Johnny Wardle. The senior professional had crossed with Burnet once too often, and the new captain – eager to instil discipline and to promote a young side – persuaded the committee to part company with their foremost slow bowler. Wardle had already been selected to tour Australia that winter but, as Brian Sellers told the gathered pressmen, 'He may be good enough for England but not for Yorkshire.'

Within days Wardle had gone into print in the *Daily Mail*, and the resulting furore cost him his place on the boat to Australia. "Peter May was distraught," Bob says. "Johnny was his best bowler in South Africa. Years later Peter told me how upset he'd been at losing him."

History has passed its verdict on these events. The young Yorkshire team, who finished the summer of 1958 in eleventh place, were county champions the following year. In fact, they were champions in seven of the ten following years, and Burnet is given the credit for masterminding the transition from ageing under-achievement to youthful fulfilment, from dissent and indiscipline to a new era of team spirit.

Bob does not share this analysis. "Sacking Johnny was the daftest decision ever made. He was at his best when he left Yorkshire. He'd perfected his chinaman and googly in addition to his orthodox slow left-arm spin. If Yorkshire had had an experienced captain, they could have had years more from him. Don Wilson was a good bowler, but he didn't quite have Johnny's competitive edge. The real reason Yorkshire started winning the championship was that Surrey were on the way down."

The summer of 1959 was the driest of the decade, and on the hard surfaces the Surrey bowlers often lacked their legendary bite. Bedser had turned forty, Laker was losing his appetite and Lock had had to remodel his suspect action. In addition, their captain Peter May missed most of the summer through ill-health. His seven appearances for Surrey that summer brought six victories, two of them against Yorkshire, but in his absence they won only six of the other 21 matches. For the first time for several years, an opportunity was there for a different county to fly the championship pennant.

"How many matches did Yorkshire win in 1959?"Bob asks.

The answer is 14 out of 28.

"We won 21 in 1955. But Surrey were at their peak at that time. I don't want to decry the achievement of the Yorkshire team in 1959 but, if Surrey had still been as strong then as they had been previously, Ronnie's side wouldn't have got a sniff of the championship."

But Surrey were not the same force by 1959, and it was Bob's lot to be one of the men whose leaving created 'the necessary elbow room' to bring in the young players who would restore the county of Yorkshire to its former glory.

"The person who doesn't get the credit he deserves," Bob says, "is Vic Wilson. He was senior professional under Ronnie Burnet. Then, when he became captain, they won the championship twice – and they were runners-up in his other year. Those years with Billy Sutcliffe and Ronnie Burnet, when the county perpetuated the amateur tradition, they were wasted years. We could have done much better, and there wouldn't have been all the trouble."

We shall never know who is right. Would Yorkshire have won those championships anyway, even with Wardle still in their ranks? Or did they need the catharsis of his dismissal?

*

Bob played his last day as a Yorkshire cricketer, on Thursday the 31st of July 1958, for the second eleven against Durham at the Feethams ground, Darlington. He bowled 15 overs and took one wicket for 36 as the home team finished on 180 for three in their second innings. 'Durham,' the *Yorkshire Post* reported, 'thanks to the bright 95 by Camburn, had no difficulty in defying the bowling of Cowan, Platt, Wilson and Appleyard.'

Bob's cricketing days were over. He was 34 years old and, though he told the *Yorkshire Post* that he was 'very disappointed' to be released, he knew in his heart that he was not overcoming his latest physical problems. A younger generation was emerging to bring fresh success to Yorkshire cricket, and he would have to concentrate on building a career in a different world.

"I had numerous offers to play club cricket from all over the country, and several counties made enquiries."

He still has the letters, from clubs as far afield as Ayr and South Shields, as well as several from dismayed supporters. Mrs Monica Pratley of Leeds tried to rally his spirits by suggesting revenge:

> Never mind, Bob, if you still fancy first-class cricket, I'm sure other counties will soon be knocking on your door if they haven't done so already. And if you decide to play for one of them, we look forward to you playing Yorks and giving them what for.

So did he consider reviving his career in the quieter pastures of Leicester or Taunton? He stiffens visibly at the thought, then speaks with an emphatic deliberateness. "I could never have played for anyone other than Yorkshire."

For Jim Kilburn, Bob Appleyard's place in the pantheon of cricket's greats was established – for his unique first summer, if for nothing else:

> Misfortune deprived him of a long career, but the history books will always carry and Yorkshire will always remember with gratitude the story of that great season in which he came and conquered.

"My first season back after tuberculosis was the greater achievement," Bob says now. "That's my greatest pride. I gave so much hope to fellow sufferers."

BOWLING FIGURES 1956

			First innings				Second innings			
Apr 28,30 May 1	Lord's	M.C.C.	24	8	38	2	20	5	66	1
May 2,3,4	Cambridge	Cambridge Univ	13	5	28	1	13	4	20	1
May 9,10,11	Bradford	Australians	18	4	44	4				
May 12,14,15	Northampton	Northamptonshire	20	7	45	3	15	6	18	0
May 16,17	Hull	Scotland	19	9	24	3	8	4	7	0
May 19,21,22	Headingley	Lancashire	34	14	45	2	27	7	78	4
May 23,24,25	Edgbaston	Warwickshire	24.3	12	37	3	26	12	38	0
May 26,28,29	Sheffield	Middlesex	17	3	59	1	15	2	40	0
June 2,4,5	Chesterfield	Derbyshire	14.1	3	37	6	35	15	69	6
June 7,8,9,11,12	**Trent Bridge**	**Eng v Australia**	**11**	**4**	**17**	**2**	**19**	**6**	**32**	**0**
June 13,14,15	Sheffield	Gloucestershire	28.4	5	78	5	19	8	24	4
June 16,18,19	The Oval	Surrey	19	7	28	3	15.3	3	31	6
June 23,25,26	Headingley	Derbyshire	39	9	105	3				
June 27,28,29	Sheffield	Australians	34.1	8	81	3				
June 30, July 2	Bradford	Warwickshire	16.5	5	48	7	17	3	50	1
July 4,5,6	Hull	Hampshire	25	5	69	5	21	8	40	2
July 7,9,10	Trent Bridge	Nottinghamshire	19.5	8	24	4	21	7	49	5
July 11,12,13	Kidderminster	Worcestershire	34	9	79	2				
July 18,19,20	Swansea	Glamorgan	26	3	76	3	12	3	35	3
Aug 8,9,10	Leicester	Leicestershire	15	6	36	2	23	5	43	2
Aug 11,13,14	Bradford	Worcestershire	8	2	27	0	6	3	9	0
Aug 15,16,17	Scarborough	Leicestershire	19	3	57	3				
Aug 18,20,21	Headingley	Nottinghamshire	17	6	35	3	7	2	35	0
Aug 22,23,24	Southend	Essex	15	5	27	1	15	2	49	2
Aug 25,27,28	Dover	Kent	15	4	26	3				
Aug 29,30,31	Scarborough	M.C.C.	1	1	0	0	9	0	29	1

Matches	*Overs*	*Maidens*	*Runs*	*Wickets*	*Average*
26	870.4	260	1932	112	17.25

BOWLING FIGURES 1957

			First innings				*Second innings*			
May 15,16	Oxford	Oxford Univ	13	6	26	3	22	8	45	0
May 18,20	Headingley	Somerset	8	4	27	0	8	4	8	1
May 29,30,31	Paisley	Scotland	27	8	48	4	16	5	43	1
June 1,3,4	Sheffield	Glamorgan	40	15	87	4	13.3	1	62	1
June 15,17,18	Lord's	Middlesex	17	3	39	3	25	7	60	6
June 19,20,21	Harrogate	Northamptonshire	50	14	98	4				
June 22,24,25	Headingley	Middlesex	39	4	96	1				
June 26,27	Tunbridge Wells	Kent	12	5	23	3	7	1	23	0
June 29 July 1,2	The Oval	Surrey	18	0	85	1				
July 6,8,9	Sheffield	Essex	12	4	36	0	17	5	45	0
July 10,11,12	Hull	Leicestershire	22	10	35	6	5	3	5	0
July 13,15,16	Bradford	Surrey	11.4	1	27	1				
July 17,18,19	Scarborough	Gloucestershire	14	3	30	0				
July 27,29,30	Worcester	Worcestershire	23	5	63	3	3	0	18	0
July 31 Aug 1,2	Hove	Sussex	13	3	39	1	14	4	35	3
Aug 3,5,6	Sheffield	Lancashire	22	5	50	1				
Aug 7,8,9	Scarborough	Worcestershire	20	3	65	3				
Aug 10,12,13	Headingley	Kent	14	4	36	1				
Aug 21,22,23	Edgbaston	Warwickshire	23	4	67	4	6	2	10	0
Aug 24,26,27	Taunton	Somerset	8	1	21	0	11.4	1	28	4
Aug 28,29	Cardiff	Glamorgan	12	5	18	5	18	1	66	4
Aug 31 Sept 2,3	Scarborough	M.C.C.	22	3	64	3	7	0	40	3

Matches	*Overs*	*Maidens*	*Runs*	*Wickets*	*Average*
22	613.5	152	1568	74	21.18

BOWLING FIGURES 1958

			First innings				*Second innings*			
May 3,5,6	Cambridge	Cambridge Univ	16	6	23	5	5	2	5	1
May 7,8	Oxford	Oxford Univ	7	4	15	0	9	0	26	2
May 10,12,13	Bradford	Hampshire	15	2	31	2				
May 14,15,16	Harrogate	Warwickshire	2	0	4	0				
May 17,19,20	Lord's	MCC v New Z.	23.1	11	36	4	13	2	40	1
May 21,22,23	Bath	Somerset	24	5	77	1	7.2	4	15	4
May 24,26,27	Headingley	Lancashire	19	7	34	0	3	1	10	0
May 31 June 1,2	Lord's	Middlesex	9	2	42	2				
June 4,5	Middlesbrough	Scotland	17	6	37	4	4	1	9	0
June 7,9,10	Bradford	Northamptonshire	14	3	44	1				

Matches	*Overs*	*Maidens*	*Runs*	*Wickets*	*Average*
10	187.3	56	448	27	16.59

CHAPTER 13

STILL BATTLING

1958–82

Cricket opened new doors.

One of the clients of Short's Lifts that Bob serviced was John Waddington Limited, the packaging and printing company who manufactured board games such as Monopoly and Cluedo. They were based in Leeds and had a close relationship with the Thomas De La Rue company, a relationship which dated back to the war. De La Rue's London factory, where foreign bank notes were printed, had been bombed, and they relocated the work to the Waddington site in Leeds, along with the vital printing of maps for air crews. "For the foreign currency, all the sheets were counted, as well as every bit of scrap. Then it all went into a caged area for the numbering and engraving. It was a very successful operation, with six or eight machines."

Both Waddington and De La Rue ran cricket teams, and they both maintained grounds with dedicated staff. Waddington's ground was behind their factory in Wakefield Road, Leeds, while De La Rue had two, one in Maidenhead, the other at their Formica factory outside Newcastle. The annual match between the two sides was a highlight of the year. "It was a really big occasion," Bob says. "Afterwards, there was a dinner at a hotel, with prizes. Everybody looked forward to it."

One day Bob was in his office at Short's Lifts when he received a call from Waddington's chairman Norman Watson. "Would I go and play in a cricket match against Thomas De La Rue, he asked. They hadn't won for five or six years. 'You'll play under a nom-de-plume, and we'll pay you fifty guineas.' Well, I'd only been paid £75 to play in a five-day Test for England, and this was just a Saturday afternoon in Leeds."

He arrived as J. Smith, with no sign of his Yorkshire or England sweater or cap, but his anonymity did not last long. "Who should I see as soon as I arrived at the ground but Jack Young, the former Middlesex and England slow left-arm bowler! He was a Fellow of the Zoological Society, a super chap. I remember we were playing at Lord's one year, and he took me to the zoo at Regent's Park on the Sunday morning, when the gates were closed to the public. By this time he was selling Formica so he was playing for De La Rue legitimately. 'What are you doing here?' he said.

"I think I got a fifty and took five or six wickets. But we still lost."

In the evening Norman Watson approached him. "Would you be interested in coming to work for us as a cricket professional? When my father started the business, we always used to have one."

Bob declined. "I'm not interested in playing cricket for a living," he said, "but, if it's a job you're offering, that's a different matter."

So it was that Bob found himself selling milk cartons for Waddington – and, like Len Hutton who was starting out as an international salesman for the engineering company J.H. Fenner, he made it his business to learn all he could about the technical processes.

"There were milk vending machines on street corners in those days. They were coloured blue and had an illuminated sign at night. For sixpence you could get half a pint of milk in a waxed carton. Our cartons weren't the best in the world. They were made up of paper board, printed, formed and dropped in hot wax. But the trouble was that, if they got knocked, the wax seal broke, and they leaked. Today it's a poly-coated board, which is heat-sealed.

"We also made waxed cartons for orange juice. In the cinemas they took them round on trays, and I think the cinemas made more profit from them than they did from the seats. But, after a few days, the wax absorbed the essential oils and, if the cinema didn't rotate the stock and sell it quickly, the orange juice would taste awful. So eventually Waddingtons moved into plastics."

They were years of rapid technological development, and Bob rose in the company. "I was a pioneer. I'd start something off, then they'd move me on when it was going well. My first major promotion was like that. Waddingtons set up a company with International Paper of America, and I took a two-year post as Sales Manager, promoting the Americans' milk cartons.

"But I was always aware throughout my selling career that I had a name as an ex-cricketer and, if I didn't perform better than John Smith from another company or if anything went wrong, I'd get the blame. There was always the danger that my reputation would disappear overnight. I always felt that I had to work a damn sight harder and do a better job than my competitors."

So what was his secret as a salesman? "It's a bit like bowling. You've got to probe, find ways of obtaining your objectives. My belief is that you've got to get to know people, build up their confidence, then you can sell them something and they'll trust you. In those days your word was your bond. It wasn't necessary to have a lawyer draw up a contract to get a deal honoured.

"But then in those days you were given time to form the friendships. You could go off and play a round of golf. You weren't put under the same pressure to achieve instant results.

"I attended a course once, and they were trying to teach all these set-down techniques for selling, from America. You went in with a spiel and, according to their reaction, you brought out another thing from a pigeon hole. I thought it was a lot of bull. I took the mickey out of them. They had a questionnaire to establish whether you were an extravert or an introvert. Well, I deliberately answered all the questions wrong so they said that I was an extravert."

Life had moved on from cricket. He had a demanding job and a growing family. By 1960, Rosemarie was eight, Elizabeth six and little Ian three. At their detached bungalow in Thornton Connie stayed at home with the three children. Bob played golf at the Halifax Club, getting his handicap down to five, and they worshipped together at the church up the road where Patrick Bronte had once been the parson.

"By then," he reflects, "I rarely ever thought about the TB."

Tragedy, alas, had not deserted him. Young Ian contracted leukaemia, and their lives became centred around blood transfusions and periods of remission. "Our world fell apart. It was especially hard for Liz, who was very close in age to Ian. But, apart from the transfusions, there was little that could be done. Norman Watson, the Waddington chairman, offered to pay for Ian to have treatment in America. It was a very kind offer, but the medical advice was against putting him through it. All we could do was pray – and prayers cannot always be answered."

Rosemarie, Ian and Liz

The lines of the poem haunted him.

I hope he will grow straight and trim
With strength of limb
And hands that deftly catch and throw.

In November 1960 their little boy died. "During the last week Connie sat with him all day while I was at work, and I stayed with him each night. Then on the last night, when we knew he was passing away, we both stayed with him."

The words do not come easily as he forces himself to think again about their grief. "It left a lasting scar. … No one should lose children before themselves."

Good friends, Pat and Neil Pullan, were a comfort – "Friendship has always been very important to me. I suppose that's because I had very few at one stage in my life" – and, despite the shadow that young Ian's death left over the Appleyard family, time moved on. The girls were growing up, and the challenges of Bob's work absorbed him.

In 1967 he fulfilled a childhood ambition by moving to Ilkley, the town where he and Connie still live.

"Every Whitsuntide when I was a boy, like many others we went on a trip to Ilkley. We'd take the tram to Saltaire, down the hill past Salt's Mills, over the River Aire bridge, then we'd get on the cable car of the Shipley Glen railway and trek over the glen to the Dick Hudson pub. From there we started the walk across the moors. As youngsters it seemed interminable but, when we suddenly got to that point on Ilkley Moor where it falls away into the Wharfe Valley, it was like another world. Across the valley you could see the fine houses dotted among the trees, a few of them painted white with flat roofs. Then, at the bottom of the valley, alongside the Wharfe, there was a small strip of flat land and on it you could see so many sports pitches: soccer, rugby, cricket, tennis. Coming to live here was a dream come true. I've never wanted to leave."

Now he could play his golf at the Ilkley club, and one day in the early 1970s he was approached by a fellow member, who thought his older son Douglas might make a good cricketer.

"He wanted me to have a look at him so we set up a net with a few boys, including Douglas's younger brother who was only about ten, a chubby little lad. At the end of the session, I said to the father, 'Your boy's not too bad, but the younger one is much better. He's a real natural with a ball.'"

Alas, the young lad never pursued his cricketing talent, preferring instead to hit a golf ball. His name was Colin Montgomerie.

Bob became the Sales Manager at the Waddington factory in Gateshead, where they started to break into the market for beer bottle labels. "We had two new Italian photogravure machines, with five or six colours, and I was approaching all the big companies. I'll never forget going down to see the commercial director for Bass Charrington, John Burr, in his Baker Street office. I'd done some machine trials and sent some samples with a quoted price of three shillings and threepence per thousand, and he was obviously very pleased with them. 'I'm going to give you an order for 30 million labels each for Pale Ale, Carling Black and Jubilee Stout,' he said. 'The price will be three shillings and sixpence per thousand. That's the price we're paying your co-supplier, and that's the price we'll pay you.'

"It was the only time anyone offered me more than I was prepared to ask, but it was very good psychology on his part. There were a lot of strikes in those days and, if there was any chance of supplies being interrupted, I always made sure that he was at the top of my list of priorities."

At the start of his spell as Sales Manager, the Personnel Department had difficulty in recruiting a secretary for him. There was full employment, and it took a suggestion by Bob to overcome the problem. "I composed an advertisement myself. 'Victorian father (according to daughters) requires secretary.' I got a lot of replies, daughters sent along by protective parents, and I finished up with a very good secretary.'

His daughters both confirm his description of himself.

"If we were going out with a new boyfriend," Rosemarie says, "he had to come to the house to collect us, to be inspected."

"He was always quoting lines from that poem 'If'," Liz recalls. "'If you can keep your head when all about are losing theirs.' That was how we had to live our lives."

"We had an old labrador," Rosemarie says, "and even he knew my father was the one he had to obey. He wasn't supposed to lie in the sitting room and, as soon as he heard the car driving up, he'd shoot back out to the kitchen."

For nearly thirteen years Bob worked for Waddingtons, living still in Ilkley but travelling all round Britain and Europe. Unfortunately, as his expertise developed, he started to become frustrated by developments at the company. "It was a family firm, and it got to the stage where there were too many grace and favour jobs involving members of the family and others."

And his cricket? "In the first year or two I played friendly matches for the company on Saturdays, but in the later years I just played once a year. Without any great success."

His great love now was golf, and it was at a golf event that he met David Perry, the former England rugby union captain who was a director of another print company that specialised in beer bottle labels, Fell and Bryant of Croydon. "He was a bit concerned that we were going to hit his preserve. I got on very well with him, and he suggested that I might join the British Printing Corporation, his parent company. I was offered the job of Sales Development Manager for the twelve companies in the group."

So began the next stage of his career in marketing. He familiarised himself with labels for Heinz Beans and Pedigree Pets, heat transfer paper printing onto cloth and polyester for the textile industry, wax and foil strips for sweet wrappers. Each year he made two trips to the States – "23 days at a time," he says, "and 15 internal flights each time."

But did his cricketing past count for anything there? "Yes, it did. The Americans didn't understand cricket, but they respected the fact that I'd played for England. They like achievers in any walk of life."

After joining BPC he became based at Maidenhead in Surrey, spending his weekends in Ilkley and weekday nights at the Farmers' Club next to the War Office on the Embankment in London. "That was fine," he says, "till the IRA started leaving bombs under cars. Every morning you had to get down on your hands and knees to inspect your exhaust. Then they restricted the parking."

His cricketing days came to a final and painful end at the Purnells ground in Paulton, Somerset. Purnells was another of the group's companies, and there he turned out for the Corporation against the Chairman of Purnells' eleven. Alongside him was Alan Moss, the Middlesex fast bowler who had played in

Bob's last Test match at Trent Bridge in 1956, limping off the field so that Bob had to take the new ball in the second innings. Moss was now managing director of a fellow company printing magazines in Nottingham and, when they took the field at Purnells, their captain was filled with excitement. "We'll open with our two England bowlers," he declared.

"I hadn't bowled for at least two years," Bob says with embarrassment. "They gave the two of us the new ball, and I couldn't hit a barn door. Alan was doing rather better at his end, but I was hopeless. I really shouldn't have played. It was one big mistake."

"We were both too old and past it," Alan Moss says. "But they were good days, before Maxwell came in."

It was in March 1981 that Robert Maxwell took over the British Printing Corporation, and quickly their working lives were transformed. "Initially," Bob says, "I thought, 'Here's a man who's extremely clever and will be good for the company.' But I soon found out that he was a crook."

In July Bob attended the Lord's Test. Ten years earlier government inspectors had concluded that Maxwell was an unfit person to run a public company. Bob had seen him in action for four months, and he took the opportunity of a chance meeting to express his growing concerns.

"The old England players used to have a room underneath the England dressing room, with lunch and tea, and in the pavilion I bumped into a senior board member of the National Westminster Bank. He had a leading position in the MCC, and we spent some time together. He was going round all these boxes – Denis Compton's, Alec Bedser's – drinking large whiskeys, and I was trying to make my halves of lager last. I said to him that I was concerned about Maxwell, and he said, 'Don't worry. BPC owed us ten million pounds. We put Maxwell in. He'll get you sorted out.'"

But Maxwell's 'sorting out' was not to the liking of BPC's senior staff. "David Perry was Chief Executive of the packaging group by then, and Maxwell used to ring him up at all hours. David was living in Oxford, and Maxwell was nearby in his rented mansion, Headington Hall. So he was summoning David to meetings from home. 'I want you down here at nine o'clock on Sunday morning.' Well, David sang in his church choir, he soon got fed up with all that, and he became very suspicious of Maxwell's business practices. So he left – ironically, to become the Managing Director at Waddingtons."

BPC ran a large golf day, where important clients were invited, and at the dinner Maxwell made a speech. "It was so embarrassing. In front of all our contacts, he was saying that there was no such thing as a free lunch and how we had to justify the day with fresh contracts."

Around this time Bob negotiated a major new contract with Nestle's, for packaging and labelling of Milky Bars, Nescafe and other products, bringing in £1.2 million a year for three years, and this brought him into Maxwell's sights. "He always wanted to be involved in the biggest accounts, and Nestle was one of the biggest we'd ever had in the packaging group."

Then came the next downturn in Bob's fortunes. At a dinner he became involved in an unpleasant argument with David Perry's successor. "He was at one end of the table, I was at the other and, in front of the group's senior executives, he started taking the mickey out of me, saying things like, 'Listen to him. He's got a bit of an order from Nestle, a few thousand pounds.' I stood up to him. Perhaps I shouldn't have said what I did, but he got very irate, and a few days later I was told that I wasn't wanted at Maidenhead. I was being transferred to Maxwell's personal staff."

"You're a self-starter," the tycoon told him. "Just go and find new markets for everything we produce."

"The whole thing was wrong," Bob says. "At first I was quite impressed by him. He used to arrive at his desk at seven o'clock and read the financial papers. So I used to go along at half past seven. I could easily get there, and he was fine. I was trying to get the business of printing the London Underground tickets. The chap in charge was a collector of cricket memorabilia. But Maxwell was too impatient. Within a month he was asking me, 'Have you sold a million pounds worth of business yet?'"

Bob's unhappiness intensified as he started to attend regular meetings with the chief executives of all the group's companies, one of whom was Alan Moss. "They were scheduled for 8.30 on Monday mornings, just to force people to travel down on Sunday night. He used to come in a bit late, make an entrance – just as Geoffrey Boycott was wont to do on the Yorkshire committee. Then he'd have a go at somebody. We used to think, 'Whose turn will it be today?' He was a real bully. But he paid good money, and a lot of the people were carried along by greed.

"He told the chief executives one week to make 20 or 25% cuts in their workforce by that Friday. Just like that. Peter Hassall at Purnells wouldn't do it. He resigned.

"I went to a meeting he addressed at our factory at Croydon. There were rumours that it was closing, and Maxwell stood up and told them that he was spending £300,000 on a new machine and that they would have twelve months to improve profits. I couldn't believe what I was hearing. I knew he'd already decided to move everything up to Accrington. Within a month he'd closed the place down."

Maxwell was a liar and a cheat but, as Bob is quick to acknowledge, he had charisma and he had a cunning intelligence.

"He was probably the cleverest man I've ever met. He could absorb information like blotting paper. Any letter to him had to be written on a single sheet of paper so that he could pick up the salient points quickly. He demanded high effort and work rate. But he was ruthless. I used to go to the local pub for a beer-and-sandwiches lunch with my fellow executives, and we'd swap Maxwell stories. There was one about this chap whom he spotted on the monitor screen in his office leaning over the reception desk, smoking a cigarette. He ordered his instant dismissal, with a pay-off of £50, and it turned out that the chap was waiting for a signature for a parcel he'd delivered.

"I remember one day sitting with Maxwell in his office. He was a big man, with glossy black hair, obviously tinted. 'All the best people have left,' he said. 'I'm left with a load of idiots.' And we looked at each other."

Bob is a tough man, he has survived worse things in his life than having a bullying crook for an employer, and he is not always sympathetic when people talk about stress. "What's stress compared with what the Battle of Britain pilots went through? They'd come back from a sortie. The plane would be refuelled, and they'd sit there, waiting for the next call. They were on call 24 hours a day. That's what I call stress. You compare that with the England players who refused to tour India after September the eleventh or said they were too scared to visit Zimbabwe. 'If you don't want to go,' England should have said, 'we'll pick somebody who does.' Mind you, I admire Henry Olonga for what he did. That's the kind of guts you need."

But working for Maxwell gave him a different outlook. "I saw a lot of unhappiness. I was lucky. We'd paid for our house. Our children were married. I could afford to take him on. But the younger men, with mortgages and children at university, had to take it. This is where stress does come into it. Somebody on his staff said, 'He's got forty ways of getting rid of people.' Nebulous reasons like unauthorised expenses or withholding information.

"He moved me into an office with a lot of people. I was supposed to be generating millions of pounds of business, and I was sharing a desk and a telephone with a junior rep. And it was the oldest desk he could find. The top left-hand drawer was missing. It does get to you. You start to think, 'Perhaps I'm not as important as I thought I was.'"

His former England colleague Alan Moss was one who did not survive. "He was a bright chap, had a lot of contacts, but he came back from holiday, and his daughter gave him this letter that had been delivered by hand. He read it, then went out on his own and walked round the garden. He'd been sacked, with immediate effect. He drove to his London office to clear his desk and, when he came out, he found his car had been broken into and his brief case, containing all his contact books, had been taken."

By summer Bob had had enough. He let his expenses rise above the thousand pound figure that required Maxwell's approval, in the hope that this would trigger a redundancy, but he had not reckoned with his boss concocting a story that, in driving a company car out of a tight parking space, he had banged into a hoarding and caused a glass door on the other side to be shattered. He was dismissed for damaging company property, with no pay-off.

"It was quite impossible that I'd done it. I took him to the Industrial Tribunal for unfair dismissal. He sent a message that he was out of the country, which apparently he always did, but somebody said, 'No, he isn't, he's here in London.' So the tribunal chairman said, 'You'd better get him here within two hours. Otherwise he's in prison.' We won that, but the maximum award was only £7,000. So I took him to the High Court for wrongful dismissal."

In the meantime he had his BPC pension to sort out. Bob took the precaution of consulting a friend working in the field and was advised that the BPC scheme was a sound one. "I remember my exact words in reply. 'I don't trust Maxwell,' I said. 'It won't be long before he has his sticky fingers in the pension fund.' I don't blame my friend; at that time nobody had ever heard of company pension funds being raided. But, needless to say, I was very glad I did move my money."

Bob was dismissed in August 1982, but it was not till April 1984 that legal proceedings were concluded. The Bedser twins had recommended a solicitor, Richard de St Croix, and letters went back and forth with regularity.

"Maxwell tried every trick. He called for 'further and better particulars'. Then he put 50% of my claim into court a month before the hearing. That meant that, if the judge decided that it was a fair settlement, I would have to pay his costs from that time on. I turned it down so he put in another 25%."

At this point Bob's legal team held a conference, and they gave him 'our strong advice' that he should accept the offer. "Richard de St Croix told me that you never get 100% at these hearings. They thought I was being reckless, particularly as I was financing my action from private funds where he had a large public company to draw on. But I said, 'I'm sorry. You know the law, but I know Maxwell. He won't turn up in the court."

Appleyard versus Maxwell, the indomitable battler versus the 'Bouncing Czech'. For 19 months and 93 solicitors' letters Bob had held his ground. "It was fairly traumatic at the time," he reflects. "It's something I won't forget."

In the end, however, as so often in his life, Bob's poor health had the final word. He was all set for his day in court, he had David Perry lined up to appear as a witness for him but, on the day before the hearing, he fell ill with a bad attack of bronchitis. "There was no way I could travel. I sent a message down. 'If he puts another year's contribution into my pension, I'll accept.' And he did. I got almost all of my claim, and he had to pay all the costs."

It is one of the great badges of honour in Bob's life, that he took on Maxwell and beat him. "I don't know of any others who did."

"I could have done," Alan Moss says. "I consulted a leading lawyer, and he advised me that I would win the case. But I wanted to get on with the rest of my life. I didn't want that hanging over me."

But Bob has never been one to give up a fight. Proudly he quotes Maxwell's remark, reported back to him by a sympathetic confidant of the tycoon. "I know that Appleyard. He's a bloody-minded Yorkshireman. He'll take me all the way."

CHAPTER 14
THE CANDLELIGHTERS

Events at home soon overshadowed the battle with Maxwell.

Rosemarie's marriage broke up, and she moved back to her parents' house with her two boys. The younger one, John, was just two years old when he was diagnosed as having leukaemia.

More than twenty years had passed since Ian's diagnosis, and the treatment at St James's Hospital in Leeds had come a long way in that time. Just as Bob had been among the first generation of tuberculosis sufferers to recover to full health, they prayed that John would win his battle with the cancer's spread.

"There was so much more hope by then," Rosemarie says.

Her older boy James was five years old, attending Moorfield School in Ilkley, and, as soon as Rosemarie shared the news of John's illness with her closest friends among the other mothers, they resolved to set up a branch of the Yorkshire-based charity, the Candlelighters, to raise money for leukaemia research.

Her sister Liz joined her in the initiative. "The Candlelighters were named after the Light of Eternal Hope," Liz explains. "Right from when Ian had died, we'd always intended to do something but, apart from sending Leukaemia Research cards at Christmas, we'd never got round to it."

With their friends they organised a coffee morning at the Craiglands Hotel. "We all made cakes and gooseberry jam," Liz recalls, "and on the first morning there was a queue out of the hotel and right down Cowpasture Road."

For a year it seemed that their prayers had been answered, as John went into remission and seeming recovery. "We really thought he was better," Rosemarie says. But the disease returned, and this time there would be long stays in hospital and no remission.

"For a long time I was away from home," Rosemarie says. "We saw my husband regularly, but James was living with my parents, being looked after by them. My father was wonderful with him. I think, with his own childhood experiences, he knew what James was going through, and he made a special bond with him. They're still close now."

John's death plunged the family into fresh grief, but Bob knew the role that he had to play.

If you can watch the things you gave your life to, broken,
And stoop and build 'em up with worn-out tools.

"My father's always been our rock," Rosemarie says. "He's always been there for us when we've needed him. People who know him through his public life see him differently, but he's a very caring man."

"We were all devastated," Bob says. "They say time heals, but it didn't seem as if it ever would."

After a while Rosemarie remarried and had two more children, a brother and sister for James.

In the meantime the coffee mornings of the Ilkley Candlelighters led on to greater things: garden parties, Christmas fairs with Santa's grottoes, flag days, fashion shows and an annual ball which, Liz says, is now "*the* ball in Yorkshire." To date, the Ilkley branch has raised more than a million pounds.

"They've done a brilliant job," Bob says. "All of them. Rosemarie and Liz and all their friends. I'm very proud of them."

"This was taken at the Scarborough Festival," Bob says. "We used to play on the outfield during the intervals. And one time we were invited to sit at the President's table at lunch, and James got to sit between Peter May and Imran Khan. He's never forgotten it."

CHAPTER 15

FIGHTING FOR THE FUTURE

Since 1982

"Maxwell wanted my car back, and the day he was sending somebody to fetch it, I was going to the Headingley Test. So I rang Don Brennan to ask him for a lift. He said, 'I'm not sure. I'm getting a lift myself.' The chap who was taking him was the Chairman of ICI Fibres, John Lister of Harrogate. He had a chauffeur-driven car, and I finished up spending the day with him. 'We might have something for you at ICI,' he said, and he asked me to go over and meet the Marketing Manager. They'd developed a plastic bottle for drinks like Coca-Cola, but they had no knowledge of the packaging industry. So they gave me a consultancy job. That was quite a turning point in my life. One door closes. Another opens. I've always believed that."

As a freelance consultant Bob was soon in demand, but he was approaching sixty and he was already comfortably off. He started to think that he would like to spend some of his time making a contribution to cricket in Yorkshire.

"I've always been grateful for the way the club treated me when I was ill, and so much of my later career I owed to my success in cricket. I felt it was time to give something back."

In the twenty-four years since he had played his last match for the county, much had changed. There had been the years of success in the 1960s, under Vic Wilson and Brian Close, but they had been followed by years of failure on a scale unimaginable to men of Bob's generation. Though there were now four trophies each year to be won, Yorkshire went through the 1970s without winning one of them and, when the 51-year-old Ray Illingworth returned as team manager to lead them finally to the John Player Sunday League title in 1983, any joy was cancelled out by the shame of finishing the championship season for the first time ever at the very foot of the table.

Throughout these years of failure the club's leading player was Geoffrey Boycott, and the committee decided at the end of 1983 that its only hope of moving forward lay in dispensing with his services. It was a contentious proposal. Boycott had become the greatest run-maker in the history of Test cricket, and all Yorkshire was immensely proud of that. Further, he had scored 1,941 runs that summer, over 800 more than any of his team-mates. But too often, his critics charged, he had used up winning time with his slow batting, and too many gifted players had left to join other counties. The cricket committee included Norman Yardley, Fred Trueman, Ronnie Burnet, Billy Sutcliffe, Phil Sharpe, Bryan Stott, Don Brennan and Ray Illingworth, and their decision was unanimous.

Bob had not been close to Yorkshire cricket in these years, but he was astute enough to see the potential danger of this showdown, particularly as Boycott had been promised a testimonial the next year. Together with John

Lister of ICI Fibres and his friend Arthur Hutchinson, later to become a judge, Bob put forward a compromise: that Boycott be allowed to play during his coming testimonial year on condition that he then retired. The proposal was known as the Appleyard Compromise and on Christmas Eve 1983 Bob, with Connie alongside him, put it to a barrister friend of Boycott, whose reaction seemed to suggest that it would be acceptable to the player.

Unfortunately the New Year meeting with the county club's officials was less successful. Ronnie Burnet, the cricket committee chairman, had had enough. Twenty-five years earlier he had led the county to the championship after parting company with his senior professional Johnny Wardle, and he and his committee were determined to bring the team together with firm action.

Boycott's supporters were well-mobilised. Their discontent had been stirred five years earlier when Boycott had been relieved of the captaincy, and many of them had lost all respect for the men running the club. They had raised the signatures necessary for the calling of a special meeting, and Bob and his two allies were filled with foreboding. Arthur Hutchinson set out their thoughts:

> It is a sobering, if not heart-breaking, thought to contemplate that the opposing factions in this war, who no doubt would each claim to have the interests of Yorkshire cricket foremost in their minds, are prepared to put the very future of the Club at risk over an issue as transient as the offer of a contract for one season to an ageing player.

Their compromise was lost in the angry showdown. The special meeting, costing £25,000, took place in Harrogate on the 21st of January 1984, and tempers quickly became frayed. The committee sat on the platform, with their president Norman Yardley in the centre, and one rebel pointed at them: 'Who would buy a second-hand car from this lot?' Sidney Fielden, a police officer, spoke with the passion of a Methodist lay preacher while Brian Walsh persuaded with his subtler barrister's skills. The motion to reinstate Boycott was carried. Then, more dramatically, the meeting passed votes of no confidence: first in the cricket committee, then – by just 3609 votes to 3578 – in the full committee.

For Bob, it was the worst of returns to Yorkshire cricket. Norman Yardley – "one of the most unselfish men I've ever met" – resigned, and in the ensuing elections most of the committee – Trueman, Burnet and Sutcliffe among them – were swept away. A committee that had contained a wealth of playing experience from the county's more illustrious past was now dominated by men whose main purpose in seeking election was to champion the cause of Boycott.

Yet in their midst were two newcomers, both elected unopposed from districts of Bradford, men not associated with the previous regime: Brian Close and Bob Appleyard. With Phil Sharpe and Bryan Stott who had narrowly survived the purge, they were the only members with first-class cricketing experience on the new 23-man committee – except, of course, that also elected, representing the district of Wakefield, was Geoffrey Boycott himself.

It was a time of great turbulence. The county finished last again in 1984, and Brian Close's first spell as chairman of the cricket committee did not see out the year. Inevitably in such divided times Appleyard the advocate of compromise soon gave way to Appleyard the fighter. The man who had got the better of Robert Maxwell was not going to come out second best to the new men in power in Yorkshire.

"When I was a player," he says, "the committeemen all had real stature. They were successful businessmen like Ernest Holdsworth, a director of the Bradford Dyers' Association, or great past players like Herbert Sutcliffe and Brian Sellers. The people who came on with Boycott had no such experience at all. They just waited to see how Boycott was going to vote and stuck their hands up with him."

Bob chuckles at the memory of a conversation between Len Hutton and Brian Close.

"Isn't this chap Walsh a QC?" Hutton asked.

"He is," Close replied.

"And Fielden, isn't he a Detective Sergeant?"

"Aye."

Len paused. "Well, what chance do we have with Boycott if he can fool a QC and a Detective Sergeant?"

The last straw for Brian Close as cricket committee chairman was a dispute about the position of the wicket-keeper. For fifteen years David Bairstow had been the county's keeper, but he was captain now and good enough to play in the side as a specialist batsman. The second team keeper, Steven Rhodes, was showing real quality, and both Brian Close and Bob thought that Bairstow should give up the gloves so that Rhodes' potential would not be lost to the county. "He was an England prospect," Bob reckoned.

Rhodes' father Billy had played for Nottinghamshire in the 1960s, and he now worked in a fruit and vegetable wholesalers in Bradford Market. Bob was not on the cricket committee but, at Brian Close's suggestion, he went at dawn one day to see Billy Rhodes, in the hope that he could influence his son to stay with Yorkshire while the matter was resolved. Alas, to the horror of both Bob and Brian Close, their efforts were in vain. Without reference to the cricket committee, the club chairman Reg Kirk gave Worcestershire permission to speak to their young keeper. As Bob predicted, Steven Rhodes did go on to represent England – but not as a Yorkshire player.

Bob's interest in joining the committee had not been to engage in such politics, not even to help run the first team. In his view his greatest value lay in his commercial experience, and he served on the Public Relations and Fund-Raising Committee. His great aim was to develop youth cricket in the county.

When in January 1988 he visited Australia for the Bicentennial celebrations, he saw their Academy and talked at length to Jack Potter the Director. With some dedicated fund-raising he thought that Yorkshire could create something on the same lines.

One of several sessions on slow bowling that Bob ran in the winter of 1987-88
Phil Carrick (Yorkshire captain), Bob, Paul Booth, Ian Swallow, Phil Berry
"I want to get the spinners thinking on attacking lines," he told the Yorkshire Post

There was general enthusiasm for the idea, and Bob's extraordinary skill as a money-raiser made it an opportunity too good to reject.

Unfortunately, in the poisoned atmosphere of the Yorkshire committee, it was inevitable that the detail would occasion division, and the detail in this case was the location: Leeds or Bradford. There had already been a similar argument, back in 1985, about the setting up of an indoor cricket school, and on that occasion Headingley had won the day. But three years later Boycott's views no longer carried automatic sway. Walsh and Fielden, QC and detective sergeant, had become disillusioned with Boycott, and further elections had altered the committee's composition.

"Sidney Fielden has been a wonderful committee member over the years," Bob says. "He's made it his job to help the members with all their problems."

The line-up on the Bradford-Leeds dispute was clear. Bob and Brian Close, with Bryan Stott, favoured refurbishing Bradford Park Avenue so that it could house the Academy. Geoff Boycott and the influential Tony Vann advocated Headingley so that it would be alongside all the other facilities of the club.

At the heart of the debate lay two problems: one, that the Headingley headquarters, though benefiting greatly from having Test match status, was not owned by the county; the other, that the Park Avenue ground had fallen into disrepair. For the advocates of Leeds, Park Avenue was a lost cause, an unsuitable site for further expenditure, a choice they felt that was born of parochial sentiment not objective analysis. For the advocates of Bradford, the Academy provided a perfect opportunity to revive Yorkshire's best stadium and to do so on a firmer financial footing than the county had ever negotiated with Headingley's owners.

Further, Bob believed, the pronounced slope at Headingley made it an unsuitable surface for bowlers to learn their trade. "It's so essential to practise on the flat. Your run-up has to become a memory. The last thing you want is to be wondering where your feet are landing."

With hindsight one can see that it was a critical time for the club, when it needed to harness all its cricketing, financial and commercial acumen to achieve a clear strategy, but the committee remained in a fractured state, lacking crucial expertise and unable to advance with a common purpose.

"We were still suffering from the effects of the Boycott revolution," Bob reflects. "Too few of the elected members had any real knowledge or experience of cricket or even business at that level, and as a result the county was wandering in the wilderness. The effects of those years really led to the financial disaster we have today."

And Bob's own contribution? "I'm not the world's best committeeman," he admits. "I'm impatient. I like to get things done. If I meet a difficulty, I seek out an expert without delay. The endless debate and procrastination frustrated me. I had no love of Maxwell, but there were times when I longed for his ability to pick out the crucial facts, draw a conclusion and take instant action."

"It was a difficult time," Bryan Stott says. "Tony Vann was all Leeds, Bob was all Bradford, and they were both running their own campaigns. It got to the point that I wrote to them both and asked them to stop. They'd both got so much to offer."

"It was a hell of a struggle," Bob says. "I wonder if any of the youngsters who have been through the Academy know what went into setting it up, all the politics on the committee, the fund-raising."

Bob is a Bradfordian to his core. He can still feel the thrill of cricket as it used to be at Park Avenue: the late afternoons as a boy when he waited with his bottle of pop for a member to take him in to watch the great Sutcliffe and Verity and to marvel at the young Len Hutton; the days as a county cricketer when he heard the roar of the crowd as he sent the visiting batsmen on their way, six South African wickets on his first appearance there, twelve against Essex the same summer. Why should he be prepared to see the ground fall into dereliction and decay, if a chance existed to revive it to its former glory?

But Bob has not fought for the ground purely out of sentiment. "You don't do things for yourself," he insists. "You do them because you feel they're going to do some good for Yorkshire."

'The best watching ground in England' is how Ray Illingworth and others describe the Park Avenue ground in its prime, but the demise of the adjoining football club, coupled with the social problems of the surrounding Canterbury estate, created a downward spiral that culminated in 1985 with the condemning as unsafe of the historic, if eccentric, Victorian pavilion. Bob had played cricket for Yorkshire at eight different grounds in the county. Huddersfield and Hull had long gone from the fixture list, and now Bradford too was abandoned.

"In the 1970s," Ray Illingworth recalls, "Yorkshire were offered the Park Avenue ground lock, stock and barrel, everything free, even the football pitch, and they didn't take it on, even though they had an independent arbiter who said, 'You could cover your costs from perimeter advertising.' You could have pulled down the football stand, extended the playing area and had a 25,000-seater ground. It would have provided a much better venue than Headingley."

Always the sticking point, it seemed, was that Headingley brought in crucial income as a Test match ground, though some did not see this as an insuperable obstacle. "We could have gone to Bradford as our headquarters," Bryan Stott says, "and still played two matches and the Test at Headingley."

The city of Bradford had a population larger than Middlesbrough, Harrogate and Scarborough all combined. It was the centre of the ancient wool trade that had created the wealth of the West Riding. Its cricket league had been the best in the world, its ground the scene of so many memorable matches in the great history of Yorkshire cricket.

"The square was still in wonderful condition," Bob says, "and it's very flat, unlike Headingley. The practice facilities were also first-class."

In Bob's view it only needed a development plan and some business flair to get the ground back in action. It was owned now by the Bradford Metropolitan Council, and Bob worked tirelessly as the 1980s drew to a close to secure a deal. He enjoyed influential support, from David Warner of the *Bradford Telegraph and Argus* to Bruce Moss the president of the Bradford League, and they persuaded the council to offer them the ground on a 999-year lease at a peppercorn rent. There was even a grant attached to assist with the set-up and running costs of the Academy.

The committee voted in favour, with the final resolution going to the Annual General Meeting of the club. Some like Tony Vann, doubting the wisdom of the location, voted against, but the members were in favour and the Academy began its life in the summer of 1989.

"It's so crucial to have good coaching at the start of a youngster's career," Bob says. "Then, when he reaches a certain level, he needs people who are qualified to take him further. I look back, and I realise how lucky I was to have Emmott Robinson and Arthur Mitchell to teach me and to play under Norman Yardley and Len Hutton. But up to the age of 26 I was only playing cricket in my spare time. My idea with the Academy was to give the youngsters three years of coaching, like being on a training ship, starting at the age of 16."

Bryan Stott wanted to bring Ken Taylor back from Norfolk to run the scheme – "He'd have put the real seal on it" – and Bob tried without success to woo Don Wilson away from his position as MCC's Head Coach at Lord's. In the end they appointed the younger Steve Oldham.

The square was renovated, practice pitches established, dressing rooms with showers and toilets, a dining room and office were all provided. It was 'a costly venture for Yorkshire cricket', according to Boycott, but Bob still possesses the accounts. In the first four years, when he was 'the fund-raising supremo', the county contributed only £15,000 a year out of a total four-year expenditure of over £260,000. Bradford Council also contributed £15,000 a year and, with the remaining £140,000 coming from donations, the project managed a surplus of income over expenditure. "Bob knew so many people," Bryan Stott says. "He had this outstanding ability to get in to see chairmen and managing directors and to come out with promises of money."

Michael Vaughan, Darren Gough, Chris Silverwood and Anthony McGrath are among many young cricketers who have benefited from attendance at the Academy, all four of them progressing into the Yorkshire side and from there being selected to play for England.

"There was a long time," Bob reflects, "when the majority of Yorkshire players served their apprenticeship in the Bradford League. That was the major breeding ground. But now it isn't quite as strong, and the Academy has opened up avenues for people all over the county. In fact, it was my original vision that it would be a regional centre for the whole of the North of England, part of a structure of regional centres around the country."

The Academy not only provided talented youngsters with cricket coaching, it was also intended to offer an education in business skills so that they would have other job opportunities beyond cricket. This initiative led Bob into discussions with the Bradford University School of Management. From his dealings with Robert McClements and Professor David Weir, and from extensive negotiations with the England Cricket Board, there emerged a course in Cricket Management and Coaching. From that there developed not only the Bradford and Leeds University Centre of Cricketing Excellence but also a structure of six such centres around England and Wales.

"Without Bob," Robert McClements says, "we would never have achieved what we have. He was responsible for bringing together all the influential people, bashing everybody's heads together. He opened so many doors into the world of business and into the highest circles in cricket. He worked tirelessly."

In July 1997 the University of Bradford awarded an honorary doctorate to Bob 'in recognition of his contributions to the sport of cricket and in particular his work in supporting the development of courses in cricketing management'. "With my background," he says, "having attended the old Bradford Technical College before it became a university, that was a very special day for me."

When the Academy began in 1989, not all its successes were home grown. Bob had written to Jack Potter in Australia, planting the idea that they might arrange player swaps, and back came a letter, asking him to arrange some playing opportunities for a 19-year-old lad from South Australia, by the name of Craig White, whose birthplace was in Morley, Leeds. Bob raised sponsorship from Yorkshire Bank and Tetley's and wrote to the youngster. He still retains the reply.

> Dear Mr Appleyard,
> Thank you for your letter concerning the possibility of me spending an Australian winter playing cricket in Yorkshire. I am thrilled with the response. ... Regarding work, I will do virtually anything! I have had bar experience in several hotels and in my

year at the Academy I have been working for a builder in his office. I would really like to work as an assistant curator at one of your ovals if it could be possible. ... I would be looking to play cricket at the highest level possible (eg County Seconds). ... Thank you so much for your assistance. I am extremely keen to do well and advance my cricket experience as much as possible.
Yours faithfully
Craig White

The young all-rounder made such an impression in a pre-season match at Headingley that he was in the full county side for the first fixture. Within four years he was playing for England, with fellow debutant Steven Rhodes.

Another initiative was the 'Find-A-Fast Bowler' scheme, for which Bob secured sponsorship from Poundstretcher. Wilf Paish, the maverick athletics coach who had worked with Tessa Sanderson the javelin thrower, was drawn into the fold, showing key parallels between the two activities and adding valuable insights into the psychology of top level sporting achievement. For Bob, the man who had practised yoga techniques and tried to achieve peak concentration in his delivery stride, this was a welcome contribution.

"The big question you have to ask of any fast bowler is, 'How much does he want to bowl? How does he react when he reaches the pain barrier?' Anyone who puts in a lot of physical effort will feel pain. But it's up to you, not your doctor or physio or coach, how you respond to that pain. Assessing a young player's future depends as much on his ability to withstand pain as on any technical ability."

His mind runs back to Don Bradman as a boy spending hours batting a ball against a wall and to his own nets at Bowling Old Lane when he would stay after all the others had finished. "I'd have three practice balls and three separate stumps. I wouldn't pack up till I could hit each stump in turn – or till darkness fell."

'Concentration – Application – Determination.' But not excessive activity, he insists. "Mark Broadhurst came through our Find-A-Fast Bowler scheme, one of the most promising youngsters to emerge in Yorkshire since Fred Trueman. But he was completely overbowled. In one Young England match, when he was barely seventeen, he was asked to bowl 27 overs in an innings. It was an outrageous demand, and in no time he was burned out."

He returns to a familiar theme. "Youngsters today don't have the same stamina that we had. They're taken everywhere on wheels. So you can't treat them like we would have been treated sixty years ago."

Another sub-committee on which Bob served tackled the problems of the Headingley pitch, which had become prone to cracking and was threatening the Test match status of the ground. "The groundsmen at different times had added different top dressings. One used Humber Silt, which set like plasticene, very pliable. Then Surrey Loam became flavour of the month, and that set like concrete on top of it. Unfortunately Surrey Loam also cracks when it dries out and, when it's watered, the edges of the cracks get soft. It starts to look like crazy paving."

Before the 1988 Test against the West Indies Bob and the groundsman Keith Boyce took advice from the Bingley Turf Research Station, and they decided that the cracking could be reduced by blocking up some of the drains. That would retain the right level of moisture at the surface.

"The day before the game," Bob recalls, "the pitch was perfect, all the cracking gone. But unfortunately that night the heavens opened and, when the ground staff mopped up, they emptied their machines into the manhole at the bottom of the square. With hindsight they would have been better taking the water to the outside drains."

Play eventually got under way, with Dickie Bird officiating at the Football Stand end, and at the start of the day's third over, as Curtly Ambrose prepared to bowl, a great spurt of water shot up out of the ground, flooding the bowler's run-up. A bemused Dickie stood there in astonishment.

"We were having a special 50th anniversary celebration of Len Hutton's 364," Bob remembers. "I was with Ray Lindwall and Neil Harvey at the time. When the water started spouting up, I said to Ray, 'What would you have done?' 'I'd have run round it,' he said."

Dickie Bird suggested sending for a plumber Then, to a chorus of boos and catcalls, he led the players off. Play did not resume for another two hours.

Bob has a profound respect for scientific research, for new materials, but as a gardener a worry lingers in the back of his mind. "I have a theory that all the treatment of the water, the filtering and the chemicals, has affected it. When you put tap water on the plants, it does keep them alive but, as soon as you get a shower of rain, they shoot up. I think it might be the same with pitches. In the 1950s, the pitches were left open to the rain and, when they were dry, they were very good, but now we don't seem able to get the same consistency."

Meanwhile the fight to revive Park Avenue had moved on from the establishment of the Academy there. The Friends of Park Avenue Cricket had been formed, Bryan Stott was negotiating with developers, and a local league side, Field's Packaging Limited, put the square back into use.

Their full dream was not realised – "The developers wanted too much of the returns for themselves," Bryan Stott says – but on August the 21st 1992 the ground welcomed the return of county cricket.

Surrey were the visitors and, according to *Wisden*, 'The pitch was not without pace but also yielded a little slow turn to assist the spinners.' Rain ruined the second day, but the ending – with Surrey's last pair scoring 21 runs to scrape home in the final over – lived up to Park Avenue's reputation: 'a memory ground', 'a place where the cricket never went to sleep'

Unfortunately, in such a troubled district, security became an issue. Ownership of the lease on Park Avenue was held by the Yorkshire CCC Charitable Youth Trust but, with the Academy on site, the county took back responsibility for the ground on a three-year sub-lease. Their supervision, in

Bob's view, fell short of what was required. "It was all political," he believes. "There was no will to keep up the ground." With a number of incidents of theft, damage to cars and vandalism, county cricket's return to Park Avenue lasted only four more years.

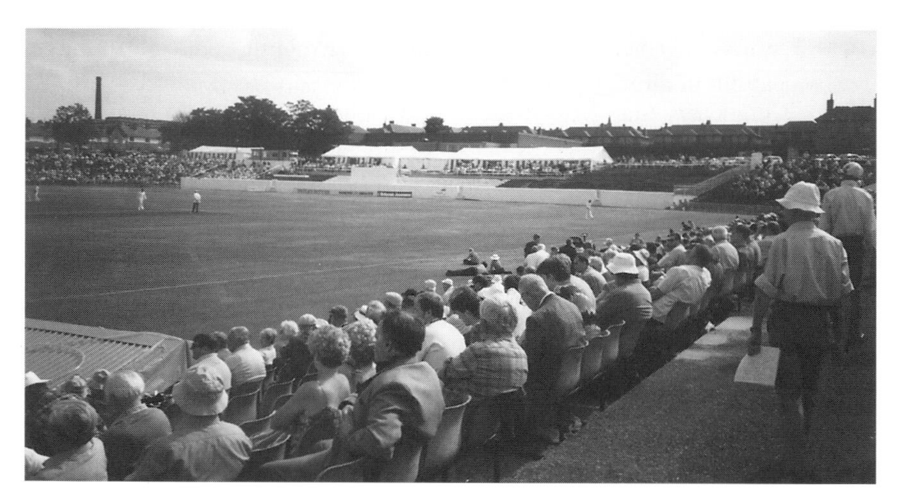

The Bradford crowd on Yorkshire's return

"I've more or less accepted that it's a lost cause now," Bryan Stott says.

Bob does not agree. "It's only because of the political meandering of Yorkshire County Cricket Club that it's in danger of extinction. It's still a first-class ground."

By 1992 Bob's years on the committee had come to an end. The committee was streamlined from 23 down to 12, with four electoral districts, and it was decided that only one former player should be allowed to represent each district. Bradford had several, and both Bryan Stott and Bob stood down in favour of Brian Close. "It was a total nonsense," Bob says. "I agree that you don't want a committee made up entirely of ex-players, but so many of the ex-players were in Bradford. Good candidates were lost."

Bob's involvement with Yorkshire did not end at this point. He was still involved with the University of Bradford and with the Friends of Park Avenue, and he continued to search for funds for the Sir Leonard Hutton Foundation Appeal, to support youth cricket in the county. The Appeal's aim is to raise £1,000 for each run scored in Hutton's record-breaking 364.

"I approached Paul Getty through Peter May and Colin Cowdrey, and he offered to start off the fund with 10% of the target and then rounded it up to a straight £40,000. And we still get £10,000 each year from Nestles, going back to the contact I made when I won the account for packaging Milky Bars. But our greatest benefactor over the last twelve years has been Charles Fenton, who lives on the outskirts of Bradford. His health didn't allow him to play much cricket, but he's been a wonderful supporter of our work."

Inevitably there has been further controversy. Bob is unhappy that the Academy has been taken away from Park Avenue to a club ground on the outskirts of Leeds. He was appalled by Yorkshire's appointment of a marketing manager with no background in cricket. And he sees the recent restructuring, forced by debts of several million pounds, as the consequence of years of mis-management by a weak and divided committee.

Most painful of all for Bob, though, was the furore stirred in the summer of 2001 by the gates that were erected at Headingley to commemorate Len Hutton. The designer, with no great feeling for the batsman, based her work on a photograph of Hutton playing a most uncharacteristic heave. Further, her attempt to create a multi-racial image, by incorporating a group of Asian women spectators, seemed to many to have little to do with Hutton himself, and Bob – never afraid to speak his mind – was among those who said so.

The controversy took an uglier term when the Chief Executive issued a statement that Bob's criticism had racist implications, and this was publicised in the national press. "I'd raised so much money for the Hutton Foundation," Bob says, still angry. "Our 'Enjoy Cricket' scheme had started in Bradford, and at least half the youngsters had been from the Asian community."

The Hutton family themselves had not been privy to the design, and they rallied in support of Bob, threatening that Lady Dorothy would not open the gates as scheduled. Within days Bob received a full, public apology. "I could have got a lot of money out of them," he says, "but what would have been the point of that? I've spent years trying to raise money for Yorkshire cricket."

Alas, the debacle did not end there, with further appalling publicity being generated when members objected to an invitation to John Major to open the West Stand on the same day. The former prime minister diplomatically stood down, and Bob sent him a private letter, apologising for the club's behaviour.

Even away from Yorkshire cricket, Bob's battling has seen him hit the front pages of the local newspapers. In the winter of 1998-99 Ilkley Golf Club rejected his request to use a battery-powered trolley during the winter months, thus preventing him from enjoying the Wednesday afternoon friendly matches that helped him to exercise his increasingly arthritic knees and ankles.

Almost half a century earlier he had climbed the hilly Halifax course four times a weekend, trying to build up stamina while – unknown to him – the tubercular hole in his lung was growing. Two winters later he had used golf to build back his post-operative fitness. For 33 years he had been a member of the Ilkley club. His golf had been a source of pleasure all his life, and now the club authorities were closing the door on him. "And on a few others. It was most unfair." He was determined that it would not shut without a fight.

"I'd been on the sub-committee at Yorkshire, dealing with the state of the ground at Headingley, and I know how quickly turf recovers from wear and tear. For a Test match, a narrow strip of turf has to survive five days of intensive use. The damage a few golfers would have caused with wide-wheeled, battery-driven trolleys would have been minimal by comparison."

He pointed out the much greater damage caused by the gang-mowers in the autumn, but it was all to no avail and, with an anger that has never fully abated, he resigned his membership on principle and concentrated his physical energy on his garden.

There, climbing vigorously through the branches of a flowering cherry, is a creamy white rose that he bought with a cheque that Lorna Smart had sent them the Christmas before she died. "She became a friend of the family. She came to both our daughters' weddings and never forgot their birthdays."

The white rose is now as tall as the cherry tree – but how much harder it has been to nurture the White Rose of Yorkshire cricket. Bob has battled away for what he thinks right, but his contribution has been, and still is, about much more than the many controversies.

"Over the last twenty years," Bryan Stott says, "Bob's really put a lot of work in. Honest, realistic work. He could have done with an MBE or an OBE. He's done so much for cricket in Yorkshire."

Tony Vann, Bob's principal opponent on the Yorkshire committee, is as quick to give praise. "There would never have been an Academy in Yorkshire without Bob Appleyard. Bob is the man who carried it through. I know we've never seen eye to eye, but my admiration for him has never altered."

"It took some understanding to play with Bob," Bryan Stott says. "I understand him more now from having worked with him on the committee. You build up your admiration over a period."

"Never mind about all that," Bob says. "When I've finished this book, I'm going to start the Friends of Park Avenue again. There's a crisis developing. If the University Centre of Excellence doesn't stay at Park Avenue, the ground could be lost forever.

"It's the best cricket ground in Yorkshire. Bradford has already lost too many recreational grounds. I know it's in a bad area, but it could do a lot to bring racial harmony to the city. People need something positive in their lives, and the Asian community are very supportive of cricket. If nothing's done, it will fall back into the same state of dereliction and disrepair as in 1989. I'm determined, even at 79 years of age, that that isn't going to happen."

If you can lose and start again at your beginnings

"Park Avenue must survive."

CHAPTER 16

SEVENTY-NINE NOT OUT

The present day

Five miles up the river Wharfe from Ilkley stand the ruins of Bolton Abbey, where 850 years ago a small group of Augustinian canons and their prior settled. Amid meadows, woods and waterfalls they lived frugally, but in time their hard work accumulated sufficient wealth for them to construct roads and bridges, set up mills and organise markets. For 400 years they were at the heart of the slow development of the area, and they built an abbey with a priory church. Then came the Reformation. Their community was broken up, their lands confiscated and the abbey reduced to ruins.

The east end of their church was destroyed, but the nave survived to form a church on its own. Though it has suffered long periods of neglect in the last 400 years, there have also been times of restoration: one during the Victorian age, another only twenty years ago when an enterprising new priest created a fresh vitality around a traditional service. A congregation that had dwindled to single figures grew to such an extent that now on Sunday mornings more than two hundred worshippers fill the church, among them Bob and Connie Appleyard, who sit halfway up the nave on the far right hand side.

"We try to get there about half an hour before the service," Bob says. "I like to sit in the pew and think about all the people who have sat there over the centuries. What they were thinking. How they were dressed. What their attitudes were.

"I look at the great stones. I think how they must have humped them about, how they got them into place. There are so many memories in a church."

More than sixty years earlier he had been a young man on a bike, occasionally passing through on a Sunday in summer, stopping with his friends to marvel at the speed at which the river raced by and to scramble up the cliff beyond.

"It was one of the places we might go for a day. We even jumped over the river. It narrows to run through a rocky gorge, there's a whirlpool, and it's very fast, one of the fastest rivers in the country. Lots of people have lost their lives in it. We must have been a bit daft – you might call it adventuresome."

Somehow, despite all the setbacks, Bob has survived into his eightieth year, still full of life, and he likes to reflect not only on the changes he has seen but on those experienced by previous generations.

"The book that got me thinking about writing this book was *Seventy-One Not Out* by William Caffyn. He was a professional cricketer for Surrey in the nineteenth century. He stayed in Australia after a tour there and, when he came back, he wrote the story of his life."

Bob draws down the volume, published in 1899, and we read from the early pages:

> What a change in the history of cricket has been brought about by the railways! What a countless number of matches have they been responsible for! … I myself have had to walk many a mile before a day's cricket in the early years. … One of the Nottingham players, it is said, used to ride on horseback to Sheffield before playing in their match, rising at an unearthly hour to do so.

"In my time it's been the motor car," Bob says, and he returns to a familiar theme. "Over the centuries the toughest used to survive, didn't they? Tuberculosis, dysentery, the plague. People walked or rode horses, and the stock was strong. Even in my life we've been through war, through food rationing, a lot more hardship than the present generation go through. And it does affect the cricket. People haven't got the same natural fitness, the same stamina, and they aren't as tough."

He sits in the pew, and he thinks of the Bronte sisters, dying of tuberculosis in Haworth. "I read *Wuthering Heights* and *The Tenant of Wildfell Hall* as a boy, and I always had a strong sense of affinity with the Brontes. When I left school and started working, prior to our taking up cycling, a group of us used to catch the bus across to Haworth. We went into the parsonage, looked at the graveyard and the pub. There were no shops selling souvenirs, no Japanese tourists with cameras. It was a deserted place. Then we'd tramp home across the moors, across to Hebden Bridge and on to Halifax and not always on the footpaths. When the mists came down, it could be fairly dangerous. People lost their bearings."

This book has gone through several titles. Initially Bob wanted to call it *A Lad's Game*.

"That's what cricket was," he says, "and what it still should be. I know society and cricket have changed and will continue to change. People need more instant entertainment, but we mustn't destroy what's good in the game: the spirit of it, the traditions, the skills."

After *A Lad's Game* came *Seventy-Nine Not Out*, a 100-years-on sequel to William Caffyn.

"I feel very privileged with the span of my life in cricket. I've met George Hirst and Wilfred Rhodes, I played with Leonard, and now I've got the pleasure of seeing the youngsters coming through, watching them as George Hirst watched us. Michael Vaughan is the nearest to Leonard that I've seen since my own playing days. He looks so good: the correct way he plays, the time he has."

Then for a while we toyed with *A Bloody-Minded Yorkshireman*. Bob is, and always has been, a combative Bradfordian, probing the enemy batsmen with a relentless determination, taking on every obstacle in his path, be it a hole in the lung, a bullying employer or a fellow committee member with a different point of view.

"I should be getting to that time of life," he says, "when I relax. But I see things that need doing, and I still want to do them."

But in the end we settled on the lines from Emily Bronte, lines she wrote over 150 years ago, before medical science found a cure for tuberculosis, when people found their hope in religion:

No coward soul is mine,
No trembler in the world's storm-troubled sphere;
I see Heaven's glories shine,
And faith shines equal, arming me from fear.

'Faith Conquers Fear'. That was the headline in the *Daily Express* when they told the story of Bob's recovery, and he still holds on to his faith to guide him through his life.

"If you've got an enquiring mind, a lot of what Christianity teaches doesn't make sense anymore. Therefore I suspect that it's a lot harder to have faith in the bible as it's written, without questioning it."

For many years, while Bob made his way in the world, he was supported devotedly by Connie, whose faith has also never wavered. She made a home for their children and gave him the loving care that he had not always had in his early life. Now it is falling increasingly to Bob to look after her, and he does so with unfailing patience.

"I tend to look on the bible as a book that shows you how to live your life. It seems a bit far-fetched in places, but there is something behind it, something we don't quite understand, something I don't think anybody understands. It's like a book of instructions. If we all lived our lives by it, the world would be a better place."

The service at the priory church is a traditional one, drawing its congregation from all over the Dales and beyond. "David Sheppard has turned up a couple of times, when he was Bishop of Liverpool and attending a retreat nearby."

Look across from Bob and Connie to the back of the aisle on the far side, and you will spot another figure from Bob's cricketing days: Fred Trueman with his wife Veronica.

"Not long after we started going, he turned up one day," Bob tells – but, like the occasion when Norman Yardley presented the two of them with their county caps, Fred disputes this order of events. "I'm sure we were already going when Bob first came."

Together, on opposite sides of the church, they gaze towards the eastern wall, with its painted flowers, and their voices rise up to the wooden beams of the high roof.

The Lord's my shepherd, I'll not want.
He makes me down to lie
In pastures green; He leadeth me
The quiet waters by.

"All the years people have sat here and worshipped. There's something solid about it, something that will last after we have gone."

The service ends, and the congregation spills out into the summer sun. Fred and Bob stand with their wives and exchange the latest news of Yorkshire cricket while the river winds its rushing path around the flat pastures where the sheep graze.

The estate is owned by the Devonshire family, and every day hundreds of visitors arrive, most of them in motor cars. There is a gift shop, a café and a garage – but, Bob says, "it's all in good taste; it hasn't been made too commercial. They've tidied it all up, blended in the new developments, and it works. I admire them for the way they're looking after the countryside."

Fred starts to hold forth about the arrogant incompetence of some of the old amateurs who ran the game. "I'm writing another book," he says with relish as he and Veronica move away towards the car park. "There's a few things I want to get straight."

But Bob is in reflective mood, the spell of the church service still with him.

"The game is at a threshold," he considers. "Those administering it have got to think about its future. It's given me a great life; I just want it to be there for the youngsters growing up now. That's what the Hutton Foundation Appeal is raising money to achieve."

He and Connie return to their car, starting the journey home through the main gate and turning towards Ilkley: past the shooting lodge and the two cottages, one now an antiquarian bookshop, the other a restaurant. A high stone wall runs down the left-hand side of the road, and he glances at the hole in it as he passes.

"It's not a proper archway. It's all jagged, more as if someone has knocked some stones out. There's a footpath beyond it, leading down to the river. I remember when we came here as boys, we used to dash through that hole. We always thought it was going to fall down. But it's still there, just the same."

Will it still be there in another sixty years?

And will a congregation still fill the church?

What countryside will there be to enjoy in sixty years' time?

And what cricket?

A BRIEF STATISTICAL DIGEST

Robert Appleyard

Born: 27 June 1924

BOWLING IN ALL FIRST-CLASS CRICKET

Year	*Matches*	*Overs*	*Maidens*	*Runs*	*Wickets*	*Average*
1950	3	83.4	18	177	11	16.09
1951	31	1323.2	391	2829	200	14.14
1952	1	16	4	28	1	28.00
1954	30	1027.3	315	2221	154	14.42
1954/55	13	264.4 †	82	656	44	14.90
1955	16	558	185	1106	85	13.01
1956	26	870.4	260	1932	112	17.25
1957	22	613.5	152	1568	74	21.18
1958	10	187.3	56	448	27	16.59
TOTAL	**152**	**4934.1** †	**1463**	**10965**	**708**	**15.48**

† *includes 187 eight-ball overs in Australia*

BOWLING IN TEST CRICKET

Matches	*Overs*	*Maidens*	*Runs*	*Wickets*	*Average*
9	239.4 †	70	554	31	17.87

† *includes 79 eight-ball overs in Australia*

SEVEN OR MORE WICKETS IN AN INNINGS

33	6	76	8	Yorkshire v M.C.C.	Scarborough	1951
9.3	3	16	7	Yorkshire v Somerset	Taunton	1954
18	6	29	7	Yorkshire v Surrey	The Oval	1955
23	8	33	7	Yorkshire v Lancashire	Old Trafford	1954
15	3	35	7	Yorkshire v Hampshire	Bradford	1954
18.1	5	44	7	Yorkshire v M.C.C.	Scarborough	1954
16.5	5	48	7	Yorkshire v Warwickshire	Bradford	1956
37.5	16	57	7	Yorkshire v Leicestershire	Leicester	1951
28.4	5	84	7	Yorkshire v Gloucestershire	Bradford	1951

TWELVE OR MORE WICKETS IN A MATCH

40.4	18	43	12	Yorkshire v Essex	Bradford	1951
38.5	10	88	12	Yorkshire v Somerset	Taunton	1954
54.5	24	93	12	Yorkshire v Leicestershire	Leicester	1951
41.3	11	94	12	Yorkshire v Somerset	Taunton	1951
49.1	16	106	12	Yorkshire v Derbyshire	Chesterfield	1956
38.1	6	124	12	Yorkshire v M.C.C.	Scarborough	1954

BATTING & FIELDING IN ALL FIRST-CLASS CRICKET

Innings	*Not Outs*	*Runs*	*Average*	*Catches*
145	54	776	8.52	80

Highest Score 63 Yorkshire v Kent Tunbridge Wells 1957

BATTING & FIELDING IN TEST CRICKET

Innings	*Not Outs*	*Runs*	*Average*	*Catches*
9	6	51	17.00	4

Highest Score 19* England v Australia Sydney 1954

BOWLING ON DIFFERENT GROUNDS

	Overs	*Maidens*	*Runs*	*Wickets*	*Average*
Bradford	308.2	96	643	69	9.31
Middlesbrough	21	7	46	4	11.50
Scarborough	350	73	862	57	15.12
Huddersfield	97.2	33	210	13	16.15
Headingley	550.3	174	1200	71	16.90
Hull	226	63	471	23	20.47
Sheffield	506.2	140	1208	48	25.16
Harrogate	114	33	262	10	26.20
Yorkshire grounds	**2173.3**	**619**	**4902**	**295**	**16.62**
Other UK grounds	**2496**	**762**	**5407**	**369**	**14.65**
Australia & New Zealand	*264.4 †*	*82*	*656*	*44*	*14.90*

BOWLERS AVERAGING UNDER 17
IN FIRST-CLASS CAREERS COMPLETED SINCE 1914

Qualification: 200 wickets

	Matches	*Runs*	*Wickets*	*Average*
H. Verity	378	29146	1956	14.90
R. Appleyard	152	10965	708	15.48
J.B. Statham	559	36999	2260	16.36
W. Rhodes	1110	69993	4187	16.71
W.E. Bowes	372	27470	1639	16.76

BOWLERS AVERAGING UNDER 18
IN TEST CAREERS COMPLETED SINCE 1914

Qualification: 25 wickets

	Matches	*Runs*	*Wickets*	*Average*
M.J. Procter *(S.A.)*	7	616	41	15.02
R. Appleyard *(Eng)*	9	554	31	17.87
H. Ironmonger *(Aust)*	14	1330	74	17.97

ACKNOWLEDGEMENTS

I took over the writing of this book after some years of work by Derek Hodgson and, although the final text has been written by me, I want to make it clear that it is built on the firm foundations laid by Derek. He is the one who took on this project when it had too long been neglected, and my involvement has only been after he had done a great deal of hard work.

We would both like to thank Bob and Connie for looking after us on so many occasions. In my case, this involved several overnight stays, sleeping in the same bed where Sir Leonard Hutton once slept.

We are also both greatly indebted to Ron Deaton, a retired cricketer from the Airedale and Wharfedale League who has assisted Bob in sorting out the mementoes of his cricketing career and who has worked tirelessly in the background to ensure that this book does justice to Bob's life. Ron's working life was spent with British Rail, supervising the production of train timetables, and I suspect that without his assistance this book would have contained many more inaccuracies. It would certainly have taken longer to produce.

Chapter 15, which includes the story of Bob's contribution to Yorkshire cricket in the last twenty years, draws on much research by Rob Mills of the *Yorkshire Post*, and we would like to thank him for this.

In researching this book we have interviewed Bob's daughters Rosemarie Fisher and Liz Paul, Trevor Bailey, Michael Barton, Dickie Bird, Mary Braithwaite, Ron Cooper of Knypersley Cricket Club, Eric Hill, the late Geoffrey Howard, Ray Illingworth, Eddie Leadbeater, Ted Lester, Robert McClements of Bradford University, Alan Moss, the Rt Rev Lord Sheppard of Liverpool, Terry Spencer, Bryan Stott, Ken Taylor, Fred Trueman, Tony Vann, Douglas Verity, Willie Watson, Don Wilson, Vic Wilson and Geoffrey Wooler, and we would like to thank all of them for their co-operation.

We would like to thank David Smith of Corsham and Douglas Miller for kindly agreeing to read and comment on the manuscript. If there are still errors of fact or grammar, then these are the responsibility of the authors. We could not have asked for a more dedicated and perceptive pair of readers.

We have made regular use of the following reference books:

Wisden Cricketers' Almanack

Playfair Cricket Annual

Bailey, Thorn & Wynne-Thomas, *Who's Who of Cricketers* (Newnes Books, 1984)

Robert Brooke, *A History of the County Cricket Championship* (Guinness, 1991)

Jim Ledbetter & Peter Wynne-Thomas, *First-Class Cricket, 1930-39* (Limlow Books, 10 volumes, 1991-2002)

Swanton, Plumptre & Woodcock, *Barclays World of Cricket* (Collins, 1986)

Anthony Woodhouse, *The History of Yorkshire CCC* (Helm, 1989)

Anthony Woodhouse, *A Who's Who of Yorkshire CCC* (Breedon, 1992)

A Century of Bradford League Cricket (2003)

We have also read and occasionally quoted from the following books:

Rex Alston, *Test Commentary* (Stanley Paul, 1956)
Trevor Bailey, *Wickets, Catches and the Odd Run* (Collins Willow, 1986)
Trevor Bailey & Fred Trueman, *The Spinners' Web* (Willow Books, 1988)
Ralph Barker, *Ten Great Bowlers* (Chatto & Windus, 1967)
Geoffrey Boycott, *Boycott on Cricket* (Partridge Press, 1990)
William Caffyn, *Seventy-One Not Out* (William Blackwood, 1899)
Brian Close, *I Don't Bruise Easily* (Macdonald & Jane, 1978)
Roy Genders, *League Cricket in England* (Werner Laurie, 1952)
Bruce Harris, *Ashes Triumphant* (Hutchinson, 1955)
Bruce Harris, *Defending the Ashes* (Hutchinson, 1956)
Alan Hill, *Johnny Wardle – Cricket Conjuror* (David & Charles, 1988)
Gerald Howat, *Len Hutton* (Heinemann Kingswood, 1988)
Margaret Hughes, *The Long Hop* (Stanley Paul, 1955)
Len Hutton, *Fifty Years in Cricket* (Stanley Paul, 1984)
Len Hutton, *Just My Story* (Hutchinson, 1956)
Ray Illingworth, *Yorkshire and Back* (Queen Anne Press, 1980)
John Kay, *Cricket in the Leagues* (Eyre & Spottiswoode, 1970)
J.M. Kilburn, *A History of Yorkshire Cricket* (Stanley Paul, 1970)
J.M. Kilburn, *Cricket Decade* (Heinemann, 1959)
Peter May, *A Game Enjoyed* (Stanley Paul, 1985)
Don Mosey, *Boycott* (Methuen, 1985)
Don Mosey, *We Don't Play It For Fun* (Methuen, 1988)
A.G. Moyes, *The Fight for the Ashes* (George Harrap, 1955)
John Reid, *Sword of Willow* (Herbert Jenkins, 1963)
Alan Ross, *Australia 55* (Michael Joseph, 1955)
Alan Ross, *Cape Summer and the Australians in England* (H. Hamilton, 1957)
David Sheppard, *Parson's Pitch* (Hodder & Stoughton, 1964)
Brian Statham, *Cricket Merry-Go-Round* (Stanley Paul, 1956)
Bert Sutcliffe, *Between Overs* (W.H. Allen, 1963)
E.W. Swanton, *Swanton in Australia* (Collins, 1975)
E.W. Swanton, *Victory in Australia* (Daily Telegraph, 1955)
Freddie Trueman, *Fast Fury* (Stanley Paul, 1961)
Frank Tyson, *A Typhoon Called Tyson* (William Heinemann, 1961)
Johnny Wardle, *Happy Go Johnny* (Robert Hale, 1957)
Willie Watson, *Double International* (Stanley Paul, 1956)
E.M. Wellings, *The Ashes Retained* (Evans Brothers, 1955)
Peter West, *The Fight for the Ashes 1956* (George Harrap, 1956)
Don Wilson, *Mad Jack* (Kingswood Press, 1992)

also from the following newspapers:
The Times, Daily Telegraph, Manchester Guardian, Yorkshire Post, Yorkshire Evening Post, Bradford Evening Telegraph

and from the yearbooks of Yorkshire County Cricket Club.

This is a story that should have been told years ago. Hopefully the long wait makes its telling now the more powerful.

Stephen Chalke
Bath, October 2003

INDEX

Bob Appleyard and his family are not included.